Key West's Civil War

Key West's Civil War

"Rather Unsafe For a Southern Man to Live Here"

John Bernhard Thuersam

Key West's Civil War "Rather Unsafe For a Southern Man to Live Here"
Copyright© 2022 JOHN BERNHARD THUERSAM

ALL RIGHTS RESERVED. No part of this publication may be reproduced, distributed, or transmitted in any form or by any means, including photocopying, recording, or other electronic or mechanical methods, or by any information storage and retrieval system without the prior written permission of the publisher, except in the case of very brief quotations embodied in critical reviews and certain other noncommercial uses permitted by copyright law.

Produced in the Republic of South Carolina by

SHOTWELL PUBLISHING LLC
Post Office Box 2592
Columbia, So. Carolina 29202

www.ShotwellPublishing.com

Cover Image: Courtesy of Monroe County Public Libraries, Florida History Dept., Key West, Online Photo Collection, 4528986104/ KW waterfront 1862.

ISBN: 9978-1-947660-66-3

FIRST EDITION

10 9 8 7 6 5 4 3 2

For Charley Reese

No one can be a philosopher who is not capable at times of looking upon the world as if it were a pageant.

—Arthur Schopenhauer

TABLE OF CONTENTS

FOREWORD I

PREFACE III

ACKNOWLEDGMENTS VII

CHAPTER 1: 1
"A Palmyra in the Desert of Waters"

CHAPTER 2: 21
"From Territory to an Independent Nation"

CHAPTER 3: 37
A Parting of the Ways - The First Year of War

CHAPTER 4: 57
"This Don't Sute Me as a Soldier" - The Year 1862

CHAPTER 5: 79
"I Have Determined To Leave Here In Disgust"

CHAPTER 6: 107
"Rebel Shipbuilders: The Brothers Tift"

CHAPTER 7: 121
"To Be Away From This Detested Spot" – The Year 1863

CHAPTER 8: 141
"The Massachusetts Idea"

CHAPTER 9: 159
"Crossing the Lines into Rebeldom" - 1864-1865

CHAPTER 10: 179
Key West's Bird of Passage – Homer G. Plantz

CHAPTER 11: 195
"Key to the Florida Pass" Caribbean Geopolitics

EPILOGUE 215
"The South Broken on the Wheel"

THE LAST WORD 225

ABOUT THE AUTHOR 227

BIBLIOGRAPHY 229

INDEX 241

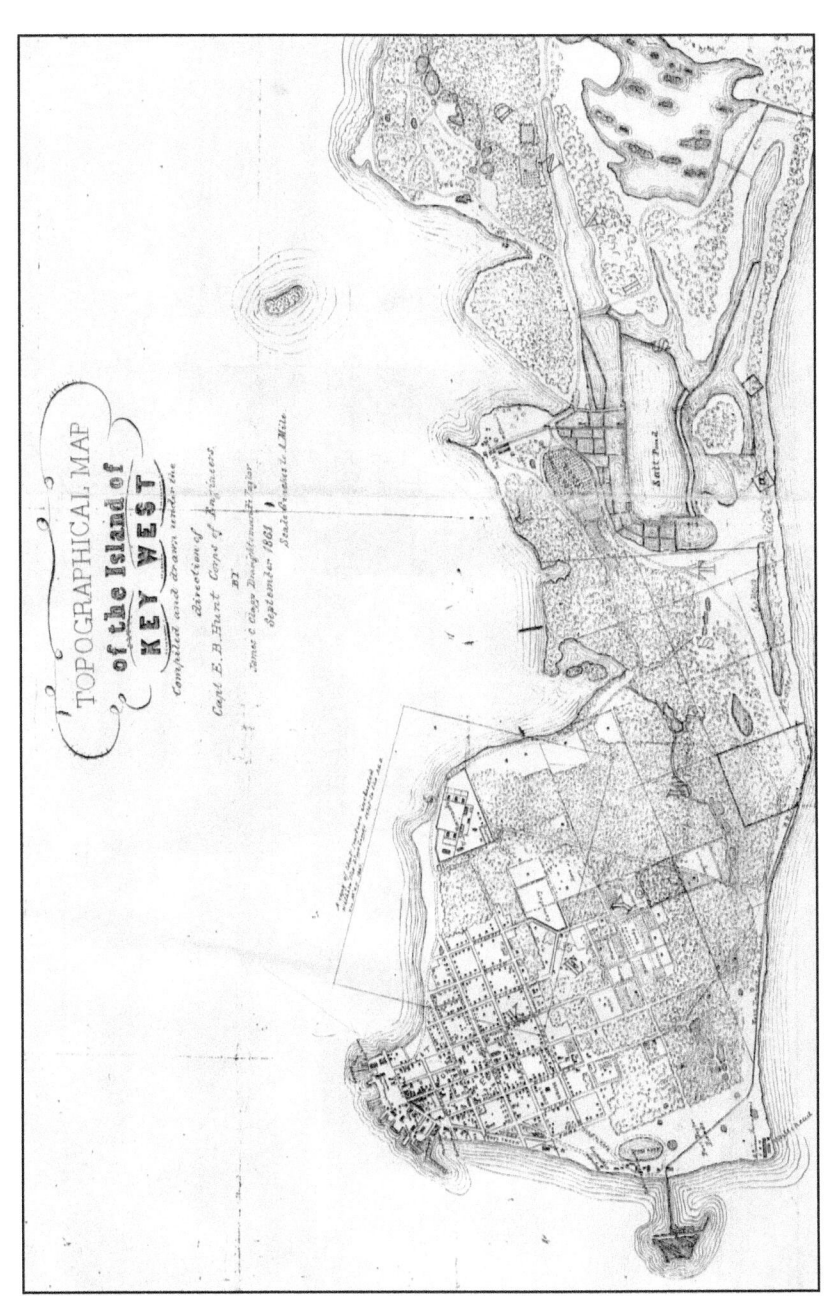

An 1861 Map of the Island.
https://www.flickr.com/photos/keyslibraries/31232115190/

KEY WEST.—A BIRD'S-EYE VIEW OF THE CITY.—THE BLACK PORTION SHOWING THE PATH OF THE FIRE, WHICH BEGAN AT THE ARROW.

View of the Island from the Northwest.
https://www.flickr.com/photos/keyslibraries/24421621115/

FOREWORD

It has been said that the great American bloodletting of 1861-65 has caused the writing of more books than any other subject except Christianity. Whether that is true or not, it is certain that the war has created a vast literature. This is not surprising. That event was larger in the scale of mobilisation and casualties, compared to the population of the time, than anything in American history. It is full of dramatic action, great personalities, and fascinating "what ifs." Its geographical range was great and it is the pivot on which the United States changed from a Union of self-governing commonwealths to a centralized Empire.

That is why it is so good to find a genuine original contribution to the war's history like Mr. Thuersam's account of Key West under occupation. Key West, a unique and southernmost American city that overlooks the vital water passage from the Atlantic to the Gulf States, is serendipitously celebrating the 200th anniversary of its founding in 2022. Mr. Thuersam's work gives a lively account of how the war acted on a considerable real group of Americans.

We academic historians tend to become routinised, lose our passion for finding what is interesting and true in the experience of mankind, and regard our calling as just another job, or, even worse, falsely claim that history is explained by some ideological slogan. It is encouraging to find a writer whose engagement with our history is still fresh and passionate. This author is a self-taught master of responsible historianship who still conveys to us the excitement of discovery of meaningful things about our past that we did not know. It will be a boon to see more of his work in the future.

Clyde N. Wilson
Emeritus Distinguished Professor of History,
University of South Carolina

PREFACE

> The museums of the world are filled with coins and trinkets that seem but broken links in that mysterious chain which connects the spirit of the living with the long-buried past.
>
> —Dickison Park, July 4, 1889

Only a few steps from today's modern landmark Green Parrot Bar lies Key West's historic Jackson Square, the seat of Monroe County government since the island's original proprietors in the 1820's established a public square bordered by Whitehead, Fleming, Southard and Thomas Streets for perpetual use by county authorities.[1]

On that public square in late 1860 stood the old courthouse where island residents met on the 12th of December to consider the question of continuing Florida's relationship with the federal union. That union was already fractious when Florida ratified the United States Constitution in early March 1845 and became a State. The topic was of such importance that it attracted the largest assembly of residents to that date and debate lasting until midnight. At its end, three delegates were elected to represent county residents at the Tallahassee convention early the following month. To put this event in perspective, this courthouse meeting occurred a little more than a week before South Carolina declared its independence, and two weeks before Major Anderson's seizure of Fort Sumter at Charleston. The latter would be duplicated at Key West a month later.

Key West at that time was a small, close-knit and highly diverse community in the northwest corner of the island. At that time the high lot at 907 Whitehead Street which prominent businessman Asa F. Tift purchased in 1850 for his family home was located "on the outskirts

---

1   Browne, pg. 59.

town."[2] The custom house at the corner of Front and Greene Streets was a small building despite the increasing maritime traffic in the harbor. Living across the street, according to a Whitehead map marked by late Key West historian Betty Moreno Bruce,[3] was the home of influential Key Wester Stephen R. Mallory, who prior to being appointed a Florida senator in 1850 had served as inspector of Customs, and Collector of Customs. The early Asa Tift home also appears near the southwest corner of Caroline and Front Streets close to his wharf; and the home of Navy paymaster Felix Senac, a relative of Mallory, was nearby. Attorney and diarist William Hackley lived on the northwest corner of Duval and Caroline; Ellen Mallory's Boarding House stood on the west side of Duval between Front and Greene Streets. Key West today bears little resemblance to December 1860 beyond remaining prewar architecture and the masonry walls of Fort Taylor, a silent witness to the time this volume revisits. Then Duval and Front Streets were the center of town with grocery, dry goods stores and businesses clustered nearby. Tift's Wharf was busy with maritime traffic and the courthouse active with shipwreck adjudications. In those distant days arriving and departing ships were the island's connection to the outside world.

A deep review of island history reveals that most if not all islanders, who were in no way homogenous, were satisfied with the status quo of late 1860 and saw no need for the great change to come. The island was friendly, neighbors knew each other and those elected usually won their office with wide, popular margins. They certainly viewed nearby Fort Taylor's presence as protection from outside threats and not a "Bastille" where citizens could be held as prisoners of conscience. The islanders had always been appreciative of the military presence and uneasy without it - only six years earlier the Seminoles were on the war path once again near Tampa and many recalled the Indian Key massacre. A quick look at Fort Taylor's original design reveals three seaward-facing sides of fortified masonry and cannon, and the landward side being unprotected wooden barracks. Of course, no cannon faced the town the fort defended but this was to change.

---

2 Fair, pg. 50.
3 Rapier, pg. 2 (marked Whitehead map.)

Preface

When Florida declared itself an independent republic on January 10, 1861 it did so with the consent of Monroe County's elected delegates. The local army captain quickly precipitated a crisis when he moved his soldiers into Fort Taylor under cover of darkness and turned his cannons on the townspeople rather than await an anticipated peaceful settlement of national political issues. President Buchanan, a former diplomat, encouraged a convention of States to settle national difficulties without bloodshed. Southern unionists implored his successor to pursue a path of patience, diplomacy and peaceful gestures to avoid war. Lincoln had options.

War brought extreme change which was mostly dictated by Key West's increasingly strategic position rather than real fears of the island's liberation by mainland forces. The European powers were already active in the late prewar period Caribbean and Gulf of Mexico which did not particularly cause international incidents, but the possibility of European intervention to assist the South's struggle for independence made the island far more important than before. This was foreseen as the reader will discover. Added to this was a new Secretary of State who became increasingly imperialistic and typical of those in command of powerful armies and navies.

The pages that follow explore the background of the islanders of that time: from where did they emigrate as native islanders were either young or nonexistent in 1860; what were their political or societal beliefs and how did they react to war and the "enemy" troops occupying their island? And what of the occupation troops, mostly men from central Pennsylvania and New York who spoke derisively of "Conchs," and wrote in letters home through the end of war that Key West was a nest of "traitors" and "secesh." Very importantly and seminal to this study: since the islanders largely supported Florida's political independence how did this interesting potpourri of Bahamian "Tories", New England Yankees and migrants from South Carolina, Georgia, Alabama and old Spanish Florida become Southern "secessionists"?

Though today's crowded island paradise receives scant attention in the many books written of Civil War Florida, Key Westers of that era – immigrant, native or transient – contributed substantially to the South's defense on and off the island. Many civilians were deported by the US military and some left to avoid martial law and in sufficient number to create a virtual Key West-in-exile community between Tampa and Clearwater by March of 1862. Some departed to become blockade runners importing needed supplies and weapons; others provided intelligence networks advising Southern authorities of enemy ship movements, military strength and operations. Local men slipped away as stowaways to enlist in Florida's Volunteer Coast Guard, later the "Key West Avengers" of the Seventh Florida Regiment, and eventually duty aboard ship with the Confederate Navy. Another left for New Orleans to build an innovative and formidable ironclad as well as other Southern warships. One prominent Key Wester emerged as the far-sighted Secretary of the Navy at Richmond, and another served as a multi-lingual paymaster in Europe for Confederate munitions and warship acquisition.

Above all it is important to point out that the "unionism" of Civil War-period Key West has been over-stated and mistaken for temporary acquiescence to intimidation and the presence of a formidable occupying power. As occurred in other border Southern towns once overrun and occupied by military force, "unionism" was more often feigning allegiance for personal profit, political gain or retribution tied to earlier local disagreements and political feuds.

There is ample evidence of Key West's resistance to military occupation after January 10, 1861 and through the war, as well as local men secretly departing the blockaded island. Key West was certainly similar to conquered cities such as Baltimore, Norfolk, Memphis and New Bern, North Carolina, officially declared "pro-Union" though under stern military occupation which lasted for the remainder of the war. Despite occupation all were able to provide troops and intelligence to support the South's struggle for independence.

The reader is invited to think more deeply about our conventional history of this period as the pages are turned. This is not a popular history of events with supporting graphs and statistics but a serious inquiry into the island's history during what we call our "civil war." And lastly, I admit apprehension to any claim of complete accuracy within these pages, despite the laborious research of nearly three years.

ACKNOWLEDGMENTS

This story could not have been told without the invaluable work of historians of an earlier age, islanders Walter C. Maloney and Jefferson B. Browne, in particular, as well as many others found in the bibliography. I am indebted to late author Lewis G. Schmidt's research of the 47th Pennsylvania regiment which was the island's longest occupier, as well as the 90th New York. His research provides a treasure-trove of letters, thoughts and opinions from those Northern soldiers which reveal pertinent sectional and racial biases to better understand them. Special thanks are due for longtime Key West historian Tom Hambright's work with the Florida Keys Maritime Historical Society and whose transcriptions provided the very spark for this book.

Most importantly I appreciate the great minds who helped educate, prepare, guide and inspire me: Dr. Clyde Wilson, professor emeritus of History, University of South Carolina; Dr. Donald Livingston, professor emeritus of Philosophy, Emory University; Dr. Thomas DiLorenzo, professor of Economics, Loyola University; and Dr. Thomas Fleming, past-editor of Chronicles Magazine and Director of the Fleming Foundation. Their work and example brought me to understand the known past as the nexus of history, philosophy and economics.

Many thanks are due Dr. C. Allen Lynn, Steve McAllister of McAllister & Solomon Used & Rare Books and Dr. John D. Fair for their invaluable assistance in obtaining key research materials for this book. Dr. Fair's deep research of the Tift family of Connecticut, Key West and Georgia helped me immensely. Valuable assistance also came from Howard Talley III & Mark A. Saulnier.

My introduction to the island's unique "Conch" culture was provided by two Key Westers now-departed from this world, Sonny and Merili McCoy of Hilton Haven. An appreciation of "Conch" architecture and its creative adaptations were learned from island architectural wizard Thomas Szuter, a man who exemplified inspired design and the pathway to a creative, if unusual life. Tom now reposes with his fathers but left us far too soon.

Lastly, a loving appreciation of my wife Kim Song Sook who entered my life at Key West after her long journey from Pusan, Korea. So very mysterious and inscrutable are life's pathways, the winding roads so often taken on whim and obscure impulse. Her infinite patience, support and quiet understanding made this literary effort possible.

CHAPTER 1:

"A Palmyra in the Desert of Waters"

> The island of Key West is four miles long and one mile at the widest. The entire area is 197 acres, including the salt pond. It is very low and flat, the highest spot on the island being scarcely more than twenty feet above the level of the sea.
>
> —*Freeman Hunt's Magazine*, January 1852

Detailed surveys of early Florida history can be found in many capable volumes and needs not be reproduced here; a list of recommended reading is found in the bibliography.

Key West had no permanent residents prior to 1821 and it was not until late March of 1822 that the United States claimed it as a territory. Before 1821 it was a Spanish possession in the island chain named "Los Martires" by Ponce de Leon about 1513, uninhabited except for infrequent visits by pirates and aborigines. The tradition among the modern Indians is that the tribes of the mainland, in conflict with those of the reef, drove the latter in a series of conflicts from island to island until the last island was reached. "Here they made a desperate stand ... a terrible battle ensued ... the islanders were overpowered, and utterly exterminated."[1] Nothing but bones were later found.

It was not until 1700 that Europeans identified south Florida aborigines as two main tribes called Creek and Calusa; the latter said to be driven to extinction at the westernmost island. This last of the Los Martires chain was called *cayo hueso*, or "island of bones," later corrupted into "Key West." The Florida peninsula would remain in

---

1   *Hunt's Magazine*, pg. 52-53.

Spanish hands until 1763, transferred to England until 1783 when the Spanish regained possession, and later restored to England in exchange for the island of Cuba.

In 1815 the vacant island was presented to Don Juan Pablo Salas of St. Augustine in recognition of honorable military service to Spain.[2] After the Adams-Onis Treaty in which Spain ceded Florida to the United States in early 1821, Salas sold the island to ship captain and wrecker John Strong for $5000 in September, 1821; then three months later sold the island to John W. Simonton of New Jersey for $2000. Strong then sold the island to Gen. John Geddes of Charleston in February 1822 for $20,000. These transactions resulted in a series of legal tangles which were finally resolved by the US Congress in late May, 1828, when it decreed Simonton's sole claim of ownership.[3]

Despite Florida being acquired and set upon the path to eventual Statehood, the Seminole tribe had to be controlled or removed. They strongly resisted European encroachments by devastating white settlements, including a brutal massacre on Indian Key, but by 1821 it was believed that Indians were no longer inhabiting the Keys between Miami and Key West.[4]

---

2   Smiley & White, pg. 6.
3   Langley, pg. 10.
4   Smiley & White, pg. 12.

The earliest Key West settlers were for the most part from South Carolina, Virginia, Alabama, Connecticut, New York and New Jersey, along with some Spanish, all of whom brought with them varied political ideals, affiliations and viewpoints on political authority and allegiances. Others attracted to the island were English Bahamians — Revolutionary War Tories who refused to be ruled by American "secessionists" and referred to as "Conchs" — those who lived on the easily found tropical marine mollusk.

The uninhabited island grew rapidly into a small town after initial surveying by the four proprietors: John Simonton, Pardon C. Greene, John Fleeming (Fleming) and John Whitehead in 1829 — to an early population of about 517 persons in 1830. The year 1840 recorded 688 souls; 2,645 in the year 1850 and a population of 2,832 by the year 1860.

In the words of historian Jefferson Beale Browne, this early Key West was "a rare aggregation" [of] "Englishmen, Bahamians, Irish, Dutch, Swedes, Norwegians, Hindoos, Russians, Italians, Spaniards, Cubans, Canary Islanders, South Americans, Canadians, Scotch, French, shipwrecked sailors, deserters and discharged men from the army, navy and marine corps; men who had knocked about all over the world and developed personalities of their own ..." [5]

Browne tells us as well that by 1845, the black population of the island "was less than two hundred, slave and free." Construction on Forts Taylor and Jefferson, both labor intensive projects, brought more black men, mostly slaves, who were leased by owners to the government. The majority of island's slaves were domestic servants held by both Northern and Southern immigrants, but it was the US Corps of Engineers which strengthened slaveholding at Key West through its fort construction projects. The 1850 census showed a black population increased to 557, of which 126 were free.

The first slaves of Europeans came after Ponce de Leon's voyage of discovery in 1513, with Spain's King Ferdinand authorizing him to colonize "La Florida" and what became known as "Bimini." He was instructed to summon the chiefs to have their people convert to Catholicism, and "if they do not wish to obey, make war, seize them

---

5   Browne, pp. 173-174.

and carry them away for slaves."⁶ African slaves became common throughout the Spanish possession of Florida, 1513-1763 and 1785-1819, as well as the British possession 1763-1784; some slaves were taken by Florida's Seminole tribe as well.

The growing town itself was a collection of busy wharfs, taverns and boardinghouses for seamen and dueling; understandably, most female residents were wary of venturing out after dark. But Browne does write of an increasingly well-informed population: "Nearly all who came had some means and were people of culture and refinement." St. Augustine, Virginia, South Carolina, New York and Connecticut had furnished many of Key West's early population, with shipwreck salvage and fishing for the Havana market being the primary sources of income." A sketch of 1831 Key West noted widely diverse "habits, manners, views and feelings formed in different schools and in many instances totally dissimilar and contradictory."⁷

News from the outside world came to islanders aboard monthly vessels, and their eagerly anticipated arrival was announced by bell-ringing at the mail agent's wharf. This was most often an occasion for a social gathering with entire families awaiting the mail, and as former Mayor Maloney, Sr., has written: "When they did arrive everybody knew it."

Key West's first post office was simply a home on the corner of Caroline & Front Streets where incoming and outgoing letters accumulated.⁸ The town received its first charter in 1828, and monthly mail service was established between Charleston and Key West in February, 1829. Shortly after this mail service between St. Marks (south of Tallahassee) and the island was arranged; and in early 1832 a contract was awarded for regular monthly mail service between Key West and Charleston. From 1848 to 1861, the "fast and comfortable" steamer "Isabel" of Mordecai & Company of Charleston brought regular mail to the island. In addition, news from New Orleans, St. Marks and other Gulf ports arrived on the New York steamer line of Morgan & Company.⁹

---

6   Davis, pg. 52-53.
7   Browne, pg. 14.
8   *Ibid.*, pg. 82.
9   Maloney, pg. 29.

Prominent newspapers of large coastal cities kept islanders informed of current political and social events, observations, viewpoints and opinions from Mobile, Tallahassee, Havana, Jacksonville, Savannah, Wilmington, Norfolk and Baltimore.

Key West's first newspaper was issued in January 1829 with editor Thomas Eastin's *Register* which lived a brief life, followed by the *Gazette* on March 21, 1831 and in print until late 1832. *The Enquirer* appeared in mid-October 1834, edited and published by Jesse Atkinson; later it was named *Inquirer* which existed until 1836. As was common with nineteenth century newspapers, Key West editors most likely reprinted articles from other papers, adding local gossip, hearsay, scandals, obituaries and sensational stories to attract readership.

Subsequent newspapers published were the *Light of the Reef* of 1844-45 by editors Eldridge L. Ware & Scarborough. In 1845 the *Key of the Gulf* began with Postmaster Ware as sole editor for several years, then resurrected by William H. Ward in the late 1850s.

Antebellum life on the island is best related through letters and diaries left to us by residents. William Hackley, a Virginia-born maritime lawyer and diarist who resided on Key West from late 1828 through 1857, leaves us an interesting record of reading material reaching him via mail ships: *Knickerbocker* (New York) news magazine, *Norfolk Herald*, New York and Charleston newspapers, the *American Law Review* and the magazines *Godey's,* as well as *Harper's & Putnam's*. Hackley spent his leisure time reading Adam Smith's *Wealth of Nations,* and *Discourses on Livy and Tacitus.*

An early riser, Hackley wrote of walking almost daily from town to the salt ponds, shooting small Key deer, doves, hawks, flamingoes, partridges, and egrets. His daily diversions included games of whist, euchre, piquet, backgammon, chess and billiards with friends and associates. He also bought chances on the Havana lottery and sent his watch for repair to Charleston.

On Sunday, August 28, 1853 Hackley writes "Comet was visible again and increases in brilliancy. It moves rapidly to the south. The light of tail pulsated or intermits." This would have been Klinkerfuss's comet, visible in the southeastern sky to the unaided eye from early August to early October 1853.[10]

Interestingly, Hackley observed that "upstanding citizens like himself constituted a distinct minority of the island's population.[11] He wrote often of fishing and hunting excursions up the Keys with fellow attorneys, town leaders, clerks and military men. Hackley married Matilda Folker of Charleston, sister of six-term Mayor Alexander Patterson, all of whom remained loyalists during the coming war.[12]

An 1829 map of the island shows the town comprising the northwest corner of the island, extending from the harbor and Front Street to just past Southard Street; from Front and Emma Streets on the west; and to White and Anderson Streets and delineating the eastern border of development. Clearly shown is Jackson Square, bordered by Thomas, Whitehead, Southard and Fleemimg (later Fleming) Streets, and set aside by the proprietors for the seat of Monroe County government.

From Southard Street southward the island was undeveloped as well as the eastern portion. At that time a large two-acre tidal pond existed near the intersection of Duval and Front Streets, running toward Duval and Caroline Streets and traversed by a wooden footbridge. Described as "a miserable stagnant lagoon" which risked flooding other parts of town, residents saw it filled naturally with silt during the hurricane of 1846. "Old Town" was then young and small and did not comprise the entire island until 1889 - this accomplished by special charter. The isolated island depended upon rainwater collected in cisterns for personal use as no natural springs were ever discovered.

The profits from the salvage of wrecked ships soon dominated island business with "wharves, shipyards and chandleries" lining the harbor as well as warehouses and auction houses that held salvaged goods for eventual sale. In 1825, Congress passed legislation that all salvage from ships wrecked in US waters must be adjudicated in an

---

10 William Hackley diary, August 1853.

11 Ogle, pg. 28.

12 Ogle, pg. 8.

American port, which benefited Key West greatly. Salt production from the salt ponds on the island's eastern side never became lucrative due to unreliable labor, early rainy seasons and hurricanes.[13]

Desiring the establishment of regular religious services on the island, proprietor William Whitehead proposed a meeting in March, 1831 for the citizens to "adopt measures for obtaining the services of a clergyman, and among the duties required of him was the opening of a school." A second school was begun by Alden A. Jackson in April 1835, among several others. In 1843 a county school was begun for those unable to afford private studies and supported by taxation.[14]

The first established church on the island was St. Paul's Episcopal, serving the entire island regardless of religious affiliation. It was led by Rev. Sanson K. Brunot of Pittsburgh, the first clergyman to hold services on Key West and arriving here just before Christmas, 1832. Those enrolled in the new congregation included prominent Key West leaders William A. Whitehead, Fielding A. Browne, John W. Simonton, Amos F. Tift, Pardon Greene, William H. Wall, Stephen R. Mallory, Philip J. Fontane, Francis B. Watlington and John P. Baldwin. Several pews were set aside for the use of black residents, both free and slave who desired worship. The emigration of Bahamians began a Wesleyan Methodist congregation led by Samuel Kemp in the late 1830s, which eventually became a church of mostly Bahamians.

A Baptist congregation began worship on the island in late December 1842, associated with the Second Baptist Church of Stonington, Connecticut. Once the Connecticut congregation learned that a member of the Key West congregation was a slaveowner, the association was dropped – an interesting irony as New England slave traders dominated the transatlantic trade which brought thousands of enslaved Africans to the West Indies and plantations of the American South.[15]

With sufficient investment in homes and commercial buildings to warrant it, Key West's "Lafayette Fire Department" was organized in October 1834 by prominent islanders, who elected Asa F. Tift and Stephen R. Mallory as officers. The town's first major fire occurred in

---

13   Langley, pg. 12-13.
14   Browne, pg. 21.
15   *Ibid.,* pg. 27-29.

mid-May 1859, during a lapse in fire department organization, which burned every house but two in the two-block area bounded by Greene, Front, Simonton and Whitehead Streets. Thanks to the heroism and selflessness of immigrant Henry Mulrennan, who blew up his own residence to block the spreading fire, further destruction of the town was prevented.

Mulrennan was a Paisley, Scotland native of Scotch-Irish ancestry who arrived in New York City as an eleven-year-old. Seven years later, in 1850, he was a Mexican war veteran assigned to Key West as an artilleryman at Fort Zachary Taylor. Henry soon mustered out and entered a business partnership with Eldridge L. Ware and George H. Carey. Mulrennan established The Louvre on Front Street, which housed several clothing stores, and served as a town alderman just before the Civil War. As a testament to his enduring popularity with islanders, Mulrennan returned from the war to be twice elected mayor – in 1868 and 1870.[16]

The small US Army presence on the island began in 1831 with two companies of soldiers encamped to the east of town near today's Palm Avenue and White Streets, where barracks were eventually constructed. Nonetheless, Key West's strategic and commanding position in relation to Gulf of Mexico sea traffic was not lost on military minds in Washington. In early 1845 a suitable site for a fortress was found some 1200 feet off the island's western shore, to be accessed by a wooden causeway. Today the fort is no longer offshore as dredged fill has been used to connect the fort to the island. In July 1845 Florida's legislature ceded land for the construction of a fort to protect the island, which was near completion in early January 1861.

From this varied and unique population – in contact with the outside world only through shipwrecked passengers and monthly mail ships — emerged a distinct sense of autonomy and self-reliance on an isolated island. This is the important lens through which to understand how antebellum Key West residents viewed their existence, and the outside political world.

The rapid growth of the wrecking industry after 1825 brought many Bahamian "Conchs" to Key West – the term arising from their regular consumption of the common sea mollusk - and who retained

---

16 Browne, pg. 151.

the distinctive, and often derisive label. These "Conchs" were for the most part the descendants of American Loyalists, or "Tories" evacuated from South Carolina and Georgia in 1782 as well as New York and East Florida after peace in 1783. They settled on Abaco and Harbour Island, often with their bondsmen, rather than submit to rule by the traitorous "American secessionists" who "in their fury had hung twenty-four Loyalists in sight of the British fleet at Charleston."[17] Some Tories began arriving in Florida after 1821 and more in the mid-1830s with their black slaves, as imminent British emancipation posed a threat to their property and prosperity, despite compensation.

Importantly, these "Tories" of the eighteenth and nineteenth centuries viewed their culture as a network of personal attachments and community, engendering respect for customs, law and rank in society. Their understanding of society was one of "noblesse oblige," wherein those with wealth and authority used their influence to help those less fortunate than they.

Though American colonists viewed Loyalists as traitors to their rebel cause, Loyalists saw the American revolutionaries as the real traitors — certainly America was a Crown colony and all British subjects owed allegiance to George III and England. These Bahamian "Conchs" were seen as simple, honest sea-folk and a very close-knit group, known for being gracious, clean living, church-going Methodists."[18] Above all they maintained a defiant Loyalist tradition with pride in their British heritage, respect for law and civilized behavior.

Demonstrating his intense desire to emigrate, in 1846, Loyalist descendant Captain Richard Roberts dismantled and shipped his home to Key West to be reassembled at 408 William Street. Also, Captain John Bartlum, Jr. and wife Sarah Lowe moved their home and family from Green Turtle Cay in 1847 to 730 Eaton Street, Key West, where it remains today.[19] By 1860, Bahamian immigration was sufficient to make Key West the most populous city in Florida, and making "Conchs" its most important and influential group.

---

17 Riley, pg. 127.
18 Smiley & White, pg. 27.
19 Riley, pg. 230.

An interesting glimpse of Key West in early January 1849 is provided by Georgia native Dr. Edward S. Aldrich writing wife Corinna from the island, praising its beauty, climate and economic potential. Originally from Portsmouth, New Hampshire, Corinna married Dr. Aldrich at Mandarin, Florida in 1837, and subsequently lived at Macon, Marietta and Newnansville, Georgia. Encouraged by town leaders to open a medical practice on the island, he relocated mid-year with the hope of an appointment as Marine Hospital surgeon. Corinne arrived mid-1849 and wrote her sister of the "money plenty" from wrecking, balmy breezes, mosquitos and sand flies aplenty, and finding a home with a "large yard full of trees – cocoa nuts full of fruit – almond – dates & tamarinds."[20]

The island was found convenient for filibustering operations to overthrow Spanish rule in Cuba. In mid-May 1850, the ship and some 600 troops of Venezuela-born, Cuban revolutionary Narciso Lopez sought safety in Key West's harbor after defeat at the battle of Cardenas and pursuit by the Spanish warship *Pizarro*. The expedition's survivors were quickly disbanded upon landing to avoid arrest and prosecution under the 1794 Neutrality Act. One of Lopez's severely wounded officers on board was Col. Chatham R. Wheat of Virginia, who had won distinction in the war with Mexico, and later as well in the Civil War.

The January 1852 *Freeman Hunt's Merchants' Magazine and Commercial Review* issue wrote that Key West in the previous year contained some "650 houses, 26 stores, 10 warehouses, 4 lookout cupolas, 11 wharves, and 4 churches" – Episcopal, Methodist, Baptist and Roman Catholic. The island's schools at this point included four private academies and one county school, the former averaging about thirty scholars each and the latter, free to children without fathers, about sixty. Additionally, the magazine reported that the harbor could accommodate ships of 22 feet draft, and that the principal business of Key West was wreck salvages, commissions and the auction of salvaged articles being brisk as well as sponging.[21]

---

20 Denham & Huneycutt, pg. 517; 527.
21 Hunt, pg. 54.

The island was also affected by the illegal slave trade carried on between Africa, Cuba and often the United States, and captures made by US Navy ships that patrolled the Caribbean. The slavers, most often captained by New Englanders, were caught off the coast of Cuba. One such ship, the *USS Crusader* and commanded by Lt. John Newland Maffitt, captured the *Echo* in 1858 and *Bogota* in 1860, both with New York registry and each with hundreds of Africans aboard. Both were brought to the United States Marshal at Key West for adjudication. It is noteworthy that slave ships built and financed at New York filled the harbors there and most adjudications at Key West against Northern companies involved in the illicit trade went unpunished. These were called "blackbirders" who frequented Sweet's Restaurant on Fulton Street to discuss bribery of customs officials and to arrange false identifications. It is reported that one of their slavers brazenly sailed under the New York City Yacht Club flag. In October 1860 the slaver *Erie* was caught and its captain tried at federal court in New York, but missing papers and the captain's uncertain nationality led to dismissal.[22]

To accommodate the increasing numbers of liberated Africans, temporary housing was constructed onshore near the fort, while the Africans, sometimes numbering as many as 1,400 awaiting repatriation, were reported to be "the recipients of many acts of kindness from our citizens. Hundreds of Key Westers visited them daily carrying clothing, food and other things for their comfort and pleasure."[23] Though their repatriation to Africa was well-intentioned, it often sent the unfortunate captives to where they were once again sold into slavery by African tribes.

Key West's early days of immigration from virtually all points, development and commercial success witnessed the emergence of many people and personalities, often playing influential roles in local politics, many of whom would help direct the independence of Florida in early 1861. Several brief introductions of the island's most colorful residents follow:

---

22 McKay, pg. 14-15.
23 Browne, pg. 17.

What is known as Mallory Square today was "Tift's Wharf" during the 1850s, a successful maritime business owned by Asa F. Tift. His father Amos moved his wife and five sons from Mystic, Connecticut to Key West in 1826 and opened Tift's Chandlery on the northwest corner of Wall Street and Tift's Alley. After Amos passed away in 1829, several sons operated the business until Asa F. bought out the others in early 1840. A leading citizen of the island in church, government and public works affairs, on December 12, 1860, Asa was appointed one of three delegates to represent Monroe County at Tallahassee's convention to consider independence.

Darien, Georgia native Walter C. Maloney was a prominent town leader, attorney, mayor 1846-1848, and early town schoolteacher. Born in 1813, he emigrated to the Keys as a young man in the 1820s and married Bahamian-born Mary Elizabeth Rigby in 1838. Widowed in 1855, in 1856 Maloney married Maria S. Dubois of New York City, officiated by then-Mayor Philip J. Fontane. Politically, Maloney most likely identified strongly with the Whig party which had dominated Florida since Statehood in 1845 – and resisted any discussion of State independence. At the County courthouse meeting on December 12, 1860 to discuss Florida's political future, he proclaimed "the Union first, the Union last, and the Union always."[24]

Herkimer County, New York native William Marvin, born in 1808, was appointed US Attorney for the Southern District of Territorial Florida, arriving at Key West in October 1835. A bachelor, he initially boarded with Ellen Mallory, mother of Stephen R. Mallory. He was later appointed Judge of the US District Court of Florida, 1839-1845, and again in 1847. Historian Jefferson Browne recalled that "Judge Marvin was a man of towering intellectuality and grandeur of character. While on the bench he published a book entitled "*A Treatise Upon the Law of Wreck and Salvage*," which became a standard authority in the admiralty courts of England and the United States, and it occupies today a unique position among the treatises on the law of salvage." Politically a Whig, though sensitive to Southern interests, he was nearly-elected one of three delegates to the January 1861 secession convention at Tallahassee. He believed Florida should await

---

24 Maloney, pg. 63-64.

the decision of the Border States before deciding upon independence. For opposing immediate secession, he and other island loyalists were denounced by newspaper editor William Ward.[25]

William C. Dennis was described as a distinguished and monied Key Wester before the war. A partner with Charles Howe in island salt production, he favored Florida independence in 1861. Reportedly owning twenty-nine slaves in 1859, he was Key West's largest slaveholder and very likely had imported them to satisfy US Army demands for slave labor at the two forts under construction.[26] Diarist William Hackley wrote in mid-February 1856 of himself hiring "a Negro woman for two months" from Dennis. Dennis died in 1864.

Philip J. Fontane came to the island in the late 1820s, the son of Felipe Juan Fontanet of St. Augustine. He operated a grocery and chandlery, was elected town alderman in 1832 and served three terms as mayor between 1840 and 1856. An 1838 map of the town shows the Fontane home adjacent to the Patterson house at the end of the old Salt Pond walk – eventually Duval Street.[27]

John Parvost Baldwin – who claimed aristocratic British ancestry - served as town mayor 1857-1860 while Collector of Customs 1853-1861 and left for the Bahamas at the outbreak of war, returning afterward. Being familiar with Stephen Mallory as well as Confederate agents in Europe, Confederate agents Felix Senac and Henry Huse in Europe. He likely engaged in lucrative blockade running business. He purchased the Patterson home at Eaton and Duval streets in 1860 - the home still stands. Daughter Annie married Philip H. Fontane, son of Philip J.[28]

Harriet, or "Hattie" Pinckney was the daughter of Dr. Theodore A. and Sibyl (Marvin) Pinckney, of Duchess County, New York, the family arriving at Key West in 1837. Mrs. Pinckney was the sister of Key West attorney William Marvin, the latter finding a position at the Custom House and Marine Hospital for Dr. Pinckney. In 1852, Harriet

---

25 Browne, pg. 65.
26 Smith, pg. 6.
27 Browne, pg. 53.
28 Naugle, online.

married army Lt. Caleb Huse, a Massachusetts native and West Point graduate, who took extended leave in Europe to inspect and evaluate the armaments of several countries.[29]

Island businessman James Filor came to the island in 1835 and dealt in real property and other investments, and built his own two-story brick "fireproof" warehouse near the waterfront. Buildings such as these were used for the storage of salvaged goods and being brick did not require insurance. With the construction of the two forts nearby and the US Army engineers interested in leasing African slave labor, Filor brought slaves to Key West for that purpose and was the island's second-largest slave holder with seventeen. Extant letters suggest he obtained slaves from Maine-native and auctioneer Ziba B. Oakes's Charleston brokerage. Filor is sometimes noted as "Honorable" and may have been appointed judge.[30]

Born in 1797, Alexander Patterson of Stonington, Connecticut was one of St. Paul's Episcopal Church first members and was elected vestrymen in 1833. An early island merchant he operated a store at the foot of Whitehead Street auctioning salvaged goods from wrecks. Patterson served as a member of the State legislature as well as mayor for four terms, 1845-1868. He initially lived at 522 Caroline Street, then the corner of Eaton and Duval Streets. Referred to as a "Tory," he was installed as mayor when federal troops occupied Key West when martial law was both threatened and imposed.[31]

Charles Howe was a native of Northboro, Massachusetts, born in 1801 who arrived in Florida in 1827, possibly acquainted with the Amos Tift family of Mystic, Connecticut. He was appointed a Monroe County justice of the peace, held property on both Indian and Duck Key and, on the latter, produced salt with his seven African slaves. In 1835 Howe was appointed Inspector of Customs and Postmaster at Indian Key, just southwest of today's Islamorada, where he lived with his family. During the Seminole attack of August 1840, his family survived by hiding on nearby Tea Table Key. After selling all he owned at auction at Key West that November, he and family removed to Dade County, then Key West in 1842. Howe was appointed Collector of

---

29 Kearney, pg. 206.
30 Browne, pg. 12; see also Smith: "Engineering Slavery".
31 *Ibid.*, pg. 27.

Customs at Key West in 1861, serving until 1869. Howe, sons Charles Jr. and Edward, were all loyalists in 1861 who joined the "Union Volunteer Corps" of Key West. [32]

Captain Francis B. Watlington was a New York City native born in 1804 who came to the island in the early 1830s. He built a home at 322 Duval Street between Eaton and Fleming Streets, now the oldest house on the island. He was employed as a pilot and wrecker, and with nine daughters his Duval Street home became a notable social center of the island - minus alcohol. He avoided strong drink and co-founded, with Joseph C. Whalton, the island's prewar "Sons of Temperance." In 1858 daughter Emeline Frances married local newspaper editor William Ward and resided in the family home. Ward left for war in 1861 and never returned to Emeline and their daughter.[33]

Merchant Fielding Archer Browne of Virginia, born in 1796 came to the island as a shipwrecked passenger enroute to Mexico to join his brother. He was elected to the town council and served as first Key West mayor in April 1836 under the town's new charter, with William Hackley as one of the elected councilmen. He was mayor for two terms, 1833-1834 and 1836-1837, as well as diplomat, Vice Consul for France and Spain. Browne owned a large warehouse and wharf, used for the storage of salvaged goods awaiting auction. He married Angelina Sophia Folker on the island in late September 1837.[34]

Jefferson Beverly Browne was born at James City County, Virginia in 1814 to John Eaton and Elizabeth Ann Browne. Browne attended William and Mary College before arriving in Key West at the age of 16 on Christmas Eve to begin employment with his uncle Fielding A. Browne. He was appointed a member of the St. Joseph Convention which framed Florida's constitution for eventual Statehood, served as territorial US marshal, clerk of the US Court in Key West, and member of the Florida legislature 1866-1870; 1875. Browne was among those supporting Florida's independence at the courthouse on December 12, 1860. Described by a descendant as "the typical Virginia gentleman, with the manners and pronunciation which distinguished them." He went on to become a very successful island merchant; town marshal

---

32 Wilkinson, keyshistory.org .

33 Browne, pg. 12.

34 Browne, Fielding A. Wikipedia accessed 2.2.22; see also Browne, pg. 52-53.

in May 1840, mayor 1870-71, and State legislator. He married Mary Nieves Ximinez of St. Augustine in December 1840, a union which produced four children including Hon. Jefferson Beale Browne.[35]

Syracuse, New York-native and Key West newspaperman William H. Ward was born about 1830 and was a graduate of the early US Naval Academy. After service in the Mexican War he resigned his commission in 1852, took up residence in Key West and in 1857 he began editing the *Key of the Gulf* . Ward married Emeline Frances Watlington in 1858 and resided in her family home at 322 Duval Street. The weekly, four-page paper provided a platform for political views on the sectionalism afflicting the country, and throughout 1860 and early 1861, was the most widely-known pro-independence newspaper in Florida. Ward's masthead proclaimed "Ask Nothing But What is Right – Submit to Nothing That is Wrong."[36]

Winer Bethel of Nassau arrived on the island in 1847 and by 1861 had practiced law and held the position of Monroe County probate judge. Historian Browne writes of him as "a portly, handsome man with a full, curly beard, and always dressing to impress." His son Livingston would follow him in the legal profession.[37] Euphemia Lightbourne came to the island with brother-in-law Winer Bethel. She immediately began a private school and began an active membership in St. Paul's Church. She devotedly ministered to those afflicted with illness and disability.[38]

Bahamian William Dennis Cash came to the island in 1858 after receiving a formal education from Dr. Duncan, Rector of Nassau's Episcopal Church. Cash then taught school on the island for several years before accepting a clerking position with William H. Wall & Company, later Wall & Pinckney and the largest general merchandise store on the island. He married fellow Bahamian Elizabeth Bartlum in 1857.[39]

---

35 Browne, pg. 91.
36 Schmidt III, pg. 44-45. See also Browne, pg. 141-142.
37 Browne, pg. 182.
38 *Ibid.,* pg. 189.
39 *Ibid.,* pg. 102.

William Pinckney, son of an early Collector of Customs and the second native-born of Key West, rose to success in 1860 as junior partner and manager of William H. Wall & Company, a highly successful mercantile and wrecking salvage business. The senior partner, William H. Wall was "a tall, slender, graceful Englishman, with the perfect diction of the cultured men of that nation." William H. Wall reportedly was retired and living in New York.[40]

Stephen R. Mallory, a self-educated, self-made man, was the son of Key West's first white female resident, Ellen Mallory, and described as highly conservative politically. After service as Key West attorney, Collector of Customs and Democrat party organizer on the island, he was appointed United States Senator from Florida with Whig support over veteran David Levy Yulee in 1850, as he was considered less a Southern nationalist than Yulee. Little-known was Mallory's support of a railroad line to the island, first advocated in an 1835 issue of the "*Key West Inquirer*." This proposal Mallory also included in an official report while chair of the US Senate Naval Affairs Committee. His prewar home was located across from the old Custom House, at the southwest corner of Greene and Front Streets.[41]

Gibraltar-native Peter A. Crusoe was born c.1820, and migrated to Key West in the late 1840s. He served as Monroe County Clerk of Circuit Court from 1851 till the outbreak of war in 1861. About 1851 he married Bahamian-native Sarah A. Roberts. She gave birth to their children Medora, Evelyn, Edwin, Clarence and Arthur. Crusoe was appointed a secretary recording the Dec. 12, 1860 courthouse meeting nominating Monroe delegates to Tallahassee.[42]

Felix Senac, a little-known Key West immigrant who played a unique role in the coming war was employed as the chief clerk and paymaster at Fort Zachary Taylor's construction site. Born in 1815 at Pensacola, he was the cousin of Angela Moreno, daughter of Don Francisco Moreno and wife of Stephen R. Mallory. It is believed that Senac's coming to Key West was the result Angela Mallory's sister Irene's influence. Irene's husband, Capt. Jeremiah M. Scarritt assumed command of Fort Taylor in May, 1852. Early Key West

---

40   *Ibid.*, pg. 174.
41   Durkin, pg. x; Browne, pg. 194; Rapier Map, pg. 2.
42   Browne, pg. 211; find-a-grave.

attorney and diarist William Hackley's frequently mentions outings with Mallory, Senac and Scarritt. Given his fluency in English, French and Spanish, Senac was commissioned a US Navy Paymaster in 1857 largely through Mallory's influence, and shortly afterward departed Key West for the high seas.[43]

Elected Key West mayor in 1852 and a year later elected Monroe County sheriff, Fernando Joaquin Moreno was a Pensacola native born in 1823. Prior to the war he was an underwriter's agent at Wall & Company's store on Front Street and became well-acquainted with clerk William Pinckney. Moreno was described as courtly, polite and with distinguished manners. Though slightly deaf he carried a silver ear trumpet at his side and was regularly seen riding his pony to the South Beach.[44]

Also employed at Fort Taylor was draughtsman James C. Clapp who produced detailed construction plans for the army engineers. Clapp additionally was an accomplished artist who augmented his three-dollar per day salary with hand-sketches of the town, many of which were lithographed in London and Paris and are highly-prized today. Clapp was elected a town alderman in 1859 and remained a loyalist, or "Tory," after war began, and was rewarded with appointment as US Marshal for the Southern District at Key West.[45]

The man known as "Mr. Marcus" in Key West was Genoa, Italy native Marcus Oliveri. Described as tall and handsome, he operated an island restaurant known for "Yankee pie-eating contests" and bowls of canned oyster stews. Mr. Marcus was an independent-minded merchant, said to be common on the island, and fond of suggesting that dissatisfied customers eat elsewhere and stating that "I don't care a shucks for your patronage." In 1860 he was reportedly employed as an assistant at the Marine Hospital, perhaps the result of restaurant customers finding friendlier island eateries.[46]

---

43 Rapier, pg. 15.
44 Browne, pg. 211.
45 Williams, Ames, pg. 8.
46 Browne, pg. 181.

Bahamian Robert Watson was a twelve-year-old when his family moved to Key West in 1847. His father may likely have been lured by the profitable wrecking business at Key West, as the Bahamian government felt it diminished the desirable "habits of steady industry" among inhabitants. In early December 1857 Watson became a Florida citizen, and obviously had profited from a good education in Key West schools as evidenced in his later wartime journal.

When the war came to the island in early 1861 this descendant of British "Tories" was employed as one of the island's skilled carpenters. Having experienced federal occupation of his town since early January and determined to defend his adopted State,

Watson's initial diary entry of September 27, 1861 reads: "Owing to the political affairs of the country, and the federal troops having possession of this place, and as it is rather unsafe for a Southern man to live here, I have determined to leave in disgust, consequently I left today in the schooner *Lady Bannerman* for the Bahama Islands, in the company of Cyrus A. Canfield, William Sawyer, Alfred Lowe and others." Watson's diary thankfully survived the war and forms part of the basis for this book, the original is in family possession. This journal and Lewis G. Schmidt's research of Pennsylvania and New York soldier's diaries were invaluable to gain an accurate picture of life on the island during the war.[47]

---

47 Campbell, pg. 5. See also Riley, pg. 227.

CHAPTER 2:

"FROM TERRITORY TO AN INDEPENDENT NATION"

> If there be any among us who wish to dissolve the Union, or to change its republican form, let them stand undisturbed as monuments of the safety with which error of opinion may be tolerated where reason is left free to combat it.
>
> —Thomas Jefferson

> When all government ... in little as in great things ... shall be drawn to Washington as the center of all power, it will render powerless the checks and balances provided of one government on another and will become as venal and oppressive as the government from which we separated.
>
> —Thomas Jefferson

Historian Jefferson Bowne wrote the following of Key West's leading men: "The influence of the cultured men who located in Key West in the early days fostered the spirit of resisting Federal usurpation [of State authority], and as early as 1832 an editorial appeared in a newspaper then published in Key West, voicing a sentiment which rings true to the Declaration of Independence."

Predicting the sentiment of the December 12, 1860 Courthouse meeting, the editorial[1] read:

> We have always thought the true value of our Union consisted in equal rights and equal protection to every citizen, and when these objects are so perverted as to become a means of impoverishment to one section while benefitting another; and when it becomes necessary to sacrifice one portion of the States for the good of the rest, the Union has lost its value to us. We are then bound, by the basic principles of our free government to maintain our rights and defend our lives and property. If we are oppressed it is a matter of perfect indifference whether that oppression be inflicted by a foreign power or our next-door neighbor. Upon the same principle we are compelled to resist both – even unto death.

The writer quoted above was clearly referring to the "tariff of abominations" which supported high protectionist tariffs for Northern manufacturing interests, while the agricultural South imported manufactured goods and paid 87% of the tariffs. Added to this disparity was Northern States wanting this money in the treasury to be used for their particular development projects.

As Florida became a US territory in 1819 and began its expected trek toward eventual Statehood in 1845, it attracted both federal and commercial investment, with railroads and port improvements important politically. The territorial political establishment represented the large landed-interests of Florida, a mostly-Whig lawyer and speculator class concentrated in middle Florida – the early cotton-planters. They desired federal money for Indian removal and internal improvements such as harbor dredging and bridges.[2]

These mainland interests were quite different than Key West, a remote community blessed with a large natural harbor and highly-profitable wrecking industry. The islanders greatly appreciated the company of US soldiers assigned there as protection against possible Seminole raids. Politically, Key West's commercial and municipal leaders would

---

1   Browne, pg. 90.
2   Doherty, pp. 2-3.

have identified as conservative Whigs and been supportive of Florida's economic improvements. Monroe County business interests opposed railroad construction and subsidies within the State, logically fearing a potential loss of port business and economic importance in Florida.

However isolated from national affairs they were, Key West residents in general, especially Bahamian Conchs, wanted to be left alone. They left the Bahamas for better wrecking opportunities and to escape an increasingly dictatorial and far-off British governing system. At Key West they wanted no intrusive government and only desired the freedom to pursue their vocation with little interference. Life for them in the 1840s was a limited awareness of Territorial, or later State government, and the US District Court which by 1828 was necessary to adjudicate shipwrecks. Beyond this contact with government were friendly relations with the few soldiers and workers at Forts Taylor and Jefferson.[3]

To better understand antebellum Key West politically it is important to view the island as not being heterogeneous, but more like a cosmopolitan New Orleans or Mobile, an aggregate of multiple nationalities and ethnic groups. To be sure, the newspapers from those cities, as well as Pensacola, Tallahassee, Savannah, Wilmington, Richmond and New York had much to do with influencing the island's prevalent political views. It was logical that older residents like Walter C. Maloney, Sr., would be Whig in their political leanings; the younger generation like his son Walter C. Maloney, Jr. were "Southerners" of the Democratic party, especially since 1850 and amid increasing sectional turmoil.

Key West benefited from the rise of islander Stephen R. Mallory, a Catholic who began his career law clerking for Judge William Marvin. He rose to inspector of, then Collector of Customs at Key West and a popular leader in Florida's Democratic party. In 1850, Mallory was selected by Florida Whigs to succeed Democrat David Yulee-Levy as United States Senator from Florida. It is interesting that Mallory was not considered, before or after the war, to be a staunch advocate of Floridian independence. He certainly sought

---

3   Riley, pg. 226.

justice and equality in the Union for Florida, as well as deprecating war. His mentor Marvin was said to be "Southern-minded" and no doubt imparted these views to Mallory.

The 1830s saw the rise of "Jacksonian Democracy" and Key West was affected as was the rest of the Territory. The Democratic party, also early-known as "Jeffersonian Republicans," was a reaction to the aristocratic Whigs and home to the "common man." It emphasized protecting individual rights and State sovereignty against usurped federal authority. Democrats were also opposed to centralized banks and high protective tariffs, the latter protecting New England industry from foreign product competition and forcing the agricultural South to pay more for imported goods – Florida included.

Though remote from the tariff controversy between New England and the American South, mail ships brought regular news of an increasing sectional divide. Between 1808 and 1832, import/export tariffs which funded the federal government were the most important economic debate in the country. The industrializing North wanted high protective tariffs, the agricultural South desired low tariffs. By 1860, nearly 90% of all federal taxes were being paid by the South, and Northern States clamored for this money to be spent on river, harbor and rail projects within their States.

Given the island's small population with little if any agricultural land and very few African slaves, Key West fell into the group of Florida counties staunchly Democratic and opposed Statehood in the early 1840's.[4] In general, island politics beyond simple municipal services were not important to most citizens, with the most serious prewar political eruption coming in 1838 when citizens were divided over Mayor William Whitehead's move to support town government with occupational taxes.

Also in 1838, island residents elected two Monroe County delegates to the St. Joseph's convention: Joseph B. Browne and Judge William Marvin. They were sent to represent the county and help frame Florida's constitution of 1845. Otherwise, the town was quiet politically until growing sectional disputes in the latter 1850s shattered the calm.

---

4   Doherty, pg. 29.

Whigs were the primary territorial political party in Florida and dominated politics until 1850. The party's supporters were the propertied and commercial interests, and their dependent classes. Voters were attracted by the simple materialistic goals of that party – banks, benefits and protections for business interests, stimulation of internal improvements, sound financial policies, and educational initiatives. By 1850, the Whigs were the party of national unity, North, South, East and West, but abolitionist, nativist and sectional forces were undermining their power. After nullification and tariff issues of the 1830s and 1840s drove wedges between North and South, the Southern wing of the Democratic party began re-calculating the value of political union with the North. From 1850 onward, the word "secession" became more commonly heard.[5]

Florida's tallies in both State and national elections reveal the political tenor of the State, as voters moved away from Whigs and toward Democrats. After Statehood on March 3, 1845, Democrat William Dunn Moseley of North Carolina became Florida's first governor, 1845-1848. Moseley was a strict constructionist of the Constitution and opposed federal intervention into strictly State affairs. It is worth pointing out that Florida's ratification of the Constitution in 1845 had more to do with expediency and commercial development rather than patriotism or nationalism. Gov. Mosely was typical of this generation which was conservative toward the growth of national powers and highly protective of their own.

In the 1848 national election, Florida, especially central and eastern, and younger men, voted 57% for the popular military hero and Whig, Gen. Zachary Taylor – 4120 votes to 3083, with Monroe County voting for Democrat Lewis Cass. An ardent advocate of popular sovereignty for the territories and leaving internal issues to local voters, Cass's name resonated with Monroe County residents who recalled him as the US Secretary of War in 1836 who sent troops to Key West for protection from Indian raids.

---

5   *Ibid.*, pg. 49.

It was the "Mexican Cession" – the outcome of the war with Mexico -- that led to Civil War as the territories gained became the battleground between Northern and Southern disputes over access and political control. It is very clear at this point that there had developed two very distinct cultures, and countries, North and South.

In 1847, influential Sen. John C. Calhoun of South Carolina denounced Northern efforts to restrict Southern labor access in the newly-acquired territories. He asked Southerners to abandon the Whig & Democratic parties, "shun their conventions" & support a Southern party. The Missouri Compromise of 1820 revealed to Calhoun the need for a strictly Southern party to counter-balance an increasingly powerful North.[6]

In 1850, despite longtime Whig control of Florida's legislature, Democrats won a majority in the State House & Senate. With the North-South divide increasing at this time, many Democrats favored immediate withdrawal from union if Southern demands for equality in the Union and territories were not agreed to. They looked hopefully for a sense of justice from the North and an end to sectionalism. Florida's US Senators then were Democrat David Levy-Yulee & Whig Jackson Morton. Yulee was a strong railroad supporter and devotee of Calhoun.

Florida's Whig Governor-elect Thomas Brown, a Virginian and War of 1812 veteran, delivered his inaugural address on October 1, 1849. He expressed grave concern over the national controversies centering on African slavery, pledging his adherence to the sovereignty of the States, the rights of the South in the Union, and strict adherence to the Constitution. He condemned the "intrigues of partisan politicians" which had made disunion and secession household words. "I believe," he warned, "that the Northern fanatics have done much to weaken the attachment and reverence of the people for the Union; and I fear as much has been done by Southern demagogues as Northern fanatics."

Brown opposed Southern conventions to discuss increasing Northern sectionalism stating that any convention "was revolutionary and inexpedient before any overt act of aggression on Southern rights in the Union were committed." Brown spoke thusly after Senator Levy-Yulee suggested to Calhoun a meeting of Southern governors to discuss a convention of Southern States "to devise means for mutual

---

6   Holt, pg. 268.

protection" and formation of a Southern political party to offset the purely sectional Republican party of the North. The Whig press in Florida approved Brown's course, while the Democratic press almost as unanimously opposed it."[7]

Though Florida's other Senator, Morton, was a Whig, his views on the sectional disputes did not coincide with most of the Whig hierarchy and were similar to his colleague, Yulee. He asserted that the Nashville Convention in early June, 1850 was designed to save the Union if possible or to save the South if it were not. Morton supported the Convention's goal and asked Brown in 1850 what it would take for him to calculate the true value of the Union for the South, presuming that the Convention would suggest such means and measures for the South to preserve her liberty and independence. Morton added "Call this revolutionary if you choose and make the most of it."[8]

The results of the election of 1850 seemed to show that Floridians were not yet ready to support the cause of secession or disunion," though the Whig party had been shaken with only two years to live. Many pro-Union public meetings were held across the State, usually organized by Whigs, though one was sponsored in Key West by strict constructionist Democrats.[9] A telling statistic which guided late antebellum political affiliations and voting in Florida was this: "Between 1850 and 1860 the number of South Carolina-born inhabitants of Florida almost doubled, and the number of Georgians increased by about 50 percent. The largest number of non-native Floridians were from Georgia and South Carolina, in that order, and together comprised about one-third of the total population by 1860."[10]

By 1850, Stephen R. Mallory of Key West had become a well-known and well-spoken Democrat active in the State's organization. Marvin was most likely consulted for his opinion on Mallory's ascent to Florida senator. As Whigs controlled the State Legislature which appointed Senators to represent Florida in the national Senate, Whig moderates were concerned in early 1850 about Sen. Levy Yulee's participation in Calhoun's Nashville Convention, called by the latter

---

7 Doherty, pp. 36-39.
8 Doherty, pp. 39-40.
9 *Ibid.*, pg. 49.
10 *Ibid.*, pp. 56-57.

to consider immediate secession. Mallory, though a Democrat but considered far more moderate than Yulee, was selected to be a Florida senator. Mallory might have been considered a lesser evil despite holding similar viewpoints as Yulee, but railroad development intrigue may have been involved as well. Monroe County Democrats interested in protecting Key West's shipping prominence were opposed to Yulee's Fernandina to Cross Keys railroad – and Florida Whigs were prominent in a projected Jacksonville to Pensacola railroad.[11]

Mallory was in good favor with Whigs given his respect for the Constitution and articulate defense of Southern equality in the union. Senator Henry Clay of Kentucky recognized this admirable trait in Mallory. The Florida Sentinel wrote on April 8th, 1851: "Mr. Mallory happened to be in Havana during Mr. Clay's late visit to the island, and in response to the hope expressed by the latter, that Florida had been fortunate in her change of Senators, securing one who would stand by the Union, Mr. Mallory declared himself a Democrat and friend of the Union, on the basis of the [1850] Compromise."[12]

1852 was a year of decisive Democratic victories in Florida, including a 60% vote tally for Democrat Franklin Pierce over Whig Winfield Scott. Pierce supported the Kansas-Nebraska Act, acceptable by the South, and in 1854 supported the Ostend Manifesto encouraging Cuban annexation if Spain refused a US offer of purchase. It was denounced by the North and in Europe, but attractive to Key West merchants and investors. Democrats consistently condemned Whigs for betraying the South's interests.

The same year Democrat James C. Broome of Leon County defeated Whig George T. Ward to become Florida's third governor, 1853-1857. A South Carolinian and strict constructionist, his numerous vetoes of the Whig-controlled legislature earned him the sobriquet "veto governor."

Florida voted 57% for Democrat James Buchanan over Know-Nothing Millard Fillmore in 1856. The secretive, anti-Catholic Know-Nothings were anathema to Key Westers, and opposed Southern migration to the Territories. Georgia's Alexander Stephens was said

---

11 Durkin, pp. 36-38. See also Doherty, pg. 143.
12 Durkin, pg. 49. See also Doherty pp. 47-48.

to be convinced that Know-Nothingism revealed the longings of New England for a Northern form of wage slavery. Stephens was fond of referring to New England's elite as the 'Cod Fish aristocracy'.

Florida's Catholic missionary beginnings date back to the 1550's at St. Augustine but the faith was not formalized at Key West until the construction of St. Mary by the Sea in 1852. This is the third oldest parish in Florida.

The year 1854 was the last statewide race run by Florida Whigs. Many moved into the Know-Nothing party as "nationalism" was the only remaining issue they could support.[13] The anti-immigrant Know Nothings and sectional Republican parties had displaced the Whigs nationally in 1855 as the only opponents of the Democratic party, and the die was cast for final confrontation.[14]

Diarist William Hackley noted in early-October 1855 his sense of a "foreign element" - perhaps Bahamian Conchs - dominating the island politically. He wrote of a recent island election for local officers and that he did not vote. "The Key Wester had a ticket which was badly beat" and that the "foreign element here is too strong for them and always will be." The population of then was about 2,000 white people, "not 200 male and female are native-born Americans."[15]

In 1856 Florida elected its fourth governor, Democrat Madison S. Perry of Alachua County. Perry was a South Carolinian, a strict constructionist of the US Constitution. Deeply concerned with the new sectional Republican party and, foreseeing secession, in 1858 he began urging the reestablishment of Florida militia in case of emergency. At the end of his term in late 1861, he served as colonel of the Seventh Florida Regiment.

The demise of the national Whig party created a grave concern that a Republican presidential candidate, hostile to Southern interests, might win the 1856 election. The *Raleigh* (North Carolina) *Standard* declaring on Oct. 4, 1856 "that the Union could not survive the election" of Republican John Fremont, and resistance advised should that party be victorious. This may well have prompted secession in 1856.

---

13 Tebeau, pg. 176.
14 Holt, pg. 805.
15 Hackley diary, October 15, 1855.

Fear of a Fremont victory was sufficient for Governors John Wise of Virginia, James Adams of South Carolina, and Herschel Johnson of Georgia to meet in Raleigh with Gov. Thomas Bragg on Oct. 13, 1856 to discuss a plan of action should Fremont be elected. It is likely that Gov. Perry would have been advised of his fellow governors' opinions.

The course that Florida would follow in 1860 was certain by November's national election date. Sixteen - and all of the largest - newspapers in the State supported Florida's independence; ten supported the Constitutional Unionists.[16]

Key West historian Jefferson Browne wrote that national political contests had not caused any serious concerns among island residents until 1860, and "that year saw the initial rumblings of national upheaval that was to destroy constitutional guarantees." He added that this "stirred our people to the depths."[17]

In the national election held in Nov. 1860, Florida voted over 62% for Democrat John C. Breckinridge in preference to Constitutional Unionist John Bell. Monroe County voted unanimously for Breckinridge; Democrats carried 31 of the 38 Florida counties and tallied at least 45% of the vote in each except three – Clay, Santa Rosa and Escambia. In the planting counties of Alachua and Marion, Breckinridge won over 75% of the vote. As an indication of support throughout the South, Breckinridge won more support in Florida than any other State except one.

In 1860 there was little enthusiasm for "unionism" in Florida as author Ralph Wooster has written regarding the State's January convention, with most ready for independence but only differing in tactics. The "cooperationists" wanted to await the action of Georgia and Alabama, while the "secessionists" favored immediate action. The former, mostly conservative Whigs, argued that should those two States not withdraw then Florida's action "would be an empty gesture." But when it came to a final vote all but seven of the "cooperationists voted for independence.[18]

---

16 Tebeau, pg. 178.
17 Browne, pg. 129.
18 Wooster, pg. 79.

Beyond the *Key of the Gulf* paper which William Ward began editing in 1857, islanders were reading the newspapers and absorbing the viewpoints found in the arriving newspapers of cities from New Orleans to New York City – the latter being a Democratic stronghold. The sectional divide was never so acute as it was true that few Northerners read Southern newspapers and few Southerners read Northern newspapers.

Key West was indeed a "Southern" town with a truly polyglot of residents from all corners of the globe, though imbibing the prevailing political opinion and sentiment of their section. Many, if not all, Florida political leaders since before Statehood agreed with South Carolinian John C. Calhoun in viewing the United States as a federated, or confederated, union of equal and sovereign States – and not a "nation." In the eyes of most Key Westers, including those from the North, Florida was a sovereign State and its citizens fully capable of determining its political relations with other States, including forming a more perfect union with those of a similar mind. And most understood "secession" as did the venerable Nathaniel Macon of North Carolina who stated that "the best guard to public liberty and to public justice that could be desired."[19]

Actions that certainly affected the views of islanders was the May 9th Democratic meeting in Jacksonville, resolving that "we are of the opinion that the rights of the citizens of Florida are no longer safe in the Union and think that she should raise the banner of secession and invite her Southern sisters to join her." Another meeting at Gainesville on May 21st resolved that "if in consequence of Northern fanaticism the irrepressible conflict must come we are prepared to meet it." Another resolved that "we would sacrifice our lives before yielding to the Black Republican Party."[20]

At the Democratic National Convention at Charleston in late April, 1860, Florida joined Mississippi, South Carolina, Louisiana, Texas and Arkansas in rallying behind the "Alabama Platform" and William L. Yancey of that State. All were convinced that their principles were in accordance with the United States Constitution and determined that northern Democrats should not dictate the party platform. The

---

19 Sitterson, pg. 32.

20 Davis, pg. 42.

issue before the Democratic Party was well-stated by the *Richmond Examiner* of March 6, 1860: "Shall Democratic minorities in Republican States be allowed to shape the policy of the Democratic party" regarding issues existing only in the Democratic States? Not only was Ward's *Key of the Gulf* printing this, but newspapers including the *Richmond Examiner* were read by islanders.[21]

Monroe County Democrats gathered at City Hall on May 23, 1860, appointing Joseph B. Browne, James Filor, George L. Bowne, Asa Tift & editor William H. Ward as delegates to the June 4th Democratic Convention at Quincy. The delegates were instructed to have Monroe County represented at the upcoming June, 1860 Democratic National Convention at Baltimore, where Key West resident George L. Browne served as one of six Florida delegates. All supported the John C. Breckinridge and Joseph Lane presidential ticket.[22]

As Floridians, islanders would hold nothing in common with the Republican platform. Many had arrived from foreign countries and feared the nativist, Know-Nothing element amongst Republicans. The party itself was a polyglot of Northern Whigs, Free-Soilers, Transcendentalists and anti-Catholic Know-Nothings – Lincoln was a longtime Whig and though concerned about the extreme nativism of the Know-Nothings, needed their political support. Republicans were charged with keeping sectional tensions alive, despite the Compromise of 1850 which was to have ended it, "for its own nefarious purposes," and "the result could be nothing but ultimate disaster for the American nation." Fearing the worst from Lincoln's victory, National Democratic leader August Belmont stated in late 1860 that "the Republican leaders are utterly blind to all dangers," and "I do not believe that the party intends making any concessions" for peace, preferring their party over the welfare of the country. Apparently knowing the candidate from his State well, the editor of the *Illinois State Register* lamented the morning after election day: "The election of Mr. Lincoln will be a national calamity ..."[23] Lincoln's plurality in November 1860 "as the first president to be elected upon the sectional issue of antagonism to the South and its institutions, stirred up the people of Key West,

---

21   Dumond, pg. 35.
22   Hesseltine, pg. 282.
23   Silbey, pg. 26; 32. See also Doherty, pg. 22.

in common with the rest of the Southland."[24] The election of the new Republican president was promptly followed by two financial panics on the New York Stock Exchange as banks in Charleston, Washington, Baltimore and Philadelphia suspended specie payments. As the South withdrew and repudiated loans to Northern banks, business failures in 1861 exceeded those following the Panic of 1857.[25]

The address by thirty Southern congressmen to constituents, published on December 14, 1860, two days after the Monroe County Courthouse meeting, was telegraphed to newspapers throughout the South. The document stated that "the Republican congressmen would make no concessions and that all hope of reasonable compromise was futile." On December 23rd, Georgia Senator Robert Toombs telegraphed Southern newspapers that "the refusal of the Republicans to accept the Crittenden amendments was indicative of their general hostility toward the South," concluding that "I have put the test fairly and frankly ... and now I tell you upon the faith of a true man that all further looking to the North for security for your constitutional rights in the Union ought to be instantly abandoned. It is fraught with nothing but ruin to yourselves and your posterity." The strenuous efforts to find compromise with Republicans reveals many "Unionist" Southerners resisting talk of independence, while Republican intransigence increased the number of Southern States scheduling conventions to discuss continuance in political union with the North.[26] The only opposition to withdrawal in Florida came from those wanting to follow rather than precede, that of Alabama and Georgia. Florida's vote for independence was passed by a vote of 62 to 7.[27]

Florida became a free and independent nation by the vote of her people through elected delegates, on January 10, 1861. In concert with other States which had withdrawn from the 1789 federation, a Southern convention was to assemble at Montgomery, Alabama on February 4 to form a provisional government, using the 1789 Constitution as a framework.

---

24   Browne, pg. 90.
25   Potter, pg. 119.
26   Dumond, pg. 192.
27   Dumond, pg. 198-199.

On February 9, 1861, the congress unanimously elected Jefferson Davis of Mississippi and Alexander Stephens of Georgia, as president and vice-president respectively, of the new American Confederacy. Importantly, commissioners were appointed to treat with the United States government for the division of territories and debts, and to arrange for future friendly relations. In particular, the commissioners were to arrange compensation for arsenals and forts constructed in the former States of the US.[28]

After Florida's independence was declared in early January 1861 James Buchanan remained US president until his successor was inaugurated on March 4th. The possibility of compromise was hoped for by those who believed that the Union could be preserved, the rights of the South preserved and a reconstructed union acceptable to that section. Buchanan thought the new president would urge a constitutional convention of the States to peacefully iron out their differences.

For the incoming Lincoln administration, the question of import and export tariffs became a paramount issue as Northern businessmen foresaw trouble in the new Southern Confederacy's virtual free tariff on goods. The South was an agricultural section and manufactured little – and Northern business had grown wealthy through protective tariffs that benefited only the North. With the revenue from Southern ports gone and the South's lower tariff attracting European shipping, disaster for Northern business was in the offing - imported British goods might be smuggled from the Confederacy to the detriment of Northern manufacturing. Southern independence could not be allowed.

By the end of February tense relations existed after the unsuccessful Washington Peace Conference earlier that month and a continuing and volatile standoff at Fort Sumter and Fort Pickens at Pensacola. Confederate States official commissioners sent to Washington were being ignored. Buchanan understood that waging war against a State was treason according to Article III, Section 3 of the US Constitution,

An attempt on the part of some States to hold, by military force, an unwilling State in the union, must inevitably lead to the worst form of internecine war. If successful, it would result in the establishment of a new and totally different union than that established by the Constitution of 1789 which was a union of consent, not of force, and

---

28 *Ibid.*, pg. 206; 211-212.

comprised of constitutional equals. The result of civil war would be a "union" of victors and vanquished joined by bayonet rule "and congealed in blood." – not of equals.[29]

Senator Stephen Mallory of Key West, prior to Florida's withdrawal, served with Senators Jefferson Davis of Mississippi and John Slidell of Louisiana (born in New York) on a steering committee which resolved on January 6, that "as soon as may be, the rest of the Southern States should leave the Union." Hearing this, Key Westers would certainly have been influenced by Mallory's high position and recommendations for their political future in or out of the union.

Mallory was no "fire-eater" and reportedly cool toward the secession resolution, lending truth to the *Charleston Mercury* of January 17th writing that some "Southern politicians have been stumbling blocks in the way of Southern advancement." Judah Benjamin of Louisiana underscored this as he wrote that public sentiment for secession everywhere in the South "certainly outran the politicians."[30]

Mallory addressed the United States Senate for the last time after Florida's independence and spoke eloquently as a Floridian and in words that certainly influenced Key Westers strongly. He stressed that his State had entered the union upon a basis of full equality with all other States, including the original thirteen, and continued to hold that view. He stated that "From the Union governed by the Constitution as the Founding Fathers had made it, there breathed not a secessionist upon her soil ..." Reluctantly admitting the impetus for Florida's actions on January 10th, he continued: "But a deep sense of injustice, inequality and insecurity, produced by causes all too well known, had been brought home to the reason and patriotism of her people; and to secure and maintain these rights which the Constitution no longer afforded them, they had placed the State of Florida out of the Union."[31]

No longer Florida's US Senator, Mallory became involved in what was known as the "Pickens Episode" after Florida troops took possession of Pensacola's navy yard, plus Forts Barrancas and MacRae. Fort Pickens across the bay remained garrisoned by US troops, like

---

29 Dumond, pg. 220.
30 Durkin, pg. 121.
31 Durkin, pg. 122.

Fort Taylor at Key West. Mallory first urged an assault upon Pickens by Florida troops, but later realized it could only be achieved "at an immense sacrifice of life and the total annihilation of the garrison."[32]

Mallory also used his prewar naval associations to ward off US warships entering the bay to avoid a confrontation, as well as to prevent the landing of reinforcements at Pickens. Had the efforts to prevent war prevailed at Washington and peaceful settlement achieved, the Key Wester's efforts to avoid bloodshed at Pensacola would have been widely praised.

The year 1861 had begun with the excitement of Florida's independence from the United States, a hopeful end to the political divisiveness that existed within the old American union. A new beginning was in store. The US Army soldiers at the barracks had become friends and customers of island merchants, and residents expected the US government to accept Florida's decision and begin negotiations for reimbursement for funds expended on the forts and other improvements made to date. A peaceful acceptance of Florida's desire for independence may have been anticipated by its citizens but was not to become a reality.

---

32 Congressional Globe, 36th Congress, 2nd Session, p. 485.

CHAPTER 3:

A Parting of the Ways - The First Year of War

> Of themselves, [forts] they can never exert and influence dangerous to public liberty; but as the means of preserving peace, and as obstacles to an invader, their influence and power are immense."
>
> –Lt. Henry Halleck, 1843

On January 10, 1861, prominent Key Westers Asa F. Tift, Winer Bethel and William Pinckney, elected by Key Westers to represent them, joined delegates from across Florida to solemnly rescind the March 3, 1845 ratification of the United States Constitution, and declare the State of Florida a sovereign and independent republic.

The idea of individual States withdrawing from the 1789 Union was not new in 1860-61. The New England States threatened secession on four occasions: the Louisiana Purchase of 1803, the National Embargo of 1807, the War of 1812 and the Mexican War. Anything New Englanders viewed as diluting their political power in the union would provoke talk of secession.[1]

After South Carolina's tariff resistance in 1832, several Southern States, which generated some 85% of federal revenue from import/export tariffs, began recalculating the value of political union with those in the North.

Prior to 1861 it was commonly held that the States were individually sovereign, since they collectively created the federal

---
1   DeRosa, pg. 292.

agent in Washington, DC to which they had delegated certain, enumerated powers to; all others they retained. To satisfy reluctant States who feared losing sovereignty to the new federal agency, the Tenth Amendment was inserted to ensure that all power and authority not specifically delegated, remained with the States. Beyond this, New York, Virginia and Rhode Island specifically noted in their ratifications that they reserved the right to withdraw from this new union if they saw fit. This is important to remember.

Many Northern newspapers supported States withdrawing from the union after the Republican plurality victory in November 1860. Horace Greeley of the *New York Tribune* wrote on Nov. 9, 1861: "We hope never to live in a republic whereof one section is pinned to the residue by bayonets." Eight days later the *Providence (Rhode Island) Evening Press* wrote that sovereignty "necessarily includes what we call the 'right of secession'" and "this right must be maintained" unless we would establish "colossal despotism" against which the founding fathers "uttered their solemn warnings." In the Midwest, Chicago's *Daily Times* editorialized on Nov. 21, 1860 that "Like it or not the cotton States will secede," and Southerners will regain their "sense of independence and honor."[2]

To underscore historian Browne's view of the town leadership as "strongly pro-Southern," the voters of Monroe County in November 1860 overwhelmingly supported John C. Breckinridge of Kentucky for president and his running mate Joseph Lane of Oregon.

The secession of South Carolina on December 20, 1860 was quickly followed by a proclamation from Gov. Madison S. Perry for a convention of the people to take into consideration Florida's present and future relations towards the Union. Former-mayor and historian Walter C. Maloney wrote of the island's response to the Governor's message:

> In pursuance of a previous notice for that purpose, the citizens of the island in larger numbers than had ever before met to discuss any question, theological or political, assembled at the County Courthouse on the evening of the 12th of December 1860. The city newspaper of that time, the *Key of the Gulf* reported:

---

2   DiLorenzo, pg. 107.

A mass meeting of our citizens was convened at the County Court House on the evening of the 12th instant, for the purpose of nominating and electing delegates to the State Convention, to assemble at Tallahassee on the 3rd day of January, 1861, for the purpose of taking into consideration the dangers incident to the position of this State in the Federal Union. After John P. Baldwin was elected chairman and recording secretaries Charles Tift and Peter Crusoe appointed, the object of the meeting was explained and several speeches followed. US District Judge William Marvin was a unionist, and thought it wise to await the Border States decision on independence, as did William C. Dennis and William Pinckney. S.J. Douglas favored a convention of Southern States to demand constitutional guarantees from the Northern States, and withdraw if refused. Former Mayor Walter Maloney was for "the Union first, the Union last, and the Union always." Connecticut native Asa F. Tift, *Key of the Gulf* editor William Ward, J.L. Tatum, Joseph Beale Browne and six others spoke in favor of Florida's independence.[3]

Described as "spirited," the meeting of residents was not over until midnight, and Maloney the only speaker in favor of remaining in the Union. Nominated to serve as Monroe County delegates were Winer Bethel, William Pinckney and Judge Marvin. The first two received near-unanimous votes, Judge Marvin achieved a bare majority and withdrew as his official position would cause difficulty as a delegate, Asa F. Tift was elected in his place.

Emily Holder, diarist and wife of Fort Jefferson's physician wrote that "the secessionists in Key West were victorious and boldly announced they would take Fort Taylor on the island. A rather decided secessionist told our Fort Jefferson commander that they would starve us out. His reply was that he would drop a cannon ball into his house ..." [4]

At Tallahassee on January 10, 1861, Bethel, Pinckney and Asa Tift spoke in favor of and voted to repeal Florida's ratification of the

---

3   Maloney, pg. 63-64.

4   Schmidt III, pg. 9.

US Constitution. The following day the Ordinance of Secession was signed and Florida became an independent nation – the Confederate States of America was yet to be formed. On that date Key West officially became a town in the independent republic of Florida, the forts within a "foreign" country and an expectation that Florida would appoint commissioners to arrange compensation to the United States for the cost of the forts and other properties. Florida would remain in its national period until April 22, 1861, when it ratified the Confederate States Constitution.

"Quickness is the essence of the war." Sun Tzu

Fort Taylor's commander, Capt. James Brannan, watched nervously as the townspeople embraced independence and sent their delegates to Tallahassee. He had written his superiors on December 11th that he heard from reliable sources of Florida's probable action – this was before South Carolina's independence – that he anticipated an attempt to seize his fort when this occurred. He added that his intention was to hold the fort at all hazards.[5] Brannan's communication with Washington took time with his letters taking a week and a half to reach Washington. He wrote that given his small command, both unfinished Forts Taylor and Jefferson were "at the mercy of a party which could be transported in a fishing smack," and ordered that several warships be stationed offshore to prevent landings.[6]

Brannan was also concerned that an armed force from the mainland might suddenly appear and seize both forts. The only resistance to such an event would be from his small company of artillerymen quartered in wooden barracks nearly two miles away near today's intersection of Palm Avenue and White Streets. Living within the fort then were paymaster Felix Senac, draughtsman James Clapp and a few laborers contracted by the government.

Brannan's true dilemma as a military officer was identifying where his fundamental "loyalty" lay and to whom or what he was obedient, and being unsure, requested orders from Washington. His education at West Point and oath taken to defend the Constitution of the United States

---

5   Camp, pg. 34.

6   Schmidt III, pg. 6-7.

would have seemed to be a sufficient guide as it had been to many other officers. One cannot defend something they do not understand. Brannan was born at Washington, DC and appointed to the academy from Indiana in 1837 and graduated in 1841 ranking 23rd in a class of 52.

A text used at the school was Philadelphian William Rawle's *A View of the Constitution* published in 1825 and hailed by a respected Boston journal as "a safe and intelligent guide" for understanding the Constitution. Rawle related that the essence of our republican institutions was the question of who can make or unmake a government, concluding that the people of a State may at any time alter or abolish the constitution they have formed. As each State individually ratified and accepted the document, each State could rescind and discontinue being governed by that document.[7] Had Brannan thought more deeply about his fortress's reason for existence being the defense of the State of Florida and its citizens, he could have regarded its decision for independence as the end of his purpose there. He would have peacefully awaited the arrival of Florida officials to take possession of the fort and negotiate reimbursement for all with the US government.

But Brannan was a 41-year-old career army officer in 1860, comfortable with following orders, influenced by other career officers commanding ships in the harbor and loyal to his employer. Major Anderson at Fort Sumter, a fellow West Point graduate and superior officer, had seized that fort the previous month and no doubt provided Brannan with a path to follow.

The fort commander's character may also be understood from an 1855-1856 diary of a US land official in the Keys, who wrote of regular army men like Brannan as "arrogant, self-conceited," as well as "generally dictatorial and over bearing in their intercourse which may be the result of habit."[8] In particular, a New York soldier at Key West later wrote of "Brannan being a good commander but a proud arrogant man."[9] He may well have reminded older Key Westers of US Navy Commodore David Porter who "ruled the island as a despot," appropriating wood and livestock at will from islanders.[10]

---

7   Kennedy, pg. 146-147.
8   Langley & Parks, pg. 16.
9   Schmidt III, pg. 190.
10   Langley & Parks, pg. 12.

Also, despite the *Charleston Mercury* imploring "the people of Florida to take possession of their coastal forts and ports" in early January 1861 -- specifically mentioning Key West and Pensacola – the "Island Guards" militia at Key West were ill-equipped to accomplish this with force if needed. Brannan's 44-or so soldiers had more modern weapons as well as the fort's cannon. Additionally, the US Navy ships in the harbor cordoned off the island and restricted news, effectively shutting off residents' communication with the outside world. Still, a rumor circulated of an expedition being fitted out at Charleston to seize one or both forts which was certainly concerning to Brannan.

Brannan had requested orders from Washington to guide his actions given Florida's impending independence, which was replied to on January 4, 1861 but did not arrive in his hand via steamer until January 27th.[11] As he socialized frequently with locals in earlier days, he well-knew the political leanings of the Monroe County delegates sent to Tallahassee and those who elected them. His Union-friendly counsel included Judge Marvin, Collector of Customs Charles Howe and former-Mayor Walter Maloney, Sr. Judge Marvin advised that local and State authorities were independence-minded, as well as most prominent Key West leaders, and Brannan was also being influenced by a fellow officer fearful "that the product of his engineering skill would fall into the hands of enemies of the Union." [12]

No doubt aware of the move into Fort Sumter at Charleston in the darkness of night nearly three weeks earlier, Brannan had clearly planned to replicate it. He initially directed workers to seal up all openings on the lower level of Fort Taylor to prevent entry.

Pressured by other officers and acting without orders, on Saturday January 12th Brannan committed to a plan of barricading his forty-four men inside the fort. So as not to arouse any suspicions in town, he attended the religious services Sunday as was his custom and at midnight assembled his men at the barracks. From there they stealthily marched in small squads south of the sleeping town to escape detection and into the fort. The move was accomplished by sunrise and Key West awoke to fait' accompli on Monday, January 14th. A soldier inside the now-barricaded fort wrote: "Great was the

---

11   Schmidt III, pg. 11.
12   *Ibid.*, pg. 13.

chagrin ... in the town." Key West had awakened to a new world that Monday morning, January 14th, their former soldier friends were now an enemy occupier.[13] The move certainly alarmed islanders – and other Floridians – and regarded as the first overt act of hostility by the federal government and beginning of hostilities.[14]

In a message to his superiors afterward, Brannan explained his actions as being "In consequence of the recent seizure by unauthorized persons of several forts and arsenals in the Southern States, I have placed my entire command in Fort Taylor for the purpose of protecting it. I shall, until orders from the General Government to the contrary, defend it."[15] He boastfully added that "the fort has seventy, 8-inch Columbiads, which will send a ball four miles; twenty 24-pound howitzers which flank the fort, twelve 12-pound howitzers, and a company of artillerymen."[16]

All had now changed. Upon their return from Tallahassee, Tift, Bethel and Pinckney found local soldiers barricaded within Fort Taylor, defensive embankments thrown up on the town-facing side with artillery trained on the residents. Any landward approach across the 1200-foot wooden causeway to the fort's reinforced gate could now be swept with murderous rifle and cannon fire. Before abandoning their barracks across the island, Brannan removed cannon barrels from the wheeled carriages there, covering the latter with tarps to complete his deception. Brannan's hostile act generated unnecessary animosity while Florida Unionists desperately sought constitutional compromise and a peaceful end to the political tensions with the North. His actions also reveal a distorted view of the island as bristling with enemies though residents owned few weapons beyond old fowling pieces, dueling pistols and knives. Key Westers were simply not in a position to contest the fort's ownership.

Brannan was no doubt relieved when a ship from Boston carrying an artillery company passed the island enroute to Fort Jefferson on

---

13 Schmidt III, pg. 13-14.
14 Wilson, pg. 137.
15 Camp, Jr. pg. 35.
16 Schmidt III, pg. 11.

January 18th to occupy the virtually-empty fortification and prevent its possible seizure by Florida militia.[17]

In fairness to Brannan's fear of being attacked, rumors were circulating that a mainland force had organized and was on the way to capture Fort Taylor in Florida's name. He also feared the "Island Guards" militia were being reinforced and armed with better weapons that would keep he and his soldiers isolated within the fort. One Fort Taylor soldier stated that "we expect a party from the mainland … we take turns on the watch and stop every man that comes along. The city folks say they will whip us – if we come to the city." In reality, Brannan not only had his guns trained on the town but also the guns of the several US warships in the harbor that would ward off any amphibious assault – which Florida's fledgling military was wholly incapable of.

Nonetheless, the navy ships in the harbor initiated a blockade to prevent islanders from providing intelligence to Florida authorities regarding ship movements, troop strength and fort weapons. While this was occurring and fearful of the island becoming a bloody battleground, many Bahamian families and others began departing for their homes.

This uneasy standoff between the town and Fort Taylor's guns continued through January 27th, when Brannan received orders from Washington approving his investment of the fort. That same date a *New York Times* correspondent within the fort wrote that "We have put ourselves on a war footing. Fort Taylor, if molested, will be defended, and it is perfectly able to make a vigorous resistance." Little changed during the month of February as the tension between fort and town did not abate. Brannan could only communicate with his government through the *USS Mohawk* in the harbor, which also had its cannons trained on the quiet town of "secessionists." [18]

In early March, Brannan reported to Washington that "everything is quiet at Key West to this date," and the anticipated attack from the mainland had not occurred. The town atmosphere remained pro-Southern as Brannan reported "flags of the Southern Confederacy raised upon the stores by various citizens," adding that it would be unlikely for any resident of the island to hold office under the US government-

---

17   *Ibid.*, pg. 19.
18   Schmidt III, 16-23.

sanction unless protected by federal bayonets. In spite of this a small and tepid undercurrent of pro-Union support appeared as several merchants and residents expressed support for Brannan's actions. The merchants especially were concerned with the loss of business and fearful that military action could cause inventory losses – and at the same time saw new customers in the arriving occupation force.[19]

In response to Brannan's actions Henry Mulrennan raised a "Republic of Florida" flag, likely the Bonnie Blue with a large white star, over his shop on March 12th, dubbing it "Fort Jefferson Davis." Addressing a note to the fort's commander he demanded the acknowledgement of the "declaration of independence on the part of the Southern States" and a salute to the "Republic of Florida" flag.[20]

Despite those supporting Brannan for political or business reasons, events since January created overwhelming support for Florida's independence on the island as those initially hesitant or opposed to secession may well have been converted by Brannan's suspicion of islanders and hostile actions. As illustrated by historian E. Merton Coulter, the sense of gaining independence "was action, promising brilliant new experiences, the romance of a new country, a future with wide horizons; Unionism could offer little more than a continuation of the evil days which had beset the South for a generation." This was certainly true at Key West.[21]

Encouraged by some merchants and civilians expressing support for he and his men, Brannan began small patrols across the fort's artillery-swept causeway to the town. One soldier wrote of officers followed by residents on the street, insulted, and threats of residents soon attacking Fort Taylor and "loud in their denunciations of the [US] government." A Navy lieutenant at this time expressed his belief that "nearly all the offices of the town are now filled by violent disunionists."

Brannan was much-relieved on March 25th when the steamer Daniel Webster arrived with 300 US soldiers aboard – 5 companies of artillerymen evacuated from Texas and commanded by Captain - soon - Major, William French who would succeed him in command

---

19 *Ibid.*, pg. 29.
20 Ogle, pg. 58.
21 Coulter, pg. 55.

of Fort Taylor. Thus reinforced and the secessionist populace quieted, Fort Taylor soldiers could now move more easily into the town as well as the entire island.

Commander W.H. Hutchings of the mail steamer *Atlantic* was providing intelligence to the new Confederate government and reported the arrival of enemy reinforcements. Asked then by US authorities at Fort Taylor to transport provisions to US troops at Pensacola, Hutchings refused as he considered it an act of treason to do so.

As this reinforcement occurred, *Key of the Gulf* editor William H. Ward traveled to Montgomery, Alabama, arriving on the first of April. He reported that US Judge William Marvin at Key West was to step down as he agreed with State secession. But Marvin quickly sided with Brannan's forces and held on to his post.

While consolidating their hold on the entire island during April, a reconnaissance of the island was made "with a view to the erection of any field works which may be required to enable the garrison of Fort Taylor ... to prevent a hostile landing" on the south shore and behind Fort Taylor. As the possibility of diplomatic recognition of the Confederate States was feared by Lincoln at this time, British warships and amphibious troops was the likely reason for considering new fortifications eventually built on the southern shore.[22]

Early on Friday morning, April 12th, 1861 came the collision at Fort Sumter in Charleston Harbor between an independent South Carolina and the small garrison of nearby Fort Moultrie, who had under cover of darkness on the previous December 20, slipped into Sumter and trained its guns on the sleeping town. This is precisely the event that Brannan duplicated. The US military on the island would not learn of the fort's bombardment until Friday, April 19th.

Despite his arrival with additional troops, French was bedeviled with open and pronounced independence sentiment on the island which he was determined to eliminate. On the day Fort Sumter was fired upon, French reported "several secession flags floated from buildings in view of the fort and upon the courthouse of the town." Frustrated, he issued immediate orders that no flag "other than our national one be permitted to fly over any public building."

---

22 Schmidt pp. 29-33.

French wrote Mayor John Baldwin on April 26th "complaining of the display of a secession flag from a building in town & displaying it on public grounds." Warning that if not stopped by the civil authority, "I have the power to do so by a summary process." [23]

After the Fort Sumter event demonstrated that no peaceful settlement was possible and French became more dictatorial, several Southern-born officers among the local fort garrisons, began resigning their commissions and departing for home. Mayor Baldwin, of British ancestry and also Collector of Customs at the time, soon departed his office for the Bahamas with his family remaining on the island. He no doubt saw dark days ahead for the island after sparring with French, and possible imprisonment for his leading role in the December 12, 1860 Courthouse meeting. His prewar acquaintance with Stephen Mallory, Felix Senac and Caleb Huse, all of whom would be involved in supplying the Confederacy from abroad, led him to profitable blockade-running ventures. His wife Amelia would eventually be deported under suspicion of passing intelligence to her husband.

Demonstrating that military intelligence continued reaching Florida authorities from the island, Capt. Francis Watlington, a New York City native living on the island since 1830, secretly relayed word to Florida Governor Perry on April 16th of the arrival of French's troops to the island.

To further strengthen his hold on the island, French met with a number of Key West citizens, including the new mayor, Connecticut-native and merchant Alexander Patterson, who agreed to cooperate with the military occupation. A recent steamer had also brought orders and commissions for new federal appointees on the island, including Fort Taylor draughtsman James Clapp who became US Marshal and whom French designated as the island's postmaster to control information coming to and leaving the island. French read his government's policy instructions to the assembled civilian appointees and, in particular, instructed acting-Mayor Patterson: "if unhappily rebellion or insurrection should actually exist at any time, you will then publish a proclamation, with which you will be furnished, suspending the writ of habeas corpus and immediately remove from the island all dangerous or suspected persons."

---

23 Schmidt III, pp. 35; 37; 42-43.

French's crackdown against Southern flags and symbols was paired with an effort to create the appearance of dominant "Unionism" on the island. The new US District Attorney, Thomas Boynton of Missouri, assisted with the formation of a "Union Volunteer Corps" on April 5, 1861 with former-Mayor Walter Maloney as group spokesman. In a well-publicized event that day, Mayor Patterson read a brief statement of their promise of loyalty to the United States government: "That we may assist in preserving the honor of our flag, upholding the laws, and quelling rebellion, do hereby agree to form a volunteer company, and hold ourselves subject to the order of the commander of the United States forces at Key West."[24]

During this solemn ceremony and after receiving their flag from Major French, "mutual expressions of fidelity [were] interchanged" and suitable entertainment provided, "the members of the company returned to the city and to their several avocations."[25] This group of primarily island merchants was to be later disbanded by a subsequent fort commander who as late as February 1863 continued to sense a dominant rebel sympathy among the populace, warning residents that "the disguised traitor merits the detestation of all loyal hearts."[26] He also disbanded elected the municipal government and returned the town to military rule.

Key West would not have a government in exile, as Pensacola later did when overwhelmed by enemy troops in May 1862. There, city leaders, official records and many citizens all relocated to Greenville, Alabama in May 1862 with the elected municipal government functioning through the end of the war.

As French continued his effort to suppress independence sentiment on the island, longtime Key West resident and chandler, Asa F. Tift, a native of Mystic, Connecticut, refused to coal the steamer *Atlantic* at his dock in late April as the vessel had been hired by the US military. As one of three Key West delegates voting for Florida's independence, Tift was notified that he was to "leave the island or be imprisoned in Fort Taylor."[27] Two days later French was infuriated by William H.

---

24 Schmidt III, pg. 52.
25 Browne, pp. 94-95.
26 Schmidt III, pg. 413.
27 *Ibid.*, pg. 41-42.

Ward's *Key of the Gulf* editorial which "was highly inflammatory as it espoused the cause of the secessionists." French spoke with several prominent residents who promised Ward would write no more editorials like this.

Throughout 1860 and into early 1861, William H. Ward's four-page newspaper, published weekly on Saturdays, was the most widely-known secession sheet in Florida – its masthead announcing "Ask Nothing But What is Right – Submit to Nothing That is Wrong." The editor broadcast in print his pro-independence views on the sectional disputes affecting the country, considering secession as a peaceful alternative to war.[28] Those like Ward saw clearly that there "was nothing immoral or evil in secession and the attempt of the South to establish its independence" or that "neither nature nor God had decreed" that a region of the earth's surface as politically diverse as America should be one nation forever.[29]

Rapidly losing patience with the highly visible pro-Southern feeling on the island, French warned the mayor on May 4th that reliable sources indicate "a strong effort to distress the inhabitants of this Key" is forthcoming, suggesting martial law, and that it was in his power to avoid this contingency. The mayor was to provide him with the muster rolls of any "military organization now existing" in Key West – meaning the "Island Guards" which he planned to disband.

French was again infuriated with Ward's early-May issue which he considered "more violent and incendiary than its previous numbers" and sure to elate the island's "rabid secessionists." French retaliated immediately by suspending the writ of habeas corpus on the island, the intent of which was "to arrest without molestation the parties suspected of uttering treasonable sentiments, etc." This allowed the military to arrest anyone, anytime, and in the sole judgement of the arresting soldier.[30] The fort commander announced a week later that he had ordered suppressed "the newspaper called the *Key of the Gulf* because it was uttering treasonable and threatening language against the judiciary and other United States officers."

---

28 Maloney, pp. 45-46.
29 Coulter, pg. 568.
30 Schmidt III, pg. 45.

French further directed the mayor to inform Ward that he was also under military surveillance, adding that "the fact of him not being in the cells of this fort for treason was simply a matter as to expediency and proper point in time ... at this date I have not deemed it advisable to follow this with any restrictions upon the municipal authorities or the citizens of the town." To underscore the tension between military and civilians, one of the fort's soldiers wrote that day that "the barbette guns on the face fronting the town are all in position ..." [31]

His newspaper outlawed and threatened with imprisonment in the fort, editor Ward bid farewell to his wife and child to serve in the Confederacy's navy. His press equipment was subsequently seized by New York troops to print a pro-Union paper. There is evidence that Ward survived the war but he never returned to the island. The island had been transformed into an armed camp filled with suspicion, informants, arbitrary arrests, petty humiliations and other indignities of military occupation. Such was the Key West of the war: dreading a knock at the door, islanders of all walks of life routinely had to endure occupation and life under military rule. One avoided being seen in public as Major French's stated policy was to remove from the island anyone appearing dangerous or suspicious.

French was unrelenting in his crackdown on residents he considered disloyal, and writing that "The sentiment on the key is strictly selfish." He distrusted residents expressing friendliness as perhaps secessionists patronizing him for favors, he came to believe that the Union man of today could well be the disunionist of tommorrow. Thinking that the solution may be the mass deportation of islanders, he "asked the mayor of Key West for lists of the inhabitants, extra mouths, etc., which will have to be fed by the United States." He ended the letter with "Extraneous people will have to leave"[32]

Additional heartburn for Maj. French and his provost marshal came from the feisty Caroline Lowe who, as legend has it often waved her Southern flag from the captain's walk above her home at Duval and Caroline Streets. Searches of the house did not locate the offending symbol as she apparently hid it in the staircase hollow newel post.[33]

---

31 *Ibid.,* pg. 46-47.
32 Schmidt III, pp. 45-46.
33 postcardsofoldkeywestblogspot.com, acc. 2.6.22.

Any official State of Florida correspondence with Key West elected officials was intercepted and French ordered the mayor to "resist with force any encroachments" by Florida authorities who might attempt any exercise of authority.[34] In May French accused Magistrate and County Clerk of Court Peter Crusoe, who had served in this position ten years, of somehow tampering with Fort Taylor's ammunition. He considered Crusoe "a notoriously designing and dangerous man" and determined to hang or imprison him in what was becoming the island's "Bastille" – Fort Taylor. It is highly possible that French was misinformed by past political opponents or enemies of Crusoe, as he had been involved in the "secession" meeting of the prior December.[35]

Many island residents saw in the arrival of French and his troops the destruction of all hope of Key West becoming part of the new American Confederacy. The war also brought into prominence a number of people of little importance who seized the opportunity to settle past political or social vendettas, as in the case of Magistrate Crusoe, and who became "very loud and offensive in their so-called loyalty to the Union." They spied upon their neighbors who supported independence and reported them to the military authorities hoping to have them imprisoned in the fort. The military crackdown was "hailed with ghoulish glee" by some. But the bulk of the population were firm in their allegiance to the Confederacy, defiant of the US military, with Southern flags flying from homes and businesses.[36]

With Key West and Monroe County in the hands of the enemy, Florida's government had disqualified all State officials there. Acting somewhat as proconsul and anxious to present the appearance of Key West's loyalty to the United States, French suggested residents hold elections and appoint officials, with both voters and candidates first taking the prescribed oath to support the US government. After voters so qualified had cast ballots for the pre-approved slate, French proclaimed on May 18th that Union men had been installed and the pliant Patterson declared mayor. He further announced that his martial law would end if municipal affairs recognized the supremacy of US laws.[37]

---

34   Schmidt III, 46-47.

35   Browne, pg. 211.

36   *Ibid.*, pg. 92-93.

37   *Ibid.*, pg. 52-54.

A sad day for the island was May 20th when former-Tampa mayor Capt. James McKay's ship *Salvor* departed with former-Magistrate Peter Crusoe, Judge Douglas and his family, as well as Asa Tift who was facing imprisonment for refusing to coal the *Atlantic*. Tift was bound for Georgia after leaving the chandlery business in the hands of his younger brother and business partner Charles Tift.

The *Salvor* soon returned for more departing islanders, including US Army paymaster Major Smith who had resigned from the US military, taking him along with others to join Florida forces at Cedar Key and Fernandina, "thirty going in one day". By the end of May French could claim to have successfully deported the "principal seceders" of Key West's population. An exception was Mexican War veteran and island merchant Henry Mulrennan, arrested on June 6th by Major French for alleged "treasonable statements" and earlier demanding the surrender of Fort Taylor to the "Island Guards" militia. He was to be imprisoned in Fort Taylor until orders to the contrary.[38]

Built at Buffalo in 1856 as a wrecker, McKay purchased the *Salvor* at Chicago in 1860. Finding her suitable but without sufficient length, he sailed her to New York to add 70 more feet of length. With this accomplished, he entered the lucrative Tampa-Havana cattle trade until war began, when he offered his ship to the CS Government which the latter found unsuitable. After transporting Tift, Crusoe and others, totaling 186 souls to Tampa free of charge, McKay returned to Key West in early June on a cattle-run to the Havana market. Believed to be loyal, a US quartermaster officer joined him on the voyage to Cuba with funds to purchase horses for army use at Key West. After unloading, McKay's crew refused to return to Key West, his ship laid up, the quartermaster told to return as best he could, McKay hired a boat to Tampa. He was, ironically, arrested for treason against Florida upon arrival as he apparently cooperated with an enemy waging war against the State for which the prosecution wanted him hanged.

After friend and Navy Secretary Stephen Mallory encouraged him to use the *Salvor* to obtain weapons and run the blockade, McKay returned to Havana to load "$400,000 cargo of guns, other war materials and merchandise," obtained with funds from Cuban investors. Heading for Cedar Keys from Havana, she was captured by

---

38 Schmidt III, pg. 57.

a blockader, towed to Key West and McKay imprisoned in Fort Taylor. The *Salvor* and her crew was taken to Philadelphia.[39]

McKay was released after taking the oath of allegiance once again, then returned to Tampa to resume his cattle-runs to Havana while frustrating all attempts by the blockading fleet to capture him. In 1863, he was appointed Confederate Commissary Officer for the southwest Florida district.[40]

The island's clergymen did not escape surveillance as it was reported that a Methodist Rev. Davis had been arrested in mid-July and confined in a Fort Taylor cell for criticizing Lincoln's government and "uttering the most seditious prayer in the presence of our soldiers." Only after the church's presiding elder pleaded his case did French agree to release Davis if he too left the island.

Despite the crackdown, muffled press and deportations, support for independence remained evident. Though a *Philadelphia Inquirer* reporter wrote in late July that "everything was quiet at Key West" and "Union feeling was entirely predominate," he added that nearly one-third of residents were secretly secessionist but kept intimidated by the fort's garrison. A month later the paper reported that the Northern troops trained (and kept residents in awe) with "artillery exercises every evening on the beach, firing blank cartridges, ever-alert to the possibility of French or British intervention on the side of the Confederacy and accompanied by an amphibious landing on the island.

The problem of military intelligence leaving the island continued when in mid-August a local merchant reported that Key Wester and now-Confederate Secretary of the Navy Stephen R. Mallory employed several express boats sailing between Key West and the Florida mainland which relayed movements of the US squadron. The cordon around the island was strengthened in late August with an order that no ship could depart island unless both captain and crew swore allegiance to the US government. If this did not stop illicit "correspondence with the rebels of the mainland," the port would be closed to any trade.[41]

---

39 McKay, Jr., pg. 9.
40 Waters, pg. 4-5; 12.
41 Schmidt III, pp. 65-74.

The military's hold over the island was enhanced with acclimated horses obtained from Cuba providing fast, mounted patrols for surveilling the entire island. Intending to ferret out remaining pro-independence residents, French issued "Order No. 82" in early September 1861 which required already oath-bound male residents to register within 10 days. Additionally, within 30 days all residents of the island were required to take the oath; after 60 days anyone who failed to or refused the oath would be deported. This applied to their families, as well as families of those who already had left to join the Southern cause. Many refused the oath as it included the words "freely and voluntarily" when they were being forced to recite it. Southern soldiers routinely referred to this oath-swearing as "swallowing the dog."

The Philadelphia paper subsequently reported that a large number of islanders were to leave with their families and household goods the following week. "All go to the first Rebel port, Tampa – a poor and unimportant town in the bay – already filled to repletion with half-starved Rebels from Key West." The writer said those few secessionists who remain "have prudentially kept quiet, but their influence is here, is exercised upon, and felt by the Conchs who constitute the principal part of the population."

Yet another order came from French on September 23rd which required residents to take an "oath of fidelity" or be sent as prisoners to New York and anyone avoiding the oath by claiming to be a foreigner would be deported. To get an idea of the islanders' compliance with the oath requirement, the *Philadelphia Inquirer* reported that out of the 3000 or so island residents only 400 have either submitted to the oath or agreed to recite it. The paper estimated that some 2000 residents were men.[42] Two weeks later reports indicated that 743 adult males on the island had taken the oath since early September and "only two have not yet, their time to do so has not yet expired."

Key Wester Robert Watson and others had endured enough of this. His diary begins on Friday, September 27, 1861 when he left the island with several friends as stowaways aboard an English schooner bound for his native Bahamas. A skilled carpenter and quite literate, he began his wartime diary with:

---

42   Schmidt III, pp.77-78.

> Owing to the political affairs of the country and the Federal troops having possession of this place, and as it is rather unsafe for a Southern man to live here, I have determined to leave in disgust, consequently I left today in the schooner Lady Bannerman for the Bahama Islands in company with Canfield, Sawyer, Lowe and several others. The schooner has on board 55 passengers in all, the most of which are women and children.

Obsessed with the search for secessionists on the island in October, French discovered that wreckers William Lowe and son William A. had obtained a permit to take their families up to Indian Key. French thought the Lowe's "rank secessionists and the most violent ones" on the island, and accused them of already violating a previous oath taken. The Lowes' subsequently appeared before Judge Marvin who was already acquainted with them, and explained to French that they were merely removing their families in accordance with his orders. The Lowe's seven slaves were held at the fort until mid-November, when they were released but ordered to remain on the island. This would allow the military to impress them as fort labor or personal servants.[43]

The ongoing threats and deportations forced some residents to avoid the consequences of not uttering it, but a US naval officer did note a paucity of oath-takers by mid-October. He reported that despite the 700 or so who have taken the oath, "I was reliably informed that there are not over 150 true Union men" in Key West. French and his provost marshal soon realized that oath-taking revealed little evidence of actual loyalty.

Island residents continued to receive smuggled news from the mainland, and in particular read a letter Gov. John Milton wrote to a prominent Tampa leader regarding the "citizens of Key West and that portion [of the State] which is cursed by the tyranny and presence of Lincoln's Vandals, [and who] have made their escape sacrificing home and property in preference to subscribing to the oath required by the enemies of the State. Their condition is such as to require immediate aid and relief. You will please take such steps as in your power to aid them."

---

43 Schmidt III, pp. 74-79.

On October 17th French ordered the arrest of Charles Tift, younger brother and business partner of Asa and recording secretary of the previous December's "secession meeting," holding him in a Fort Taylor cell. Charles had reportedly taken the prescribed oath and though not suspected of "treasonous" statements or actions, French nonetheless believed him somehow involved with the suspicious actions of Capt. McKay and his *Salvor*. Charles was apparently not held long as he is reported to be overseeing brother Nelson's business interests at Albany, Georgia while the latter and Asa began their ironclad construction operations at New Orleans.

In early November, French welcomed US Vice Consul-General at Havana, Thomas Savage, who visited the island on official business. Savage informed the fort's commander that Southern agents in Havana "laughed at the blockade" while reading recent newspapers from Charleston and New Orleans commonly found in Cuban hotels and restaurants. Most disturbing to French was learning that those newspapers carried accounts of many Southern battlefield triumphs which "highly elate our Spanish enemies."

Through the last two months of 1861 island residents continued to chafe under Major French's martial law, oath-taking and the hard-hand of military occupation. In late November twenty-eight Key West residents bravely petitioned Judge William Marvin to order free elections be held for the purpose of sending a delegate to Congress for proper representation. Five days later their petition was denied.[44]

---

44 Schmidt III, pp. 82-90.

CHAPTER 4:

"This Don't Sute Me as a Soldier" - The Year 1862

> I regret to say, from all I see and hear, that many of the most wealthy and influential men of this place, although they have taken the oath of allegiance, are still at heart as strong secessionists as when they hoisted the Rebel flag over their stores and dwelling houses ... Permitting such persons to remain among loyal people is wrong, especially so in a community like ours.[1]

So wrote a *New York Herald* correspondent of Union-held Key West on January 10, 1862, precisely one year since Florida declared its independence, and despite martial law, loyalty oaths, banishment and a steadily increasing force of armed troops occupying the island, Key West was still strongly "secessionist." The reporter continued:

> Many of the citizens here, those known as "conchs," are natives of the Bahamas, and ... are friends of Secession ... These people should be driven from the place and never permitted to return ... if it is still their wish to carry on their present [commercial] traffic, it should not be under the protection of the flag of the United States.

This reporter's view of being "driven from the place and never allowed to return" was not uncommon among many Northerners and similar to that of Tennessee Unionist Parson Brownlow. In a fit of anti-South hatred, Brownlow told a pro-Lincoln audience in New

---
1   Schmidt III, pg. 99.

York that he would like to see Ben Butler's troops crowd every rebel into the Gulf of Mexico and drown them as the devil did the hogs in the Sea of Galilee." Abolitionist Wendell Phillips received cheers in Brooklyn's Plymouth Church in early February 1863 when he called for no peace until 347,000 men of the South are either hanged or exiled."[2] Another abolitionist, Ralph Waldo Emerson declared, "If it costs ten years, and ten to twenty to recover the general prosperity, the destruction of the South is worth so much." Radical Pennsylvania Congressman Thaddeus Stevens was straightforward regarding the South's independence: "If their whole country must be laid waste, and made a desert, in order to save this Union from destruction, so let it be. I would rather, sir, reduce them to this condition where their whole country is to be repeopled with a band of freemen than to see them perpetuate the destruction of this people through our agency."[3] Additional thoughts on dealing with the South came from Illinois politician Orville Browning who suggested the South's subjugation, the white people exterminated, a black republic established there with Northern troops to protect "the Negroes while they raised our cotton."[4]

In July, 1861, both houses of Congress, by an almost unanimous vote, affirmed that the War was waged not to interfere with the institutions of any State but only to maintain the Union. The War, in the words of the House resolution, should cease "as soon as these objects are accomplished." It is forgotten that the Emancipation Proclamation, issued on Sept. 23, 1862, was limited and provisional: slavery was to be abolished only in the seceded States and only if they did not return to the Union before the first of the next January.[5]

Northern periodicals like *Harper's Weekly* of June 14, 1862, offered opinions regarding reconstructing the South in their own image, which would include Key West:

> If we restore the Union feeling there, we can do it throughout the South. If we cannot succeed there, the bulk of the white people of the South will have to be

---

2 Scruggs, *Times Examiner*.
3 Cong. Globe, 37 Cong., I session, 415.
4 Thayer, pg. 110.
5 Warren, G., pg. 60-65.

exiled, or got rid of in some way, in order to reconstruct the Union and secure the safety of the North ... We must then show them that if they persevere in rebellion they cannot escape hunger and misery, that they will be outcasts without property or rights of any kind; that it is a mere question of time how soon they will be hunted down; that it is simply due to our forbearance that the negroes have not been armed for insurrection; whereas, on the other hand, if they return to their loyalty ... [they may] start afresh in a new and wholesome career of industry.

Still a relative unknown in the Western Theater of the war was the ruthless Gen. William T. Sherman, who writing his brother in August 1862, said that "to attempt to hold all the South would demand an army too large to even contemplate." Believing that the Southern people must be driven out and replaced he added: "We must colonize and settle as we go South ... enemies must be killed or sent to some other country." [6]

At Key West more troops from New York, New Hampshire and Pennsylvania had arrived to occupy the island and the initially empty and unfinished Fort Jefferson 70 miles westward. Quickly manned to keep it out of Florida – and Confederate States – hands, it would as well serve as a base to project United States power into the Caribbean. During the war it developed into an American "Devil's Island" holding the worst court-martialed Northern soldiers used for labor on fort construction and maintenance.[7] These criminals frightened Emily Holder, wife of Fort Jefferson's surgeon Dr. Joseph Holder, who wrote of the soldiers confined there: "The Zouaves were men enlisted at New York City, some of the most undisciplined, dangerous characters, who under the influence of liquor would be desperate and uncontrollable. Some of the [fort's Northern] workmen were little better ..."[8]

---

6 *Confederate Veteran*, November 1896, pg. 87. "Letter of Sherman to brother John," August 13, 1862."

7 Manucy, pg. 315.

8 Schmidt III, pg. 117.

In mid-January 1862 the 90th New York Regiment under Col. Joseph Morgan disembarked as Key West's initial occupation force. The regiment was comprised of three-year enlistees primarily from New York City, Brooklyn, Unadilla and Long Island. After sufficient time to make generalizations, one newly-arrived New York soldier and diarist wrote of there being "some 'Secesh here but they keep very quiet."

On January 16th the *New York Herald* reported the military order to seize the property of the then-departed Asa F. Tift adjacent to the navy wharf. Tift was described as "a recreant son of New England" as he was at New Orleans supervising the construction of "rebel gunboats." [9]

Five days later, now-Brigadier General Brannan was assigned to Key West and instructed to "repress all disunion movements in Key West" and authorized to "occupy any land or buildings needed to implement its defense." The effect was that the island was placed under martial law and life at the pleasure of the military.

Key Westers saw the arrival of its primary occupation force in early February, 1862, the 47th Pennsylvania Regiment. The year 1862 would also see two New York regiments on occupation duty as well.[10] For them it was not necessarily strenuous duty on the island but as the months of occupation wore on the troops became weary of the warm, tropical tedium. Lamented one, "this don't sute me as a soldier" and the only thing soldiers came to fear were outbreaks of yellow fever.[11]

The islanders one soldier met while gaining a sense of his new surroundings led him record that "[although] the people of the community were not exactly Union, they had taken the oath of allegiance." But it will be seen that the taking of oaths of allegiance were not certain indicators of loyalty. The military build-up of Key West was initially to hold the island for the Northern government, and also anticipated a sea-borne attack "mounted by a substantial sea power," such as was threatened by England during the Trent Affair crisis of late 1861. With this in mind, the men were trained with heavy

---

9   *Ibid.*, pg. 99-100.
10 Schmidt III, pp. 141-143.
11 Ogle, pg. 63.

coast artillery and fully engaged in improving the fortifications and adding the two Martello towers, small, round masonry forts of mid-century 16th Corsican design, on the island's southern coastline.[12]

As previous chapters deeply scrutinize those who settled the island - their ethnicity, religious and political views – it is proper to do the same for those - primarily Pennsylvanians - who became the island's master from 1862-1865.

The Pennsylvania regiment was comprised of men from the Lehigh Valley who served the longest as Key West's occupation force. Roughly 70 percent of the 47th Pennsylvania's soldiers came from the Lehigh Valley – men from the towns of Easton, Bethlehem, Allentown, Catasauqua and Sunbury – communities that were not unanimous in support for Lincoln's war. The unit was comprised of natives of Germany or second-generation with names such as Gausler, Kohler, Lutz, Mennig, Fatzinger, Weiss, Bohlen, Leisenring, Minnich, Fetherolf, Goebel, Weisbach, Brobst and Junker. Their commanding officer was Col. Tilghman Good, grandson of a Swiss immigrant and employed prewar as a hat and shoe salesman. For news and political viewpoint they read German-language newspapers such as Der Unabhangige Demokrat and Der Unabhaegiger Republikaner. About half of the region's newspapers were printed in German with the Pennsylvania-Dutch variant being the common tongue at homes and in church.[13]

The Pennsylvania Germans being a different people than the varied islanders already discussed, it is important to understand the political, social and racial viewpoints brought with them, and how these affected daily interaction with Key West residents. We thankfully find those viewpoints in the letters and diaries of the New York and Pennsylvania soldiers as well as newspaper accounts, and military orders.

It is interesting that 36 years earlier Key West lodging house proprietor Ellen Mallory sent her son Stephen Mallory for schooling in a Moravian academy at Nazareth, Pennsylvania, not far from Allentown. Though his mother was barely able to pay tuition with her meager earnings, this is where he received instruction in Greek and Latin, obtained a lifelong love of music and developed his "delicate

---

12 Schmidt III, pg. 124.

13 *Ibid.*, pg. 165

sense of chivalry toward the fairer sex." Beyond his brief education at Nazareth, Mallory was largely self-educated and rose to be United States Senator and Confederate Secretary of the Navy.[14]

Like Monroe County, the Lehigh Valley was a Democratic stronghold though many iron-industry voters were drawn to the Republican party's high protectionist tariff position. Pennsylvania's Democrats and Republicans both claimed to be more protectionist than the other, with the shrewd Andrew Curtin running for govenor in 1860 as a "Peoples Party" candidate. Democrats rightly identified him as a Republican in disguise. It would be accurate to state that voters voted Republican for tariff reasons, but at the same time could be Democrats who valued State sovereignty. The extreme Radical Republican side of Pennsylvania politics was led by iron manufacturer and protectionist-tariff man Thaddeus Stevens of Lancaster County, a Whig and anti-Catholic Know-Nothing stronghold. His anti-Southern views were well-known as he wanted slaves armed and incited to insurrection to give the rebels a real taste of civil war.[15]

Quasi-Republican Andrew Curtin won Pennsylvania's governorship in 1860 on a protectionist tariff platform after an economic recession depressed Pennsylvania's iron industry. Previous Gov. William Packer, a Democrat, agreed with President James Buchanan that States could not voluntarily withdraw from the Constitution of 1789, both recommending that the nation's differences should be addressed in a national convention of States.

Pennsylvania founder William Penn was a devoted slaveholder who established his colony in 1681, with Delaware added in 1682. Penn wrote of preferring black slaves to white, indentured servants who would eventually be released from contracts, "for then a man holds them while they live." The original Quakers had no moral qualms holding slaves and by 1758 some 70% of Philadelphia and Chester County slaveowners were Quakers. Several prominent Philadelphia Quaker families actively imported slave cargoes from Barbados and Jamaica.

---

14 Durkin, pp. 14-15.
15 Brodie, pg. 157.

Many German and Scots-Irish immigrants were being lured to the colony by 1720 with 4 to 5 year indentured servitude contracts paying for their passage across the Atlantic. Once the immigrants paid their debt, they became the Quakers preferred farm laborers as African slaves required lifetime housing, health care and feeding. The immigrants were paid wages only, and by 1758 the Quakers shed themselves of African slaves after considering them a worldly luxury and "bad influence on their families."

In the mid-1700's many of these "Pennsylvania Dutch" departed southward down the Cumberland Valley and further still down the Shenandoah Valley, and eventually across the Blue Ridge to the fertile western counties of North Carolina. These migrants became the sturdy farmers of this region, were deeply religious and held on to their language and ways for generations.[16]

Black people in colonial Pennsylvania "led severely circumscribed lives" and could be returned to slavery for laziness or petty crimes. These early "Jim Crow Laws" forbid Africans, free or slave, to gather in "tippling-houses, carrying arms or assembling in companies."

The influx of free, white labor after the Revolution fueled Pennsylvania's abolition debates in 1778 as keeping African slaves became an exorbitant expense, and more importantly, after Delaware became independent in 1776. This "secession" from Pennsylvania solved Quaker concern about slaveholding being a luxury, left three-fourths of "old Pennsylvania" slaves unaffected by acts of the Pennsylvania Assembly, and one "disturbed" by slave ownership could sell them to Delaware farmers or farther south at a handsome profit.

In 1780, a gradual emancipation act passed which technically maintained slavery until 1848, but with free black people denied the vote or service in the militia. Post-abolition tracts regarding Pennsylvania's past have written about slavery times in a self-serving way, suggesting that it was "of a mild character" and that slaves "enjoy as much liberty as their masters."[17]

---

16   Hahn, pp. 10-11.
17   Harper, SlaveryNorth.com.

The Lehigh Valley did not record its first black residents until the 1820s – about the same time as Key West. Their arrival coincided with the Valley needing canal, coal and pig iron labor. After the canal was completed, black laborers became canal-boat mule drivers with a few finding homes in the Valley. Though Allentown and Easton were the valley's major population centers with some 10,000 people, the 1860 census listed only 16 and 85 black persons, respectively. More would be attracted to this industrializing area as railroad workers and domestic servants.[18]

But the prevalent racial views of Pennsylvanians were on display in 1838 when an anti-black mob torched the Pennsylvania Anti-Slavery Society's headquarters at Philadelphia. Also, after John Brown was hung for treason against Virginia in 1859, an abolitionist vigil in the city was jeered by a mob of some six thousand Philadelphians; the mayor would not allow the train containing his body for burial in New York to stop in the city. Wisely, a duplicate train was used to throw off the expected Philadelphia mobs. Two weeks later when a New York abolitionist spoke at Philadelphia's National Hall, a loud, rock-throwing crowd of five thousand shouted outside. And after Lincoln began accepting black soldiers in his army, Governor Curtin refused permission for black troops from other States to pass through Pennsylvania on their way southward.[19]

In addition to those with black skin, the Lehigh Valley's German Protestants did not welcome the Irish Catholics who emigrated into the State after 1830, considering them loyal subjects of the Pope. This was the State from whence came those who would rule over the island for most of the war.

Pennsylvania newspapers in general, just before and after the outbreak of war, provide a clear window into prevailing political sentiment. Sensing the country's disquiet, the *Pittsburgh Post* of October 10, 1860, opined that it "is simply absurd to say that Disunionism is confined to Southern fire-eaters - Northern Sectionalism, as manifested by the Black Republican party, is as hostile to the Union, in fact and in purpose, as Southern Sectionalism is now, or ever has been. If Mr. Lincoln were President ... the Union would be

---

18 www.wfmz, accessed 12.12.20.
19 Paradis, pp. 6-7.

in danger from that hour." On April 2nd, 1861, the same paper wrote that "The Republicans have divided the country ... and called for that party to acknowledge the great mistake of sectionalism."

On November 22, 1860, the *Philadelphia Daily News* wrote of its concern regarding what to do with "our free colored population ... a very prolific race and increasing to such an extent as to excite serious apprehension for the future. The two races can never exist in conjunction except as superior and inferior." Being of the same mind as this editorial, Lincoln soon began serious efforts to find appropriate lands in the Caribbean for the colonization of black freedmen.

Two weeks prior to Major Robert Anderson's overnight move into Fort Sumter, the *Harrisburg Daily Patriot* of December 6, 1860, wrote of "organized agitators" and sectional elements which grew in the North, culminating in "the formation of a sectional Northern political party, "thoroughly imbued and entirely controlled by hostility to the institutions of the Southern States." It continued that the Republican party "cannot escape direct responsibility for what it promotes or encourages," being naturally judged by the Southern people from its fruits," and not from its moderate-sounding platforms.

The same newspaper published President James Buchanan's December 1860 message to Congress, stating that "secession" was not a remedy conferred upon any State by the Constitution against federal encroachments. He admitted it being a revolutionary step, only justifiable "as the last desperate remedy of a despairing people, after every other constitutional means of conciliation has been exhausted." This could be said of the American colonists in 1776.

Presciently, the editorial asked: "Suppose a State can be coerced, how are we to govern it afterwards? Shall we invite the people to elect Senators and Representatives after they had been subdued and conquered? Or shall we hold them as subjects, and not as equals. How can we subdue the unconquerable will, and how can we practically annul the maxim that all governments derive their just powers from the consent of the governed?

The *Allentown Democrat* editorialized at the same time: "What has provoked the popular hostility for Lincoln? We answer: The belief that he really means to destroy, while affecting an anxiety to save, the Union." It continued that "Democrats of the Lehigh Valley opposed the Republican administration's war. They were suspicious of the shifting justifications for it. They weren't interested in fighting to free anyone. They denounced the president's restrictions on civil liberties. And they predicted the bloodshed would lead to bigger disasters."

Contrasting the two American presidential inaugurations was the February 18th issue of Philadelphia's *Morning Pennsylvanian,* which referred to Jefferson Davis as "a gentleman, a scholar, a soldier and a statesman ... his name is the very synonym of purity and honor ... without fear and without reproach." The editorial added that the President-elect of the United States is neither a scholar, a soldier, nor a statesman. He has some experience as a *Nisu prius* [general law] lawyer and local politician ... and as a flat boatman and a rail splitter."

On March 18th the *Pittsburgh Post* wrote that "Compromise only can save this Union of States. War can only result in dissolution and desolation." Addressing the issue of Southern forts like Fort Zachary Taylor at Key West which had already been seized by Lincoln's military, the paper suggested abandoning them to allow a peaceful cooling off period. It continued:

> These forts were built to protect the States where they are located against foreign aggression, not to be used against the people of the States themselves. If their occupancy by federal troops irritates the people and makes them antagonistic to the general government, and their evacuation would tend to bring back the South to allegiance, it is certainly the best policy to abandon them and thus remove a preliminary difficulty in the way of settlement. There is no humiliation in abandonment. The reason of it will be fully appreciated by the nation and by the world. It will be regarded as willingly offered, a voluntary peace measure, magnanimously adopted to save the Union.

The editorial concluded: "None but the Republicans would object to this course. They seem to feel as though they had something in the shape of vengeance to wreak against the South."

The *Allentown Democrat* wrote of its alarm over Lincoln's arrests of "disloyal" political leaders and shutting down opposition newspapers. It wrote that Lincoln's war was unlawful as the Constitution gave no authority to the federal government to keep a State in the Union – a belief shared by President Buchanan. After the September bloodbath of Americans at Sharpsburg, the paper editorialized that Lincoln and his administration were "firm in their convictions as ever that the insane policy of extermination and emancipation is the only one that can end [the war]. The editor later decried Lincoln's emancipation decree and rejected the idea or black equality to white, writing that "Lincoln's policies had already burdened the North with the cost of caring for thousands" of displaced blacks.[20]

At the very same time the three Monroe County delegates solemnly cast their ballots at Tallahassee supporting Florida's independence on January 4, 1861, and nearly a week before Capt. Brannan was training his fort's cannon on the peaceful town, the *Harrisburg Daily Patriot* in Pennsylvania editorialized:

> "Our government is one of public opinion," and was it not great crime "to force an odious government upon protesting citizens of sovereign States at the mouth of the cannon and point of the bayonet?" It insisted that force cannot be used "without destroying the freedom of citizens and undermining the very foundation of our republican system of government"

The *Pittsburgh Post* of March 18th, 1861, opined that "Compromise only can now save this Union of States and it is a bitter pill to the ultra-Republicans. The medicine will do them good and teach them that a President is subject to laws," not "partisan platforms or the insane desires of his followers." The paper urged Lincoln's party to seek a peaceful end to the impending strife.

And finally, approving of the Confederacy's improvements to the US Constitution used as its governing document, the *Philadelphia Morning Pennsylvanian* of March 21, 1861, lauded the South's framers for limiting presidents to one term of six years - ineligible thereafter - thus eliminating "that distracting, corrupting and dangerous evil

---

20 Warner, pp. 5-6.

which now prevails at Washington – the wild hunt after office." The paper assailed the Republicans for their failure to offer conciliatory measures to save the Union, and suggesting that if the Montgomery Constitution were submitted to the Northern people, it would be accepted "with joy and unexampled unanimity."

On the day South Carolina batteries opened fire on Fort Sumter, April 12, 1861, Pennsylvania's *Bedford Gazette* wrote: "The so-called "peace policy" of the Lincoln administration has been turned into one of blood and horror ... When this sectional conflict shall rage, when the Northern man shall be called upon to bathe his fraternal sword in his own blood flowing in the veins of his Southern brother, let it be remembered that this unjust and unholy war could have been avoided, but that Mr. Lincoln and his Cabinet refused to make any compromise with the Southern people ... stolidly insisting upon construing the Constitution as they please."

Lincoln's administration and sympathetic newspapers framed the calculated and logical result of the armed expedition to Fort Sumter as an insult to the US flag and government authority. The new President relied upon his Republican governors to supply him with an army while avoiding Congressional approval, and Pennsylvania Gov. Andrew Curtin responding quickly. The Lehigh Valley's Democratic newspapers appear to have been allowed past Republican censors at least until early 1863 though War Department censors did limit access to the mails.

To fully understand the Pennsylvania's response to Fort Sumter and the subsequent 90-day enlistments in Pennsylvania and other Northern States, they must be seen in the light of the stated intent of "preserving the Union," the aftermath of the Panic of 1857, still-struggling industries and an economic recession caused by the Southern trade embargo with the North. In a State with a lower-than-average median income of only $500, and expectation of clothing money, food and health care while in uniform and $49 pay (if it lasted the full three months) when mustered out at the end of the expected short "war," brought many into the blue ranks for an anticipated early capitulation of the South.[21]

---

21 Marvel, pg. 26.

The economic impulse to enlist was underscored by a Northern prisoner telling his Tarheel guard after the First Manassas battle that he and others were in the Union army because "they are out of employment and had nothing else to do." Another from just east of the Lehigh Valley enlisted for the $49 as he was an unemployed miller heavily in debt. There perhaps existed a patriotic impulse but the money helped make the decision.

The desperate need for personal income was not to last as the demand for Northern war materiel accomplished industrial recovery by the summer of 1862 to compete with the army's low pay. This took many men who had not enlisted back to work in the textile, clothing and shoe industries. An example was the colonel who founded the 47th regiment, a hat and shoe salesman who saw an income and prestige in forming a regiment. Now the quick war had become a protracted event with measures beyond militaristic slogans required to get able men into uniform, and communities, counties and State providing substantial bounty money for men to join, and remain in the ranks.[22]

Pennsylvania ultimately supplied Lincoln with 34 regiments for nine months service. For political reasons, Gov. Curtin chose to recruit more short-term than three-year troops as did Gov. John Andrew of Massachusetts who favored nine-month regiments "as a refuge for some of the State's more privileged sons." Both leaned on Secretary of War Edwin Stanton to assign favorites to quiet theaters of the war, which Key West was to be for the 47th Pennsylvania. This unit had relatively easy duty interrupted only with its brief excursion to Pocotaligo, South Carolina where the inexperienced unit was badly bloodied in October of 1862.

Though the men of the 47th may have been predominantly Democratic, some were unhappy with the antiwar views of many at home. Despite them seeing virtually no action, they saw their service "to save the Union" being undermined at home. They recalled Congress affirming in July 1861 that the war would not interfere with the particular institutions of any State and a goal of maintaining the territorial Union of States, and should cease "as soon as these objects are accomplished."[23] This would change after Lincoln's emancipation edict.

---

22 *Ibid.*, pg. 27; 51; 97.
23 Warren, pp. 60-65.

The antiwar rhetoric continued in the Lehigh Valley as news of Northern defeats – when and if the administration admitted such - and increasing numbers of war-dead coming home for burial could not be ignored. The frequent newspaper editorials opposing the war and enlistments were now resulting in attacks by mobs who destroyed printing presses. Specifically, the *Easton Sentinel, Argus* and German-language newspaper *Unabhangige Demokrat* suffered at the hands of Republican mobs for editorials criticizing the war and believing the papers not sufficiently Unionist. The majority of the mob were soldiers who had completed their ninety-day enlistments and thought the civilians unappreciative of their brief sacrifice. The newspapers defended themselves and the *Allentown Democrat* organized a 200-man force to protect it from incendiaries, and the German-language *Der Republikaner* doing the same. The latter had openly-accused Lincoln of prolonging his bloody war to profit his Republican friends in New England.[24]

Back at Key West, soldiers were busily putting the island on a "war-footing" in early 1862 as they cut through thickets and undeveloped areas for roadways to improve military access across the island. Residents continued to supply the mainland with information as Robert Watson's brother George Watson got a message to now-Capt. Henry Mulrennan at Tampa of rumors that "all the trees on Key West are to be cut down and all the principal houses in the place are to be occupied by the soldiers."[25]

But lingering local secession sentiment was still found even in the Episcopal Church congregation which was being infiltrated by Northern soldiers. After the Unionist reverend had closed his sermon with a prayer for Lincoln, incensed members closed their hymnals and remained silent to quietly express their disapproval. Quickly informed of this, the fort's commander responded by requiring all parishioners to take the oath of allegiance to the government or be forbidden to worship in the church.[26]

---

24 Schmidt II, pp. 18-21.
25 LGS3, pg. 144.
26 Schmidt III, pg. 144-146.

Sensing the true sentiment on the island, a *New York Herald* reporter wrote in mid-January 1862: "I regret to say, from all I can see and hear, that many of the most wealthy and influential men of this place, although they have taken the oath of allegiance, are still at heart as strong secessionists as when they hoisted the Rebel flag over their stores and dwelling houses ... Permitting such persons to remain among loyal people is wrong, especially so in a community like ours."[27]

In late February the *Philadelphia Inquirer* wrote that "There are strong grounds for believing there are secret emissaries of the Confederates here in Key West, since scarcely a movement is made by the naval vessels from this point that is not known to the secessionists in Havana, who arrange for the departure of Rebel vessels from that port upon the information which they obtain. As Havana is only eight hours sail, Confederate spies can easily inform them."

A month later the US military announced that a group of "political prisoners" it had been holding within Fort Taylor would be paroled and swear to not to take up arms nor aid an enemy of the United States. Shortly after this occurred one Pennsylvania soldier wrote in his diary of "the deluded followers of Jefferson Davis" appearing before the Clerk of District Court to take the oath, [then] get a pass to leave the island and at the first opportunity travel north to join the Rebels." He was aware of the flimsy meaning of paroles and oaths in time of war.[28]

The soldiers themselves – and officers - took advantage of the island's black population, free and slave, viewing them as "contraband" and theirs for the taking. Black slaves were used as personal servants to clean tents, black boots, for cooking, sewing and running errands. The fort commander issued an order that this was a "degradation upon private property ... committed by the troops of this command." The order further stated that "Negro slaves shall on no account be harbored in the quarters or encampments of the troops."

The soldiers continued the "war-footing" transformation of the island through late March as two batteries of mobile, horse-drawn field artillery arrived. New uniforms were issued with brass shoulder plates to protect crews from cavalry sabers, indicating concerns that enemy troop landings were possible. One soldier diarist wrote: "The

---

27 *Ibid.,* pg. 99.
28 Schmidt III, pg. 148.

trees are all being cut down, while artillery roads, thirty feet wide, are being run from one part of the island to another, at different points." This soldier further wrote that "our men have been working hard, but daily expect 500 contrabands from Port Royal, when we will have easy times." indicating the value and usage of the freedmen to the Pennsylvanians.[29]

Another military newspaper emerged on the island in early April with the publication of *The New Era*, the mouthpiece of the 90th New York regiment. Ironically, *The New Era's* masthead touted it as a defender of "a strict construction of the Constitution" in which it would not differ with its pro-independence predecessor. While calling for slavery's abolition with owners fully compensated, the paper reported continued resistance to occupation as "persons sympathizing with the Confederate cause had been escaping from the island of Key West" to Tampa. The newspaper's masthead read: "To show the misled and deluded of the South that we are fighting for their rights as well as our own," while disparaging independence-seeking Key Westers as "Owls."

At the same time in April Key Wester Lizzie Wall's husband Julian Myers was a Confederate Navy lieutenant at Mobile Bay and under attack by Northern warships. He commanded the floating battery *CSS Huntsville* during the engagement, and when the enemy attempted to board the *Huntsville*, Myers acted quickly to scuttle it. Lizzie was the daughter of island merchant William Wall; Julian a native of Savannah.

In mid-April Brannan reported to his superiors that the island's new military roads would be completed by the first of May but complained that promised contrabands from Port Royal had yet to arrive and both forts needed 600 laborers for heavy fortification work. He closed his letter with this need being an "absolute and urgent necessity." Previously-mentioned was the US Army Engineer Corps need for labor causing the influx of slaves to Key West with then-Capt. Brannan overseer of fort construction and slaves.

Citing "disloyal actions and statements," but certainly an act of vengeance, new US District Attorney at Key West, Thomas Boynton of Missouri asked Judge William Marvin to strike Winer Bethel from

---

29 *Ibid.*, pp. 172; 185; 194-197; 205; 217.

the rolls of the island's practicing attorneys. Bethel was an elected delegate from Monroe County in the early January 1861 convention, voting for independence. Marvin refused to strike Bethel's name.[30]

It was about this time that Northern soldier Jacob Mail deserted from the island's occupation force, finding passage to Tampa to join the Key West Avengers. He was with Robert Watson and other islanders in the Seventh Florida regiment in Tennessee, then later deserted back to the Yankees. Watson expected him to be shot for his duplicitous loyalties.[31]

The Northern military on the island was aware of now-Capt. Henry Mulrennan's coast guard at Tampa which had been attracting many island men and satisfied the fort commander since the leading "secessionists" had been leaving. On April 24th Mulrennan informed his men that he had permission to go to Key West under a flag-of-truce to bring their families to Tampa. This would further swell the growing Key West community-in-exile forming there.[32]

Yet another weekly newspaper of the occupation troops was published on May 24th, 1862, this one named the *Key West Herald* and the work of the 47th Pennsylvania, intending to utilize the press and type of William Ward's suppressed *Key of the Gulf*. As these were the private property of Mrs. Ward, the two soldiers responsible obtained a confiscated press from Jacksonville.

The consequences of islanders publicly announcing their preference for independence could be deadly. On a Sunday in early June, one soldier of the New York regiment wrote of "a Secesh who lived here on the island got to boasting of his secession principles and that he could whip anyone in the company." He indicated that the man was beaten to death by several other soldiers. The non-lethal consequences of being accused of "aiding and abetting the Confederates" was imprisonment at New York, the steamer *Baltic* having arrived there with six Key Westers on June 2nd.[33]

---

30 Schmidt III, pg. 202.
31 Campbell, pg. 131.
32 Campbell, pg. 32.
33 Schmidt III, pg. 233; 245.

The "Key West Avengers," or Company K, Seventh Florida Infantry, left Tampa in late June to join the Army of Tennessee in the Western Theater of the war. Many ladies turned out to witness their departure waving handkerchiefs and shedding tears while the men gave three cheers. They marched most of the way to Chattahoochie, by steamer to Columbus, Georgia, and by railroad to Chattanooga. They were to join Gen. Braxton Bragg's army for a bold strike to liberate Tennessee as well as Kentucky.

At Key West the Pennsylvania regiment was being transferred to Hilton Head where it remained until late September, then was sent to the Jacksonville area. In October the 47th joined several other Northern regiments near Pocotaligo, South Carolina intent upon the destruction of important railroad bridges. An ensuing battle was soon after lost to poorly-armed South Carolina forces who numbered half their strength, forcing a headlong retreat to their boats and Hilton Head. After this dismal trial under fire, the 47th Pennsylvania returned to Key West the following month where it would spend 1863 as the island's primary occupation force – six companies at Fort Taylor and four at Fort Jefferson. The regiment then remained on the island until March of 1864 when it joined the ill-fated Red River Campaign in Louisiana, and did not return to Key West for the remainder of the war.

About the time of the 47th's departure, merchant William Pinckney of Wall & Company and Judge Winer Bethel were both arrested in mid-June and held at Fort Taylor in close confinement. After several months passing without trial, they were sent to Fortress Monroe and imprisoned for nearly a year. Still considered "unpunished secessionists" who may have refused to submit to the hated oath, both were elected delegates to the Tallahassee convention and cast their votes for independence with Asa Tift. Two weeks after their arrest, the *New York Herald* published a venomous letter from Key West expressing hope that Pinckney and Bethel would receive swift punishment, and sufficient "to strike terror among those who desire to do as these two have done." Key West historian Jefferson B. Browne commented that this letter "fairly portrays the feeling of the Northern sympathizers in Key West towards those who were true to their homes and native Southland." The occupation had succeeded in turning islanders against each other.[34]

Soon after and likely the work of the 90th New York's Col. Morgan, Pinckney's fellow employee William D. Cash was arrested and imprisoned in the Fort Taylor "Bastille" for two weeks without a hearing until he signed his parole and released. He refused to sign the parole until it specifically stated that he was under duress to do so. Morgan was very unpopular with his own officers who lavishly entertained Cash after being released from captivity.[35] At this time the military's *Herald* was writing of "many problems regarding loyalties in Key West" uncovered by the suspicious Col. Morgan who was determined to ferret out any and all perceived disloyal conduct.[36]

Despite the occupation, arrests and oaths, blockade running still offered a path to a relatively-quick profit if one had the investment money, ship and connections – and often involving Northern officers. In July 1862 the schooner of Jewish merchant Newman Leopold of Tallahassee, was captured by Northern blockaders and brought to Key West for adjudication. Leopold "promptly swore an oath of allegiance and applied for a permit to go to New York" where he likely took on more Northern goods to take through the blockade and perhaps with Northern investors. No one was immune to the lure of quick profit.[37]

As Key West's harbor filled with captured blockade runners in early August while awaiting adjudication, Morgan's suspicions were raised by the many crewmembers arriving from the "rebellious States" aboard them. The accepted policy was for them to take the oath and be released, but Morgan sought approval to use them for fortification labor. He failed, but knew the crews would depart to again serve aboard runners given the lucrative pay.[38]

---

34 Browne, pg. 94.
35 *Ibid.*
36 Schmidt III, pg. 249-250.
37 Weinfeld, pg. 111.
38 Schmidt III, pg. 300.

In early August the prayers of some "Key West Avengers" were answered when orders arrived transferring ten of their number – six of them Key Westers - to the CS Navy. The letter of Peter Crusoe to Secretary of the Navy Mallory gave hope to the rest that they would be next to experience sea duty.

Morgan was an abolitionist-minded officer and perhaps even more so to please his superior at Hilton Head, Gen. David Hunter. Advised of Lincoln's initial emancipation edict, in mid-August Morgan's quartermaster seized "twenty Negroes from their masters and setting them to work for Uncle Sam."[39] Morgan also took advantage of those slaveholders who had left the island, considering their slaves abandoned despite being left in another's care. Though employed by the US government on fortifications, Morgan refused to pay their owner's agent. In early September he issued a directive to his officers to not accept as servants any slaves who leave their island owners. It is recalled that the base reason African slaves came to the island was due to the US Army leasing slaves for fortification work.[40]

The fort's commander may have been abolitionist-minded, but issued unusual orders regarding the "employment of persons of African descent." He noted that "the men of this [90th New York] regiment have been doing work that should have been done by the Negroes of Key West; the consequence is that they are now unfit to perform their necessary duties ..." Morgan proclaimed that slavery on the island was now ended and seized the black workers from the islanders owning them, making them free to work for the US Army in the same condition.

Indicating the tenor of the common Pennsylvania soldier regarding the commander's emancipation efforts, Christian Boye wrote his family on Sept. 23rd that "the abolitionist's are determined at any hazard to let the slaves free, without compensation for his loss, they are also determined to make the South a wilderness and give the N***** more privileges, than the white man ..." Boye related that should one be abused by freedmen, they may report you to the Provost Marshal as an aggressor and claim you spoke treason against the US, etc."

---

39 *Ibid.*, pg. 305.
40 *Ibid.*, pp. 311; 314.

Most Key Westers had become accustomed to the occupation and avoided interaction with soldiers which might lead to arrest and imprisonment if one misspoke. But despite being under this watchful eye, islanders remained a compassionate people and helped nurse soldiers stricken with yellow fever when possible. In late September 1862 one soldier wrote home of being "taken with the yellow fever ... a family with which I was acquainted ... carried me to their house [on Duval] ... I was ... watched, attended, and fed as an infant, and every wish anticipated." Though not naming the family except to say that they were natives of New York, it was evident that he had been taken into the Watlington home on Duval Street. The father was a blockade runner with Southern sympathies, and one daughter married to Massachusetts-native Caleb Huse, a Confederate agent in Europe.[41]

Additional Southern sympathy was discovered on the island when the Provost Marshal seized the schooner *Amelia Ann* on October 6th, secretly under construction in Key West. Found within was a "rebel" flag and a letter of congratulations for saving "her from confiscation by those infernal Yankees." Other letters found described its intended use, and comments such as: recent glorious victories in favor of the cause made it certain that all soon return to Key West and drive every Union man from the island and into the sea."

Incensed at the blatant and continued disloyalty present on the island, Morgan ordered that "every householder shall return to these headquarters by October 20th," a list of each inmate of his or her house, of the age of eighteen years, or upward, which list shall contain the following particulars: The name, age and occupation of each inmate; whether an alien who has taken the oath of allegiance to the United States, or one who has neglected or refused to take the same." Morgan additionally ordered that "all householders neglecting to make such return, or making a false return, will be punished by fine or imprisonment, with hard labor, or both, and be regarded as a sympathizer with the so-called Confederate States, and registered as an enemy of the United States."[42] Once again, taking the oath of allegiance had not proved to be a true indicator of loyalty, but all other methods of reading the minds of townspeople had failed.

---

41   Schmidt III, pp. 323-324.
42   *Ibid.,* pp. 328-329.

Under his watch Morgan endeavored to stamp out "disloyalty" on land, but it also extended to the waters as a Northern admiral reported in mid-December that "The matter of selling prizes at Key West under the direction of the district court has become a great evil." He perceptively noted that captured runners were being sold at auction to those who intended their quick return to blockade running and serving the Confederacy.

At this moment at St. George's Harbor, Bermuda, batteries of field artillery were stowed aboard the blockade runner *Harriet Pinckney* ready for the voyage to Wilmington and then shipped by rail to Lee's army at Richmond. This ship's name was familiar to islanders - the daughter of Theodore and Sybil Pinckney of Key West, wife of New Englander Caleb Huse and Confederate purchasing agent in Europe.

The island had welcome news before Christmas as the 47th Pennsylvania regiment returned after its ill-fated action at South Carolina, and greeted by a populace who intensely disliked the impetuous Morgan who would soon be detested even more.

Describing a far different island than of December 1860, one member of the 156th New York regiment wrote that "Key West is quite a pleasant little island of about 4000 inhabitants [including military] ... it is now under martial law and has been for the past year. No liquor is allowed to be sold here although it is occasionally smuggled in. Very few women appear to be here and about 2/3rds of the inhabitants are males."[43]

The year 1862 now past showed a continuation of support for independence among islanders, clandestine communication with the mainland and more young men stowing away aboard ships to "join the resistance." The New Year saw the same as one New York sergeant wrote of young "Confederate sympathizers" slipping past patrol boats bound for Tampa and "the Rebel army."[44]

---

43 Schmidt III, pg. 348.
44 Schmidt III, pg. 427.

CHAPTER 5:

"I Have Determined To Leave Here In Disgust"

He fought, but not for love of strife; he struck but to defend;
He stood for liberty and truth, and dauntlessly led on.[1]

—Mary Elizabeth Dickinson, 1890

Mexican War veteran and Key West merchant Henry Mulrennan was likely leader of the "Island Guards" when the "Republic of Florida" flag flew above his Front Street store on March 10th, 1861, referring to it as "Fort Jefferson Davis." Demanding the recognition of Florida's independence and surrender of Fort Taylor he became a steady thorn in the side of the local military and was arrested in late May for alleged treasonable utterances. After release from a Fort Taylor cell on condition he depart the island, Mulrennan became a lieutenant in Florida's Volunteer Coast Guard at Cedar Key in early November. He encouraged other islanders to join him, which they did, often by difficult and circuitous routes. This Coast Guard was based at several signal stations along the coast to watch for enemy landings and transmit information by mounted couriers. Their detachment crewed three 35-foot single-sail boats, the *Kate Dale, Mary Jane* and *Mollie Post* - with oars and sail, armed with muskets, cutlasses and bow-mounted 4-pounder cannon. In mid-December they were mustered into State service at Tampa then transferred to Point Pinellas. In January 1862 their sobriquet "Key West Avengers" was adopted.[2]

---

1 Dickison, pg. 62.
2 Fandom, 7th Florida Regt.

Diarist Robert Watson interestingly describes his company as "cosmopolitan" with a rich mix of "Yankees, Crackers, Conchs, Englishmen, Spaniards, Germans, Frenchmen, Italians, Poles, Irishmen, Swedes, Chinese, Portuguese, Brazilians, 1 rock scorpion [Peter] Crusoe; but all are good Southern men. There are also Scotchmen, Welshmen and some half-Indians, surely this is the greatest mixture of nations in a small company that I ever heard of."[3]

Their reasons for serving Florida centered on defending their homes from invasion and seeing the issue as the North enforcing a union from which the South had respectfully departed. This caused the invasion and had nothing to do with liberating any slaves. Those who resigned from the US military consistently based their decision on not bearing arms against their States.[4]

A month later most of the unit was taken into Confederate States service for three years or the duration of the war, designated Company K, Seventh Florida Infantry on April 25, 1862, under command of now-Capt. Mulrennan at Cedar Key. The term "Key West Avengers" became synonymous with Company K and those reporting for duty received $50 bounty plus clothing allowance. Soon Mulrennan was promoted to regimental quartermaster with the rank of major and Pennsylvania-native Captain Robert B. Smith assumed command.

For lifelong seamen to be assigned as infantrymen was an understandable disappointment, but the resourceful "Avengers" took action by asking former Key West Magistrate and now-private Peter Crusoe to pen a letter to the Navy Department on their behalf.

Crusoe's letter of Thursday, May 1, 1862, was addressed to friend and now-Secretary of War Stephen Mallory "From the undersigned Marines, Citizens of Key West, Fla.," requesting transfer to "a Gun Boat or other vessel of war where they may have a chance to meet the enemy and strike for their Country's cause." The letter closed with the names of the following men:

> Seamen carpenters Robert Watson, George V. Rickards and J.P. Williamson [Willemsen]; and ordinary Seamen Charles H. Berry, Joseph E. Cole, Jules Chebert, Samuel

---

3   Campbell, pg. 27.
4   Whittle, pp. 14-15.

Morgan, James Barnett, A. P. Lowe, William Sawyer, Charles H. Chapman, John B. Sands, John Dupuy, M.A. Oliveri, J.H. Moss, Edward Dorey, Joseph Fagan, Manuel Monte de Ocha, Thomas Burns, Rofino Fales, William D. Curry, Jacob Weatherford, Francisco Diaz, William Josselyn and James Levitt.[5]

The "Avengers" request was answered in early August with the transfer of 10 men to the gunboat *CSS Chattahoochie*, then under construction at Saffold, Georgia. Another 21 men were transferred to sea duty between August 1862 and March 1864, serving aboard the warships *CSS Charleston, Columbia, Macon, Georgia, Sampson, Spray, Tallahassee* and *Savanah*. All but a few were eventually transferred to naval service.

Though disappointed at losing half of his command, Capt. Smith knew his "beached mariners" were elated to be serving aboard the ships rather than fighting in Tennessee. Not all transferred quickly as the Confederate Navy was building and converting ships, and it was not until early March 1864 that Key West seaman-carpenter Robert Watson and another seventeen "Avengers" received transfer orders when most were assigned to the *CSS Savannah*.[6]

After the evacuation of Savannah and scuttling of the *CSS Savannah*, these men without a ship marched on foot to Charleston to serve briefly on the *CSS Columbia*. They then went to Fort Fisher below Wilmington in early January, in time to help man Battery Buchanan's Brooke naval guns against the second massive Northern naval assault. Though reassigned to Richmond, the previous executive officer of the Battery was George Arledge, last seen at Savannah aboard the Tift brothers *CSS Atlanta*. As the fort's flag was being lowered, Watson and his comrades were ordered to boats and crossed the river to Fort Anderson, then to Battery Campbell below Wilmington where they remained until February 22nd. Travelling by rail to Greensboro and Richmond, they were assigned to Commander John R. Tucker's Naval Battalion at Drewry's Bluff. After Lee's withdrawal from Richmond in early April, 1865 the battalion was surrounded and captured near Farmville, Virginia on April 6th 1865 and paroled.

---

5   Fandom, 7th Florida Regt.
6   Campbell, pg. 97.

These men who departed the island to serve the Confederacy were a varied lot from many places, like the local population itself. Many were seamen earning a living sailing cutter-rigged smack fishing boats up the west coast for fish to sell at the Havana market. They would fight for Florida's independence in diverse ways and the following brief biographies help describe their journeys. Included are some who they met along the way – as well as the husbands of Key West ladies who helped defend their Southern homes. The source for most if not all below is the excellent resource: https://militaryhistory.fandom.com/wiki/Company_K,_7th_Florida_Infantry_Regiment

One who did not leave the island was Walter C. Maloney, Sr., a prewar Whig and Darien, Georgia native who declared at the December 12, 1860 Courthouse meeting: "the Union first, the Union last, and the Union always."[7] He later led the "Union Volunteer Corps" of loyalist Key West merchants and residents, instigated by Fort Taylor's commander.[8]

Maloney's son Walter C. Jr. was an early Keys native likely born on Indian Key and a 21-year-old sailmaker in 1860. Settlement of the island began in the early 1820s but settlers became more numerous in the 1830s and '40s. By 1860 young men like Walter Jr. were among the few "keys natives" who were among the migrants from elsewhere referred to as "Key Westers."

In September 1861, young Walter, friend A.N. Pacetti of New Smyrna and others escaped Key West's blockade to join Florida's forces assembling at Tampa. By the end of January 1862, Walter had joined Mulrennan's Coast Guard and later "Key West Avengers." He resigned his lieutenancy on October 26, 1864, ending the war with the Washington Siege Artillery at Adams Run, South Carolina. Returning to Key West postwar he read law and rose to be collector of revenue, mayor, city attorney, and newspaper co-publisher with his father.

Private Benjamin R. Albury was born on Royal Island in the Bahamas, September 6, 1811. He came to Key West in 1852 with his wife and children, working as a fisherman. In November 1861 he departed with other islanders to join Mulrenan's Coast Guard, then

---

7   Maloney, pp. 63-64.
8   Browne, pg. 221.

transferred in late April, 1862 to the "Key West Avengers." Being 51 years old he was discharged in Tennessee due to "old age and debility." Returning to the island, he passed away in 1865.

Bahamian-born Key Wester Capt. Augustus "Gus" Azariah Archer relocated to Key West with his family in 1839 at age ten. By 1860, both he and **John Thomas Lowe** owned and captained their own vessels and left Key West to settle up the coast at Anona, near Tampa. It was there he joined the Key West Avengers, 7th Florida Infantry as a private for a period of 3 years or the war's duration. Captured in early 1862 and paroled in Kentucky in early September, he was apparently captured again near Tampa four months later, transported to Key West and perhaps paroled. Postwar, Archer sailed a schooner carrying lumber cargoes from Cedar Keys to Tampa and other coast towns, but enchanted with the wild areas near Tampa, he gathered his family and headed to Tampa. He died in 1904, near Seminole, Florida

George Henry Arledge, nephew of island merchant James Filor was born in Georgia on July 6, 1836, and on the eve of war was a clerk in his uncle's office. Sent on an errand to Apalachicola with $1500 in gold in April 1861 for lumber he was captured by Florida forces and the boat and gold seized. Arledge then joined the Confederate Navy, appointed acting master mate and assigned to Norfolk. He was later transferred to the ironclad *CSS Atlanta*, originally the Scottish-built steamer *Fingal*, reworked into an ironclad by Key West's Tift brothers in their Savannah shipyard. In June 1863 the nearly-finished *Atlanta* steamed out to meet and attack two enemy ironclads and ran aground, its crew captured.[9] Arledge was not exchanged until October 1864 and then assigned to Battery Buchanan below Fort Fisher. In February 1865 Arledge commanded the *CSS Beaufort* below Richmond and shortly after the *CSS Fredericksburg*. He scuttled the latter upon Richmond's evacuation on April 4, 1865, and cut off from Lee's retreating army, he followed Admiral Semmes Naval Brigade to Greensboro where he was paroled in May 1865. He lived near Savannah as a farmer in 1868, then in Virginia until 1870 and at last a cotton broker at Galveston, Texas, 1874-1896. He died March 16, 1898 and was buried at Washington, DC.[10]

---

9   Campbell, pg. 195.

10 George Henry Arledge, Confed. Navy (1836 - 1898) - Genealogy (geni.com).

Joseph S. Bartlum was born on Green Turtle Cay in the Bahamas on June 28, 1838, arriving at Key West with his family in the early 1850s and likely employed in wrecking. Joseph married Mary Elizabeth Roberts on Oct. 22, 1857, producing six children. He escaped the island to enlist in the "Key West Avengers" in late April 1862, and was wounded at Missionary Ridge seventeen months later. Bartlum may have transferred to the *CSS Savannah* in early 1864 with other Key Westers but no official records of service exist after February 6, 1864. Postwar he returned to the island and worked in carpentry and cigar making, passing away on September 19, 1903. Mary Elizabeth applied for and was granted a Confederate Widow's Pension for her husband's service.

Charles H. Berry of Key West escaped the island between May and November 1861 to join Mulrennan's Coast Guards at Tampa, then enlisted in the Seventh Florida Regiment in late April 1862. Transferred to the CS Navy in early August and assigned to the *CSS Chattahoochee*, he was among the 16 crewmen killed by a boiler explosion on May 27, 1863, all of whom were interred with the ships remains.

Winer Bethel came to Key West from Nassau in 1847, became an island attorney and in 1861 was a probate judge. Both Bethel and William Pinckney, the latter the second native-born of Key West, were described in late 1860 as "outright secessionists."[11] They, along with Asa F. Tift were elected to represent Monroe County at the early-January 1861 Tallahassee convention to consider Florida's independence. Pinckney was then junior partner and manager of Wall & Company, a highly successful mercantile and wreck salvage business, as senior partner William H. Wall had retired and was living in New York. According to Fort Taylor's commander in May 1861, Pinckney actively promoted independence, voted for and signed Florida's Secession Ordinance, and upon returning to Key West actively solicited subscriptions for Confederate bonds at his business. For their part as Monroe County delegates Bethel and Pinckney were arrested in mid-June 1862, held for several months in close confinement in Fort Taylor, then imprisoned at Virginia's Fortress Monroe for nearly a year without a hearing.

---

11 Camp, pg. 33.

Concluding the final paragraph of a letter to his superior condemning Bethel and Pinckney and noting their local popularity, an officer wrote: "I cannot close this letter without protesting the sympathy shown them by local government officials when arrested yesterday. They appeared to vie with each other to make them comfortable, and take away from the arrest as much of its character as possible. This is all wrong and should not be countenanced by the government."[12] Bethel returned to the island and elected Key West mayor in 1872.

John A. Bethel was born on the island July 21, 1834, his family were previously early settlers near St. Petersburg. An island schoolteacher when war came, he left for Tampa to join Mulrennan's Coast Guards in November 1861. He was promoted to coxswain two months later, then enlisted in the "Key West Avengers" for 3 years or the war. Rising to the rank of lieutenant, he resigned in May of 1864 due to chronic poor health. Postwar he fished and operated a small store at Point Pinellas, drawing a Confederate pension; Bethell died on April 12, 1915.

Thomas Burns joined Mulrenan's Coast Guard in late November 1861 and mustered into the "Avengers" for the war. He was transferred to the CS Navy on August 8, 1862 and assigned to the *CSS Chattahoochee* as an ordinary seaman and survived its later boiler explosion.

Cyrus A. Canfield departed Key West with Watson and others in late September 1861 as stowaways aboard the *Lady Bannerman* and reached Jacksonville by early December. Here Cyrus signed on to the *Olive Branch* to run the blockade between Jacksonville and Nassau and paid $50 per month wages. On January 26th, 1861, Robert Watson writes that the *Olive Branch* has been captured by the enemy and *Canfield* taken prisoner by "the damned black republicans."[13]

Charles H. Chapman joined Mulrennan's Coast Guard as a seaman on November 27, 1861. He remained in this unit until mustered into the "Key West Avengers" in late November. He was promoted to corporal in early August 1862 when islander Samuel Morgan transferred to the *CSS Chattahoochee*. Reported on detached duty to the city police at Knoxville from December 2, 1862, until March, 1863, he remained in Tennessee until late February 1864 when

---

12 Browne, Appendix O, pp. 220-221.
13 Campbell, pp 10; 20.

transferred to the *CSS Savannah* as a seaman and shortly after, the *CSS Sampson* which destroyed a railroad bridge across the Savannah River in November 1864 to prevent an enemy crossing.

Jules Chebert was born in France in 1820 and arrived in Florida about 1848. Before the war he lived in Key West with wife Missouri, nee Roberts, and the first of three children born in 1861. He left the island in late November 1861 to join Mulrennan's Coast Guard at Tampa as a coxswain. Jules was transferred to the CS Navy in August 1862 to join the crew of the *CSS Chattahoochee* until its deadly boiler explosion. He was afterward assigned to the *CSS Savannah* and shot through the body while participating in the capture of the *USS Water Witch*. After the war Jules returned to Key West and was employed as a seaman until his death in 1873.

Joseph E. Cole was mustered into Mulrennan's Coast Guard on November 27, 1861, as a coxswain, then enlisted in the "Key West Avengers" in late-April. Records indicate he was transferred on August 8, 1862, to the ill-fated *CSS Chattahoochee* as quartermaster. Injured in the boiler explosion of late May, 1863 he likely remained in CS Navy service. He returned to Key West postwar where he lived with wife Georgianna, and passed away on March 12, 1889.

Peter A. Crusoe was born c.1820 at Gibraltar and arrived on the island in the late 1840s. He married Sarah A. Roberts in the mid-1850s and served as Clerk of the Circuit Court at Key West, Florida, from 1851 to 1861. In December 1860 he was appointed as one of two secretaries assigned to record the meeting held to nominate delegates to the State secession convention which assembled in Tallahassee the next month. On May 20th 1861, he faced the choice of imprisonment or exile and sailed for Tampa to join Mulrenan's Coast Guard. He later enlisted in the "Key West Avengers" but discharged soon after - the reason stated is illegible in the records. According to Robert Watson's diary Crusoe is known to have then returned to Tampa to engage in blockade running until that town was occupied by the enemy in May 1864. He was taken into custody for refusing to take the oath of allegiance. Postwar, Crusoe returned to Key West to again serve as Circuit Court clerk from 1865 to 1868. He died at Key West on March 5, 1873.[14]

---

14 Schmidt III, pg. 53.

Edmund Curry was born at Key West on July 4, 1846. He mustered in the "Key West Avengers" on May 4, 1862, and only four months later was diagnosed with malaria. He was discharged in Kentucky in October 1862 and settled in Hillsborough County where he married in December 1867. Curry drew a Confederate pension until his death on June 14, 1925, at St. Petersburg.

Henry Curry was mustered into Confederate service on April 25, 1862, enlisting as a private in the "Key West Avengers" for a period of 3 years or the war. He was reportedly discharged from service prior to July 8, 1862 with the reason not specified.

Joseph Curry was born March 8, 1841. He married Frances Johnson on December 7, 1859. He was mustered into service as a seaman on October 14, 1861, with Capt. Noyes Florida Coast Guard at St. Marks, then as a private in the "Key West Avengers." Reported absent on Confederate records from April 1862 through 1863, he is reported at occupied Key West on sick furlough in late 1862. The Provost Marshal reports Curry had left Key West to visit his father at Manatee in June 1863 but apparently left to join the Confederate army. He was known to be chronically sick or disabled while in service and later an invalid in a Confederate Hospital. Curry died at Key West, Florida, on July 9, 1912.

Samuel George Curry was born on the island March 22, 1843. He joined the "Key West Avengers" in late April 1862 and two years later was transferred to the *CSS Chattahoochee* as a seaman, then the *CSS Savannah* until its scuttling in late December 1864. Postwar, Curry settled at Manatee where he married Amanda Melvinia Andress on September 20, 1866. He later served as commander of a local United Confederate Veterans Camp, drawing a Confederate pension until his death on April 5, 1925, at Bradenton.

William D. Curry was born in the Bahamas on May 6, 1840 and came to Key West as a young boy. He escaped the island's blockade to join the "Key West Avengers" on April 25, 1862, as a private. Often hospitalized with illness in Tennessee and Georgia, he is reported present on the company muster roll in early 1864. There is no further record of his service but he drew Florida's Confederate pension from May 3, 1886 until his death at Key West on August 13, 1886.

Born at Ferrol, Spain c.1840, Manuel Francisco (Frank) Diaz came to Key West in mid-1850s. He may have left the island with Robert Watson and others in the fall of 1861 and by late January had joined Mulrennan's Coast Guard at Tampa. He was transferred to the *CSS Savannah* in March 1864 and served aboard her until scuttling. Postwar found him back in Key West working as a seaman, then proprietor of a foreign fruits and grocery store at the corner of Thomas and Julia Streets in the 1880. He married Ascunsion Cabeza in 1888. Along with his wartime comrades he was a member of the Franklin Buchanan Camp of the United Confederate Veterans fraternal organization until his death in 1910.

Edward Dorsey likely left the island with Robert Watson and joined Mulrennan's Coast Guard in early January 1862. He joined the "Key West Avengers" in April 1862 and served in Tennessee and Georgia before being transferred to the *CSS Savannah* in February 1864.[15]

John Dupuy enlisted at a private in the "Key West Avengers" in late April 1862 and served in Tennessee. Badly wounded at the Taylor's Gap battle near Atlanta in early 1864, he received a notice of transfer to the CS Navy. Reported two weeks later as "in good spirits and doing well" by visiting Key West diarist Robert Watson, he died of his wounds on March 7, 1864.[16]

Joseph Fagan was born c.1846 at St. Augustine and in 1860 he was a laborer living at Key West with parents Henry and Ellen Fagan, and one brother. While smack fishing for the Havana market off Manatee County in the autumn of 1861 with John T. Lowe, they were boarded by Florida Coast Guards and encouraged to join their forces. Fagan mustered in as a seaman in early December and later joined the "Key West Avengers." Captured at Missionary Ridge in late November 1863, he was imprisoned until March 29, 1865. Postwar he resided at Tampa where he married Mary Aurelia Bourquardez in October 1869. A member of the UCV Camp Loring No. 1126, at Tampa, he drew a Confederate Pension until his death on June 4, 1911. Mary was denied a Widow's Pension as Joseph took the US oath prior to the official cessation of the war.

---

15 Campbell, pg. 97.
16 *Ibid.*, pg. 101.

Rofino Fales, b. 1834, was mustered into Mulrennan's Coast Guard on December 1, 1861 where he served aboard the *Mary Jane* until enlisting in the "Key West Avengers" in late April 1862. He served in the Western Theater until transferred to the CS Navy on February 25, 1864, and duty aboard the ironclad ram *CSS Savannah* until it was scuttled. He was briefly a crewman aboard the *CSS Columbia* at Charleston then followed the others to Fort Fisher and Drewry's Bluff in 1865. It is unclear if he returned to the island postwar.

"Avenger" Henry Fagan was born at St. Augustine in 1839. In September 1860 Henry was serving aboard the sloop *USS Richmond* as assistant engineer. At the outbreak of war in 1861 he resigned and was first assigned to the *CSS MacRae*, then the *CSS Louisiana* which were both at New Orleans. He was aboard the latter when it was captured by the enemy. Imprisoned at Fort Warren, he was exchanged at the end of July, 1862 and assigned to the *CSS Chattahoochee* in Georgia. Henry was among the 16 crewmen killed by the ship's boiler explosion in late May 1863 and interred with the ships remains.[17]

The husband of islander Harriet "Hattie" Pinckney was Lt. Caleb Huse, whom she met and married in 1851 after his post-West Point graduation artillery assignment to Fort Zachary Taylor. Hattie, born in New York, was the daughter of Dr. Theodore A. Pinckney and Sibyl Marvin Pinckney -- the latter sister of Key West district judge and wartime loyalist William Marvin. Huse was a Newburyport, Massachusetts native, born in 1835 and who entered West Point at age 16, graduating seventh in his Class of 1851.[18]

Huse soon returned to West Point as instructor of chemistry, minerology and geology, and in 1854 was granted a long leave to travel through Europe inspecting the armaments of several countries. Given the unsettled condition of the country in early 1861, he resigned his commission in February when told to report for active duty. After the outbreak of war he was asked by friend and Navy Secretary Stephen R. Mallory of Key West to be the Confederacy's chief purchasing agent in Europe. Huse was personally commissioned a major by President Davis.[19] Sent to England to obtain munitions and weapons, he met

---

17 Find-a-grave.com, henryfagan.
18 Browne, pp. 190-191.
19 Rogers, pg. 9.

with great success in securing rifles, cannon, powder, percussion caps, blankets, shoes, medicines -- and was credited with furnishing more than half of the six-hundred thousand small arms – most of them excellent Enfield rifles – shipped from Europe to arm Southern regiments.[20] The South's military successes from mid-to-late 1862 are attributed to his extraordinary abilities in acquiring arms for the Confederacy.

In late 1862, Huse obtained one of the South's most productive early blockade runners, the side-wheeler, twin-stack *Cornubia*. In service for almost a year before being captured, she completed eighteen runs which brought much-needed supplies into the Confederacy.[21] Another fast ship procured by Huse in England was the *Harriet Pinckney*, named for his Key West wife and intended as a blockade runner. With her deep draft, she eventually served as a supply ship between England and Nassau. In the postwar Huse returned to New York where he established an academy at Highland Falls, New York, preparing young men for West Point. One of his students was future General John J. Pershing. The union of Caleb and Hattie eventually produced 13 children, including son, Rear Admiral Harry McLaren Pinckney Huse, born at West Point in 1858, and Medal of Honor recipient for bravery under fire at Vera Cruz, Mexico in April 1914. Huse passed away in 1905.

William A. Josselyn initially mustered into Mulrennan's Coast Guard as a seaman on New Year's Day 1862 and was assigned a crewmember of the *Mary Jane*. He remained in this unit until mustered into the "Key West Avengers" in late April 1862. Chronic illness led to his discharge under a Surgeon's Certificate shortly afterward, he may have returned to Key West.

James Lovitt was likely a Nova Scotia-born smack fisherman at Key West who left the island about July 1861 to join Capt. James McMullen's Infantry at Clearwater Harbor for three months service, then mustered into Mulrennan's Coast Guard on December 20, 1861. James then enlisted in the "Key West Avengers" and was listed in Crusoe's letter to Mallory requesting transfer to the CS Navy. He was present for duty in Tennessee until discharged for an unspecified illness on October 22, 1862 – expiring the following day at 53 years of age.

---

20   Rapier. Pg. 123.
21   Carr, pg. 161.

Alfred Percival Lowe was one of several stowaways on the English schooner *Lady Bannerman* in the fall of 1861, doing so after being denied a pass to leave the island and refusing to take an oath of allegiance to the US government. The son of William and the feisty, Southern flag waving Caroline E. Lowe, he was born on Green Turtle Cay, Bahamas on July 20, 1840. A constant companion to Robert Watson, Alfred joined Mulrennan's Coast Guard in December 1861 and eventually rose to sergeant in the "Key West Avengers" He transferred to the CS Navy in March 1864 and assigned to the *CSS Savannah* until it was scuttled, then sent to Fort Fisher and Drewry's Bluff. Returning to the island postwar, he married Mary Jane Whitehurst in 1867 with their union producing eight children. He was a member of the Franklin Buchanan Camp, United Confederate Veterans, No. 1214, at Key West, until his death in December 1921.[22]

William E. "Butcher Bill" Lowe, born on November 23, 1839, at Nassau, Bahamas, was living with his parents and brother, Alfred at Manatee County, Florida in 1860. He was mustered into the "Key West Avengers" on May 1, 1862, and transferred to the *CSS Savannah* on March 3, 1864. Lowe was discharged from service due to injuries by Surgeon's Certificate the following June. He passed away at Key West on April 26, 1926.

Bahamian-immigrant John Thomas Lowe was born on Green Turtle Cay February 15, 1830, migrating to Key West by 1847 where he married Laura D. Meares in 1853. Working prewar as a wrecker, merchant seaman and fisherman,[23] the latter with friends Joe Fagan and Augustus Archer fishing Florida's west coast for the Havana market. After enlisting at Tampa in the "Key West Avengers," he rose in rank to Sergeant on March 1st, 1863. He transferred to the CS Navy and was first assigned to the *CSS Tallahassee*, then the *CSS Savannah*. Lowe participated in the daring capture of the *USS Water Witch* on June 3, 1864, the Savannah was guided by black pilot Moses Dallas who died in the attack. After scuttling the *Savannah* in December 1864, Lowe is recorded as paroled at Tampa and employed postwar as a merchant

---

22 Browne, pg. 97.
23 Campbell, pg. 189.

seaman and pilot. In 1883 Lowe established "Lowe's Landing" near the town of Anona (near Largo), named for the sweet apples imported from Key West. Lowe died at Clearwater, FL, Aug 5, 1921.[24]

Diarist Watson records the desertion of Union Soldier Jacob Mail at Key West in early 1862, from either the New York or Pennsylvania regiments. Mail may have escaped as a stowaway to Tampa where he joined the "Key West Avengers" on May 1, 1862, serving with the regiment in Tennessee until the following October when he deserted to the enemy in Kentucky. According to the diary, Mail was later found among a group of some 1,000 Union prisoners at Savannah, Georgia in late September 1864. Watson records that no one would have noticed him but when he offered to enlist in grey he was discovered. "Avenger" Joseph Cole reported Mail to an officer who sent him to the stockade. Watson expected Mail would be shot "and deserves it."[25]

Probably the most accomplished Key Wester is Stephen R. Mallory who came to Key West in 1820 with his parents John and Ellen, she, Irish-born and the only white woman on the island.[26] His father John Mallory was a construction engineer from Connecticut who passed shortly after their arrival as did his older brother John. Stephen's mother then ran a boarding house for seamen to make ends meet and try to pay for Stephen's education, sending him for three years to a Moravian academy in Nazareth, central Pennsylvania.[27] Beyond that formal education Stephen buried himself in books, spending time with Seminole companions up the coast, learning good moral habits. In the early 1830s he became island attorney William Marvin's law clerk and learned wreck and salvage jurisprudence which was a large part of the local economy. He rose to inspector of customs, was elected town marshal, collector of customs and Democrat party organizer on the island. Mallory had become sufficiently influential to be entrusted with power of attorney for the wealthy Asa. F. Tift, and by this time had become fond of remarking of the future: "nous verrons" – in French, "we shall see." In 1838 Stephen married Angela Moreno of

---

24 Browne, pg. 97.
25 Campbell, pg. 131.
26 Durkin, pg. 11.
27 *Ibid.*, pg. 14.

Pensacola, a Catholic like he who was fluent in French, Spanish and English – and musical. Through this marriage he became related to Angela's cousin, Felix Senac.

His prominence in State politics was instrumental in his appointment as United States Senator from Florida, with Whig support over veteran David Levy Yulee in 1850, as Mallory was considered less a Southern nationalist.[28] In the US Senate he gained prominence with his 1853 appointment to chair of the Naval Affairs committee which foreshadowed his future in the Confederate government. Once war began Mallory needed to quickly assemble a navy. He promoted ironclad ships – as he did prewar as chairman of the Senate Naval Affairs Committee – also conceiving the highly successful strategy of Southern commerce raiders to destroy Northern shipping. So successful was this strategy that by 1865 the Confederate privateers had all but destroyed the US merchant marine. Mallory was instrumental in gaining the transfer to the Confederate Navy of a number of Key West seamen who escaped the occupied island and were assigned to a Florida Infantry regiment. After his release from prison in 1866 he was forced to apologize to the US Secretary of War and President. He lived postwar in Pensacola where most of his former slaves returned to work for him. Unable to support themselves on the generous wages he paid them, Mallory supplied them with quality foodstuffs gratis.[29] Mallory passed away quietly at home on November 12, 1873.[30]

Born October 7, 1829, at Nassau, **William Brownell Meares** came to Key West with mother Meriem on June 30, 1838, and naturalized there in July 1852. He is believed to have sailed to "Lowe's Landing" (now Anona, Hillsborough County) with his mother in 1859; an old family friend, Capt. "Gus" Archer, is reported to have traveled with them. Meares was mustered into the "Key West Avengers" in mid-May 1862 at Tampa, but was discharged the following month due to loss of an eye and other disabilities. He married Sarah Roberts July 9, 1866, at Lowe's Landing. William died October 18, 1894 at Anona; Sarah applied for and was granted a Confederate Widow's Pension for her husband's service.

---

28 *Ibid.*, pg. 38.
29 *Ibid.*, pg. 398.
30 *Ibid.*, pg. 414.

Manuel Monte De Ocha was born ca. 1845 at Hillsborough County, Florida. He is mentioned by Robert Watson as being a member of Mulrenan's Coast Guards, and listed as a Marine and citizen of Key West by Peter Crusoe in his letter to Navy Secretary Stephen Mallory. De Ocha joined the "Key West Avengers" on April 25, 1862, then later transferred to the CS Navy and service aboard the *CSS Savannah* from early March 1864 until its scuttling. Postwar he married Matilda Willingham on January 17, 1867, at Tampa, Florida. Manuel died at Fort Meade, Polk County, Florida, in March, 1876. Despite having remarried twice after his death, Matilda applied for and was granted a Confederate Widow's Pension for her Manuel's service.

Samuel Morgan was another Bahamian-born Key Wester who escaped Northern gunboats blockading the island and mustered with Mulrennan's Coast Guard in late November 1861. He afterward enlisted in the "Key West Avengers" until transferred to the *CSS Chattahoochee* as a sailmaker. After a boiler explosion sank the vessel in late May 1863 he transferred to the *CSS Savannah* in the same position. After the scuttling of that ship in December 1864, he likely followed other crewmembers to Fort Fisher, then Drewry's Bluff and Sayler's Creek. Postwar Morgan returned to Key West with historian Browne noting he was for many years an invalid in the Marine Hospital, where he died June 16, 1904.[31]

Joseph Henry Moss was born in the Bahamas on November 17, 1845, and by 1860 was living with his mother Sarah at Key West. He mustered into Mulrennan's Coast Guard as a seaman on November 27, 1861, and five months later the "Key West Avengers." In the midst of battle at Chickamauga, Moss earned high distinction for "most conspicuous ... gallantry and good conduct." He transferred in late February 1864 to the *CSS Savannah* and served aboard her until it was scuttled. Paroled on June 15, 1865, he returned to Key West where he was employed as a carpenter and married islander Lydia Esther Pierce on February 17, 1873. He later was employed as assistant keeper at the Jupiter Inlet Light Station at Dade (now Palm Beach) County about 1880, where he died on May 22, 1885. Wife Lydia applied for and was granted a Confederate Widow's Pension for her husband's wartime service.

---

31 Browne, pg. 98.

Described by historian Browne as a "witty, rollick-some, boisterous person," ³² Irishman Henry Mulrennan was a successful island prewar merchant and considered one of the "cultivated and wealthy citizens, all strongly pro-Southern. Henry's prewar secessionist activities are already noted which caused the fort's commander, apparently a friend, to offered him either imprisonment or deportation. Henry arrived at Tampa and joined the growing militia forces at Cedar Key monitoring enemy activity and encouraged other Key West men to join him. Lt. Mulrennan rose to captain a year later, rose to quartermaster major in late April 1864 and later engaged in blockade running between Havana and Tampa. Captured in mid-May 1864 and imprisoned at Forts Delaware and Lafayette, he was not released until several months after the war ended. Henry was nearly hanged on the charge of having disguised his men as Negro contrabands to attract Northern gunboats closer to shore, and then unleashing a masked battery to destroy the enemy boats. Only through the intercession of former New York Mayor Fernando Wood and publisher James Gordon Bennett was he finally exonerated and released.³³ This event was probably the work of South Carolina-born Capt. John W. Pearson, who became Fort Brooke's commander at Tampa in June 1863. Pearson was retaliating for the *USS Sagamore's* earlier indiscriminate shelling of Tampa civilians on June 30 and found an opportunity the following March to set a trap for his enemy.³⁴

Henry returned to Tampa in the early postwar, then brought his two sons to Key West after wife Sarah passed away in December 1866. As a fitting testament to his popularity on the island he was forced to leave in 1861, Henry was elected mayor twice: 1868 and 1870. He died in 1874 at the age of 44, "A short life to have passed through so many vicissitudes!"³⁵

After Genoa, Italy native Marcus Oliveri was denied as pass to leave Key West in September 1861, he stowed away on the British schooner *Lady Bannerman* with Robert Watson on Friday, Sept. 27. Mustered into service in early December 1861 with Mulrennan's Coast Guards,

---

32 Ibid., pg. 178.
33 Warner, pg. 248.
34 Waters, pg. 11.
35 Browne, pp. 177-178.

he was soon assigned to the long boat *Mollie Post*. He entered the "Key West Avengers" but was soon discharged with a Surgeon's Certificate. He was afterward engaged in blockade running. Olivieri passed away on the island on Oct. 5th, 1887.[36]

New Smyrna-native A.N. Pacetti (1829-1913) was a second-generation Minorcan-Italian who served as a boatman in the US Navy during the Seminole Wars in Florida. After Florida declared independence in January 1861, Pacetti was captain of a boat carrying stranded Northerners to Union-occupied Key West which was seized upon arrival. While awaiting trial for alleged treason, he escaped with other stowaways on the *Lady Bannerman* on Sept. 27, 1861. He afterward enlisted in the Confederate Navy and captained vessels at Tampa and Mobile, Alabama. At war's end Marcus returned to St. Augustine and married his second-cousin, Amelia Monson, living at 56 Marine Street in a home which stands today. It is believed Pacetti was proprietor of Capo's Bathhouse located on Bay Street, a Charlotte Street confectionery, and also served as St. Johns County Sheriff 1877-1881.

Key Vaca-native John Pent was born February 4, 1845, and was nearly 17-years-old when he escaped the island to enlist in Mulrennan's Coast Guard in mid- December 1861. In late-April 1862 he enlisted with other island men in the "Key West Avengers" for infantry duty in Tennessee. Pent suffered a right-hand wound at the battle of Missionary Ridge in late November 1863 and was afterward assigned to a reserve unit for the remainder of the war. He was paroled and returned to Key West where he married Elizabeth Bowe in 1880, and with whom he sired five children. His application for a Confederate pension in 1907, witnessed by Robert Watson and Alfred Lowe, notes he was employed as an "Overseer of Prisoners" by the City of Key West. A member of Key West's Franklin Buchanan Camp No. 1214, UCV after 1889, he passed away on June 27, 1919; wife Elizabeth died less than a month later.[37]

George Victor Rickards was born at Yorkshire, England on August 18, 1836, and came to the US sometime in 1853, Key West about 1855. Employed as light keeper at Egmont Key at the mouth of Tampa Bay at the onset of Florida's secession, Rickards found himself caught

---

36 *Ibid.*, pg. 97.
37 Find-a-grave.com – Laurie Knotts Gilbreath.

in a struggle for control of the lighthouse. The Unionist collector of customs at Key West was at odds with the collector at St. Marks, siding with an independent Florida. Feigning allegiance to Union blockading ships near his key until their absence allowed him to flee, Rickard's crated-up Egmont Light's important Fresnel lens and left for Tampa with the crate, his family, and as many supplies as he could transport. On December 24, 1861, he joined Mulrenan's Coast Guard and was assigned to the *Mary Jane* until mustered into the "Key West Avengers" on April 25, 1862. Rickards was listed on Crusoe's list for transfer to naval service and as a citizen of the island. He served in Tennessee and gained promotion to 1st sergeant in mid-1864. Rickards was captured near Atlanta on July 22, 1864 and imprisoned at Camp Chase, Ohio where he died on April 17, 1865. He is interred in the prison cemetery.

Richard Roberts was a Bahamian-born sea captain employed as a wrecker since 1829 who married Amelia Curry in 1834. He was granted citizenship in 1840, the same year their first-born Mary Elizabeth, was born on the island. Their home at 408 William Street is said to have been disassembled in the Bahamas, shipped and reconstructed at Key West after the 1846 hurricane. He likely pursued lucrative blockade running and, according to his family, ferrying Florida men from occupied areas like Key West to join Southern forces. In August 1863 he was detained on suspicion of blockade running near Punta Rassa and arrested for refusing to take the oath of allegiance to the US government. Taken to Key West as a prisoner, he was later released on parole. He returned to Key West postwar and died 11 November 1878 - buried in Key West cemetery.[38]

Ship's carpenter John W. Russell was born on January 28, 1832, at Green Turtle Cay, Abaco, Bahamas, coming to Key West with wife Caroline and two children in 1860. He joined Mulrenan's Coast Guard as a seaman on January 1, 1862, then mustered into the "Key West Avengers" on April 25, 1862. After initial service in Tennessee, he transferred in late-April 1864 to the *CSS Georgia*, then the *CSS Macon* on October 6, 1864. Though no further record of him exists and as the *Macon* withdrew to Augusta after Savannah's capitulation, he likely remained with her crew. He survived the war, passing away on May 1, 1903.

---

38 Viele, pp. 86-89.

Bahamian immigrant John B. Sands was born at Ragged Island in 1841 and was likely employed in wrecking at Key West prewar. By late November 1861 he had escaped the island blockade to muster into Mulrennan's Coast Guard, then joined "Key West Avengers" in late-April 1862 for duty in Tennessee. Sands was transferred to the CS Navy in early August 1862, sent to the Navy Yard at Columbus, Georgia, then served aboard the *CSS Chattahoochee*. Escaping injury during its deadly boiler explosion in late May 1863, Sands transferred to the *CSS Savannah* until it was scuttled in December 1864. He was briefly a crewman aboard the *CSS Columbia* at Charleston then followed the others to Fort Fisher and Drewry's Bluff in 1865. He was captured after Richmond's evacuation and paroled on April 9, 1865; he returned to Key West where he married Eliza Demeritt on March 17, 1872. John died on October 25th, 1899.

Samuel Young Sawyer, born on January 7, 1837 at Green Turtle Cay. There he worked in wrecking and came to Key West about 1850 where he married Amelia Curry in early September 1857. He left the island to muster into the "Key West Avengers" on March 5, 1862 at Tampa. He was promoted to sergeant in early August, likely due to vacancies after numerous transfers of other Key West men to the CS Navy that month. In early November 1862, he was reported sick in Knoxville, Tennessee where he died on January 18, 1863 amid conflicting reports of "disease" and "drinking too much water after a long march."

William Oliver Sawyer, born in 1837 in the Bahamas and worked as a Key West seaman at the outbreak of war. He escaped the island to join Mulrennan's Coast Guards at Cedar Key on December 13, 1861, and the "Key West Avengers" in late April 1862. After reaching Tennessee William died in camp at Knoxville, Tennessee, perhaps of typhoid fever, after the regiment joined the Confederacy's western forces. He is buried at Bethel Confederate Cemetery, Knoxville.[39]

Felix Senac was a relatively unknown Key West immigrant who played a unique role in the war. Diarist William Hackley mentions him in September 1853 and Senac could have been on the island as early as 1847 as chief clerk and paymaster at Fort Zachary Taylor's construction site. Felix was a native of the Spanish Florida's city of Pensacola, born in 1815, cousin of Angela Moreno who was the

---

39 Browne, pg. 98.

daughter of Don Francisco Moreno and wife of Stephen R. Mallory, then Collector of Customs at Key West. One of Angela's brothers is Fernando J. Moreno who was a clerk at William H. Wall's Warehouse and later Key West mayor, 1852-1853. He was certainly well-acquainted with fellow clerk and future "secessionist" William Pinckney. It is believed that Senac's coming to Key West was the result Angela Mallory's sister Irene's influence, whose husband, Capt. Jeremiah M. Scarritt assumed command of Fort Taylor in May, 1852.[40]

According to the William Whitehead map of Key West marked by late Key West historian Betty Moreno Bruce, the Stephen Mallory home was on the southwest corner of Greene and Front Streets, across from the old Custom House where he was Collector. The Asa Tift home was near the northeast corner of Caroline and Front Streets, close to his wharf, and the Senac home was nearby.[41]

In mid-1857, Senac was commissioned US Navy Paymaster through Mallory's influence, noting Senac's fluent French and Spanish and departs Key West aboard ship for the Pacific. In late March 1861 he is in port at Italy where he learns of Florida's independence and Mallory's resignation from Congress as well as appointment as Confederate Secretary of the Navy. Senac resigns his commission on April 1, 1861 along with his Captain, Maryland-born George N. Hollins, and other officers who accept equal rank in the new CSA Navy.[42] Entering Confederate service as Paymaster in mid-August and sent to New Orleans to oversee financial disbursements for the new *CSS Louisiana* and *CSS Mississippi*, he found the latter was being constructed by Asa and Nelson Tift. Senac was visited often by now-Commodore Hollins, commander of the Mississippi River Fleet and fascinated by the innovative ironclad design of Nelson Tift.

In May 1863 the multilingual Senac is assigned to Europe as a Confederate munitions purchasing agent to assist Henry Hotze, but cannot escape port on a blockade runner to England until mid-June from Wilmington, North Carolina. He departed this port in the

---

40 Rapier, pg. 15.

41 *Ibid.*, pg. 2.

42 *Ibid.*, pp. 29; 49.

company of Arthur J.L. Freemantle of the Coldstream Guards and exiled Ohio politician Clement Vallandigham, who was journeying to Canada via Bermuda.

Secretary Mallory explained Senac's presence in Liverpool in a message to Confederate Navy Agent James Bulloch: "Should you stand in need of reliable assistance in your efforts in France, you may, I think, derive it from Paymaster Senac of the Navy, who has been ordered to Liverpool to pay officers, etc. He speaks French with purity and elegance, Spanish also, possesses fine business capacity, and is a gentleman of ripe judgement and rare merit."[43]

Senac was being advanced funds by Secretary Bulloch for purchases, such as an order for 2,000 C. Girard & Company grape shot revolvers for Navy use. He also oversaw purchases and payments for the advanced ironclad rams *Sphinx* and *Cheops*, to be delivered to some other nation and then delivered to the Confederacy. The Confederate Bureau of Provisions and Clothing sent Senac a schedule of articles, most importantly shoes, coats and trousers, blankets, plus beef and foodstuffs, with purchases paid for by cotton and tobacco. In addition, his purchasing missions took him to England as well as Scotland.[44]

It was now too late to build another Confederate Navy. Despite all the effort and expenditure to purchase a fleet of modern naval vessels, only the ram the *CSS Stonewall*, and commerce raider *Shenandoah* was aquired, and the latter not being a formidable warship. Though the Confederate government received full refunds for ships not delivered and money was available, the US government had shut down all possible avenues for shipbuilding in Europe. The provisions and supplies Felix was obtaining were not reaching the Confederacy as Wilmington was closed by enemy land and sea attack in mid-January 1865, and Charleston was effectively blockaded. By the end of February the South was cut off from the outside world, except for Matamoros, which proved to be a distant and ineffective route.

---

43 *Ibid.*, pg. 127.
44 *Ibid.*, pg. 151-155.

Mallory sent orders for Paymaster Senac to remain in Paris to handle the Confederacy's remaining accounts.[45] When the long-at-sea Shenandoah docked at Liverpool on November 6, 1865 to surrender to British authorities, Senac arrived to hand captain and crew their backpay with Confederate government funds still on deposit. To the consternation of US authorities, the British granted Capt. James Waddell and his crew political asylum.

With the war now over for Felix Senac, he and his family left Paris for Weisbaden. He had regularly corresponded with Angela Mallory expressing hope for an early release of Stephen Mallory from prison. Senac thought he might pursue a career in stock farming after a visit to South America – and possibly join the "Confederados" in Brazil – those who would not submit to Northern rule.

Felix Senac passed away in Wiesbaden on January 27th, 1866, and was interred in the old churchyard on Platter Strasse -- his grave did not survive two world wars and was not preserved. Wife Mary Louise and daughter Ruby relocated to Paris where the latter taught languages and was courted by former Confederate agent Harry Hotze who remained in Europe. They were married on December 9, 1867 in Paris. While Nelson Tift was in England on business in 1874, brother Asa wrote that he must surely visit Mary Louise, Ruby and husband Harry while in Paris.[46]

William H. Ward was born about 1830 near Syracuse, New York, and was a graduate of the early US Naval Academy. He served in the Mexican War, resigned his Navy commission in 1852 and took up residence in Key West. He began editing the *Key of the Gulf* newspaper in 1857 which provided a platform for his views on the increasing sectionalism afflicting the country. In 1858 he married Emeline Frances Watlington and made their home at 322 Duval Street. Throughout 1860 and early 1861, his weekly, four-page newspaper became the most widely-known pro-independence newspaper in Florida with the masthead announcing "*Ask Nothing But What is Right – Submit to Nothing That is Wrong.*" In early April, 1861, Ward traveled to Montgomery via Pensacola to report on military movements and strength at Key West.[47]

---

45 *Ibid.*, pg. 180.
46 *Ibid.*, pg. 203.
47 Schmidt III, pg. 33.

Ward returned to Key West to publish a few more editions, with the April 27th issue infuriating Fort Taylor's commander "as it espoused the cause of the secessionists" and being "more violent and incendiary than its previous numbers." Threatened with imprisonment, he departed the island in early May as habeas corpus was suspended by the military "in order to arrest without molestation the parties suspected of uttering the treasonable sentiments, etc." [48] Ward was appointed lieutenant in mid-March 1862 at New Orleans and was aboard the *CSS Louisiana* during the enemy siege. Captured and exchanged in late April 1862, he then served as executive officer of the *CSS Palmetto State*.

In the middle of 1864, Navy Secretary Stephen Mallory was determined to increase commerce raiding against the North, using light draught, fast steamers such as the British-built *Atalanta*. This already-successful blockade runner was designed by a Royal Navy expert, with twin propellers driven by two 100 horsepower engines, and virtually invisible with its light gray paint. Mallory bought her for an overpriced 25,000 pounds, but thought it worth the price considering the havoc she could wreak against enemy commerce.[49]

The *Atalanta* was armed with several rifled cannon, rechristened *Tallahassee* and commanded by John Taylor Wood, grandson of Zachary Taylor and nephew of Jefferson Davis. The ship's second-in-command and boarding officer was Lt. Ward. Steaming past Fort Fisher below Wilmington in early August 1864 and out to sea between two blockading ships on a moonless night, within four days a merchant ship was captured and several more prizes taken as the *Tallahassee* sailed northward. After setting New England and New York City in a panic the raider steamed to Halifax for bunker coal and minor repairs, then back to Wilmington in late August. After nearly three weeks at sea the *Tallahassee* had captured thirty-three enemy merchantmen, destroying twenty-six, all accomplished while eluding powerful Northern ships in search of her.[50]

---

48 *Ibid.*, pp. 44-45.
49 Luraghi, pg. 309.
50 *Ibid.*, pg. 310-311.

The raider left Wilmington again on October 26th, under the command of Lt. Ward. It was rechristened the *Olustee* to commemorate the early-1864 Southern victory in Florida and also to deceive the enemy. During this brief cruise Lt. Ward captured and destroyed six merchantmen off Delaware's coast and fought off five enemy ships before reaching the safety of Fort Fisher. When the massive enemy fleet arrived off the fort in mid-January 1865, Ward was in command of the raider *CSS Chickamauga*. His path to the sea was blocked and after the fort's capitulation he steamed up the Cape Fear River and scuttled the ship and apparently joining the naval battalion forces at Drewry's Bluff.[51] Records indicate he was captured near Appomattox, imprisoned at Johnson's Island and paroled; he never returned to Key West. A gravestone for William H. Ward is found in Elmwood Cemetery in Columbia, South Carolina, giving the date of his passing as April 17, 1920.[52]

Capt. Francis B. Watlington was an early island resident from New York City and well-situated to prosper as a blockade runner. His Confederate Navy record does not begin until 1863. He was first commissioned lieutenant aboard the *CSS Tennessee* in the Mobile Bay Squadron in early May 1863 and served with Admiral Buchanan during the later battle there. At war's end he surrendered at Nanna Hubba Bluff, Alabama on May 10, 1865.[53]

George Watson came to Key West from the Bahamas with brothers William and Robert in 1847, residing with their Griffith relatives on the island. George was able to learn a vocation as office clerk. George departed the island with brother Robert in mid-September 1861 for the Bahamas, though George remained at Harbour Island when Robert left for the mainland a month later. The latter was to learn that George returned to Key West where his wife remained. He was for many years an island auctioneer, and later tax collector, residing on Whitehead Street. Wife Laura passed in 1874.[54]

---

51 Hairr, pg. 22.
52 Csnavy.org, accessed 2.14.22.
53 Porter's Naval History, 785; Register 1864, FL CSA file; JCC 4, 122.
54 Campbell, pg. 6.

Robert Watson was a twelve-year-old when his family left the Bahamas for Key West in 1847 and ten years later obtained his citizenship. Apprenticed to carpentry, the war's beginning found him a skilled craftsman as well as seaman. Having had enough of martial law and military occupation by early September, 1861, he arranged outbound passage as a stowaway with several other local men on the English schooner *Lady Bannerman* bound for Nassau. Beginning a wartime diary upon his departure, the first entry on September 27, 1861 is as follows:

> Owing to the political affairs of the country, and the Federal troops having possession of [Key West], and as it is rather unsafe for a Southern man to live here, I have determined to leave in disgust, consequently, I left today in the schooner *Lady Bannerman* for the Bahama Island, in the company of Cyrus A. Canfield, William Sawyer, Alfred Lowe and others.[55]

Robert's view of the forces waging war against the South is revealed in his description of the enemy as "Lincolnites" and those who captured his blockade running friend Cyrus Canfield as "damned black republicans."[56]

After reaching Jacksonville in mid-November Robert boarded a train for Lake City; at a stop at Baldwin he found Henry Mulrennan and Walter Maloney, Jr. who were bound for the same destination. (at Lake City there were "63 Key West smacksmen" being held prisoner and awaiting interrogation," unaware of their compatriots passing so close to their jail).[57] At Tampa in mid-December, Robert found the Coast Guard there already organized and commanded by Mulrennan and Maloney, Jr., which Robert, George Rickards, Peter Crusoe, William Sawyer, Alfred and John T. Lowe, Marcus Oliveri, John Bethel and other comrades joined – wages were $20 per month for privates. Many Key West men noted in this chapter were either crewmembers of the *Mollie Post* guard boat or assigned to other boats.

---

55 *Ibid.*, pg. 5.
56 *Ibid.*, pg. 20.
57 *Ibid.*, pg. 9.

After service in the West and having been transferred to the CS Navy in early 1864, Watson was assigned to the *CSS Savannah* with other Key Westers until it was scuttled in December 1864. Briefly a crewman aboard the *CSS Columbia* at Charleston, he then followed the others to Fort Fisher and Drewry's Bluff in 1865. He was captured and paroled on April 14, 1865, along with Alfred Lowe, and refused to take the forced oath. Postwar Watson returned to being an island carpenter and on March 10, 1868, married Caroline Elizabeth Kemp, together raising six children. A year later he began construction of a house at 522 Simonton Street – his family residence until 1886. He and brother George had acquired most of the homes and lots in Tract 13 of the city; of them Robert owned 7 and the area was named Watson Street. Robert was a member of the Franklin Buchanan Camp, United Confederate Veterans, No. 1214, at Key West. He died in 1911.

Key West merchant William H. Wall's daughter Elizabeth "Lizzie" Wall was married to US Navy Lt. Julian Myers of Savannah. Despite his parents' objections, Julian enlisted at age 13 in 1838 and excelled in his naval career being twice-promoted for bravery by act of Congress. When war came in 1861, Myers promptly resigned his commission, was arrested and confined at Fort Warren for his decision. Paroled in mid-January 1862, he was commissioned lieutenant in early February 1862 and served at the Richmond station. During the attack and engagements at Mobile Bay in April 1862, Myers commanded the ironclad floating-battery *CSS Huntsville*. Rather than allow her to be boarded and captured by the enemy, he scuttled his ship. Postwar Myers refused to take the oath of allegiance to the Northern government. He and Lizzie made their home at Savannah. He is buried in Savannah's Laurel Grove cemetery.[58]

Jacob Weatherford is listed among Crusoe's Key West men requesting transfer to naval duty while serving with Mulrennan's Coast Guard in early 1862 at Point Pinellas, and in charge of men detailed for coast watch there. He mustered into the "Key West Avengers" on April 25, 1862, and was sent to Tennessee. In late-September 1863 he is absent and a month later listed as a deserter.

---

58   Browne, pg. 189.

Of German birth in 1816, John P. Willemsen was a resident of Manatee County in 1857 and married to Irish-born Sarah Jane. Perhaps originally a Key West smack fisherman prior to his Manatee County residency and drifting northward, John mustered into the "Key West Avengers" in late April, 1862. In Tennessee with the Seventh Florida Infantry through early 1864, he was one of the Key West seaman named in Peter Crusoe's letter to Navy Secretary Mallory in May 1862, requesting transfer to navy duty. This came in late February 1864 but no additional mention of active service remains though he did survive the war. He may have continued with others to the *CSS Savannah*, Battery Buchanan and eventual parole. It appears that postwar he returned to Manatee County working as a pilot. He died at Bradenton about 1904.

CHAPTER 6:

"REBEL SHIPBUILDERS: THE BROTHERS TIFT"

On Thursday, April 25, 1861, Mr. Asa Tift, sympathizing with those who are in array against his country refused to sell coal to a steamer in Government employ ... He was warned to leave the island or be imprisoned in Fort Zachary Taylor.[1]

Given this ultimatum by Fort Taylor's commander Asa put his maritime business empire in the hands of younger brother Charles to sell and departed on the *Salvor* with this family on May 20, 1861. Sold the following December to an island partnership, the property was seized by the US Government in mid-January 1862 while the town was under martial law.[2] By that date, Asa was at New Orleans with brother Nelson superintending construction of the ironclad *CSS Mississippi*.

One of the most successful and prominent early immigrants to Key West after it became a Territory was Asa's father, Capt. Amos Tift, who arrived with his wife and five sons from Mystic, Connecticut in 1826. It was common then for New England fishermen to fish the warm Florida coast waters in winter and Amos believed he could establish a general merchandise store on the island. This he built and operated, with additional income coming from transporting mail and freight

---

1 Schmidt, pg. 41.
2 *Ibid.,* pg. 101.

between Charleston and the island on his schooner *Lily*. But during his last visit home to Connecticut only three years later, he passed away after being infected with yellow fever on the island.[3]

With their father dead, oldest son Amos, Jr. continued the business with Asa F. for 11 years before returning to New England. The second oldest son, Nelson, sailed for Georgia and new opportunities in 1830. Younger brothers Lucius B., a deaf mute, and Julius A. assisted in the family business which Asa ran after Amos, Jr. departure in 1840. Lucius worked in the office while Julius auctioned Key West salvaged goods at Mobile. After Amos Jr. left for Mystic in early 1840, Asa F. ran the family business.[4]

As a successful island merchant committed to the betterment of his island community, Asa had earlier helped bring Rev. Brunot of Pittsburgh to be the first clergyman to hold services on the island in 1832, in St. Paul's Episcopal. This congregation served the entire island regardless of religious affiliation, including Stephen R. Mallory, a Catholic.[5]

Asa F. was described as a tall, fair-skinned, slender and broad-shouldered man with blonde hair and blue-eyes. He had a knack for shrewd business decisions and was said to be a very firm gentleman who stayed to himself. Now known as the Amos C. Tift Company Chandlery, located on the northwest corner of Wall Street and Tift Alley, a very wise purchase was the former US Navy warehouses and wharfs after its anti-piracy squadron left Key West in the 1840s. The business was expanded to include a mail agency, shipping, chandlery, commission merchant, warehousing, coal, water; also established the first ice-house with shipments coming from Mystic. He also built three cisterns to hold rainwater which he could supply to visiting ships.[6]

To protect the small community from devastating fires, Asa was involved in organizing the island's first fire company in October 1834, named the LaFayette Fire Department. He and Stephen Mallory were members of the election committee for officers and a hand-engine was purchased by public subscription. Unfortunately, the hand-engine was

---

3   Fair, pg. 27.
4   Fair, pg. 37.
5   Browne, pg. 27.
6   Heinlein, pg. 5.

found to be near-useless when a fire it was brought to fully demolished the building. Angered by the device's failure at the critical moment, the citizens hurled it off a wharf.[7]

Though not in the wrecking business, Asa and his men arrived first on the scene to claim and salvage the cargo of the Portsmouth merchant ship *Isaac Allerton* which sank in five fathoms during a hurricane in 1856. The cargo worth saving amounted to $50,000, considered the richest salvage operation in the Keys to that date. Also to his benefit in the wrecking industry was appointment as Monroe County auctioneer in 1841.

Though rather well-off financially by the mid-1840s, the hurricane of October 1846 devastated his entire complex of buildings and wharf. This storm also wreaked havoc with the work commenced upon Fort Taylor off the western end of the island. Work restarted the following year. Asa cleared the debris on his property and built two new stone bonded-warehouses, as well as two new wharves, coal platform and other amenities. While rebuilding his business Asa married sixteen-year-old Annie Wheeler in 1847, of Camden, South Carolina and soon became the father of three children: Anna, Cora and Maurice. To provide a permanent home for his growing family Asa purchased a high lot at 907 Whitehead Street for a future home, one that he would not build until 1876.

Tragedy struck Asa's family in May, 1854 as he lost son Maurice to yellow fever on the 14th; daughter Cora on the 19th; and then wife Annie on the 20th. Before her death, Annie had given birth to another child, Maurice on the 16h of May, but another epidemic claimed his life one year later. Adding to this tragedy was a severe lightning strike on his office complex in September 1855 which stunned Asa and shocked others in a counting room. Shortly afterward another fire consumed his store, stock and a steam pump, but the stone warehouses still stood. In the aftermath of his family and business disasters, the latter which he would recover from.[8]

The eve of war found Asa one of the wealthiest Floridians possessing personal property worth $57,000 and real estate holdings valued at $40,000, though he was a widower raising a nine-year-old

---

7   Browne, pg. 151.

8   *Ibid.,* pp. 49-52.

daughter alone. The increasing political sectionalism of the late 1850s may have given Asa pause in considering his small empire's future security, but the island's isolation has a tendency to insulate residents from mainland problems.[9]

At the same time in southern Georgia, brother Nelson Tift through "Yankee enterprise" had accumulated both great wealth and was fully-assimilated into his adopted home. After leaving Key West following his father's death, he established a "Fish and Grocery" store at Savannah in 1830, then moved to Augusta; by mid-1836 Nelson had formed a partnership with five others to establish a new town at the head of the Flint River which eventually became Albany, Georgia. By May 1837, Nelson had become the sole remaining founder and incorporated the town in 1838. With his wealth expanding through wise business deals, land speculation and increased trade on the Flint River, he purchased the steamer *Mary Emeline* and a few years later the *Edwin Forrest*. Finally settling down in 1838 to start a family, Nelson married Wilkes County, Georgia-born Annie (Nancy) Maria Mercer in May of that year, their marriage producing seven children.

After gaining much prominence as a leading citizen of his region, Nelson was elected to the Georgia House of Representatives in 1841 – and re-elected three times. During and after his public service he also edited and published the *Albany Patriot* (with partner S.N. Broughton) from 1845 to 1858, a paper which promoted "democratic principles."[10]

How two Mystic, Connecticut natives came to put their lives and fortunes on the line for the American South can be explained only through the culture they adopted, families and many friendships made over time. Nelson, Asa and Charles all had profited greatly in business while absorbing and coming to understand the rich, patriarchal culture around them. With Southern wives and families, all risked their lives and fortunes in defense of the South in the coming conflict but were among the many who deeply believed that secession could be accomplished peacefully. After all, President James Buchanan opposed the withdrawal of States but was well-aware of his constitutional powers as president, which did not include waging war against any of "them," as stated in Article III, Section 3 of the

---

9   Ibid., pg. 59.

10 Ibid., pp. 40-47.

Constitution. Like their Southern neighbors who surrounded them, Asa, Nelson and Charles understood that the citizens of a sovereign State, North or South, had every right to decide its own political future.

Nelson was not a "fire-eater" in favor of secession, but perhaps saw it as inevitable given his distaste for fanatical abolitionists in the north. He patriotically assisted in Georgia's defense after declaring independence, and was appointed captain in the Confederate States Navy supply department, producing hardtack and beef at his facilities near Albany, and at Palmyra in Lee County.

Nelson held period views of the black slaves in his midst and held Northern abolitionists in contempt, stating in 1845 that "many things that had been told him by the Abolitionists were false, that the Negroes are mostly comfortable, contented and happy." Owning twenty slaves himself and considering the new Republican party an enemy that he labeled "Fanaticism at the North ... threatening to pollute the Constitution itself."[11]

Asa's views on African slavery are not known, though he likely possessed perspective allowing him to view the institution as something existing in his native Connecticut since the mid-1600s. He would also be aware as a Mystic mariner that New England, by 1750, dominated the transatlantic slave trade; that there were three times as many African slaves in Connecticut as there were in Georgia and that Massachusetts held four times as many slaves as Georgia. By the time of the American Revolution, Connecticut *had more enslaved Africans than any other state in New England. It was not until March 1, 1784 that Connecticut legislated gradual abolition,* but slave children born after that date remained enslaved until age 25. This allowed Connecticut owners to sell their slaves before being forced to emancipate.[12] In the end, it was no more immoral for Southern people to own slaves than for Connecticut people to have brought them from Africa as slaves.

Being one of Key West's most prominent men and politically a Democrat, Asa was appointed a delegate to the June, 1860 State convention at Quincy, Florida, along with residents Joseph B. Browne, James Filor, George L. Bowne, and newspaper editor William Ward. Asa's affiliation with the latter would have reinforced his sense of duty

---

11 *Ibid.,* pg. 55.
12 Mitcham, pg. 11.

and loyalty toward his adopted section. The five delegates were sent to ensure that Monroe County was represented in the upcoming national Democratic convention.

After the Republican victory in November, a meeting of County residents was scheduled for December 12, 1860 at the courthouse. Its purpose was to appoint three delegates to represent the County at the Tallahassee convention in early January, taking into consideration the dangers to Florida if it remained a member of the current federal Union. This was largest meeting held in Key West up to that time. Said to be a spirited session, it lasted until midnight.[13]

Mayor John P. Baldwin served as meeting chair while Charles Tift and Peter Crusoe were appointed recording secretaries. Speakers were called on to offer opinions with former-Mayor John C. Maloney the only voice favoring the Union; Asa Tift, Joseph Beale Brown and six others spoke in favor of independence. District Court Judge William Marvin agreed with independence, doing so only after the Border States had decided to withdraw from the 1789 Union.

After the discussion concluded two island businessmen, Winer Bethel and William Pinckney, and Judge Marvin, were placed in nomination, but believing Marvin's official capacity to be an issue, Asa F. Tift's name was submitted and approved by the body. Marvin was a New York native whom historian Browne considered to be a man of strong Southern sympathies, but after the occupation began Marvin sided with the Northern troops and retained his federal position.

So appointed to represent the County, Bethel, Pinckney and Tift journeyed to Tallahassee and on January 10, 1861, all spoke in favor of, and voted for, Florida's independence. The next day Florida's Ordinance of Secession was signed and the State declared itself an independent nation.

Asa and his fellow delegates returned home to find the fort barricaded and that soldiers had erected sand embankments on the shoreward side with cannons aimed toward the city. Florida was now independent, but faced hostile troops in Fort Taylor.

---

13 Maloney, pg. 63.

The uneasy standoff between the fort and town was ended when 300 US troops arrived from Texas in March. The island changed dramatically as US Navy ships dotted the harbor and horizon and increasing numbers of soldiers marched through the streets. Fort Taylor's new commander, Major French, complained to Mayor Baldwin of "Republic of Florida" flags flying from commercial buildings and homes, warning that if he did not stop it the military would. He threatened that a severe crackdown would soon come if the citizens were not controlled - suggesting martial law, houses and persons searched, and imprisonment of anyone deemed suspicious.[14]

Asa was headed for a collision with military authorities. In late April and not long after Fort Sumter had been bombarded he refused to sell coal to a steamer in the service of the US Government, forcing it to sail to Havana for fuel. Asa clearly refused to cooperate with those warring upon his State and people – Florida was no longer a part of the United States.[15]

The *Key of the Gulf* editor left the island by May 5th to avoid imprisonment and the writ of habeas corpus was suspended the following day "in order to arrest without [constitutional] molestation the parties suspected of uttering the treasonable sentiments, etc." French busied himself that month with plans to deport islanders he believed "seditious" or "extraneous."[16]

Asa was faced with the same decision as editor Ward as his past pro-independence activities also targeted him for imprisonment. He began making arrangements to move his family to be near Nelson at Albany, Georgia, and gave control of the business and power of attorney to younger brother Charles with instructions to sell all or part of his property on the island.

Leaving the island on May 20th, 1861, aboard Captain James McKay's *Salvor*, Asa and daughter Annie likely headed for St. Mark's, Tallahassee and northward to meet Nelson at Albany and decide how the two of them might assist the new Confederacy since it lacked of a navy.

---

14   Schmidt, pg. 43-44.

15   *Ibid.,* pg. 41-42.

16   *Ibid.,* pg. 45.

Fortunately for Asa, his attorney found an interested party for his wharf property and closed in December, 1861. The buyer was James Filor & Partners who agreed to pay $18,000 in total, some of which was on demand and the balance scheduled later – ultimately received in July 1865. Though the US Navy quartermaster coveted Tift's Wharf and amenities for its own use and made several attempts to lease it from Filor & Partners, he was steadfastly refused. This impasse was overcome by the fort's commander who threatened to seize the property in January 1862 for government use unless the lease was issued. Though the quartermaster officers arranged a $6000 per month lease of the property and took control, no monies were received by the partners as the US Government claimed the quartermaster possessed no authority to approve such an expenditure. Filor and Partners eventually brought suit in December 1869 to recover their monies.[17]

Ironically neither brother had any previous experience with shipbuilding though Asa owned an island maritime repair shop, and Nelson, president of a railroad company, was only conversant with the problems of ironwork. Nonetheless, they developed a plan for river-defense ironclad gunboats to offset the US Navy's obvious advantages.

Nelson designed a simple green-pine vessel with triangular ends that could be cheaply built along the South's coast, armed with 16-cannon, 8 per side, and one end reinforced for ramming. Asa and Nelson travelled to Richmond in August 1861 to present Nelson's scale-model for review by Key West-friend and now Secretary of the Navy, Stephen Mallory, and the Confederate Navy's Board of Naval Officers, which included chief naval constructor John L. Porter and his engineer. The brothers received resounding approval and support.[18]

In a letter to Mallory in late August, the brothers proposed to superintend construction of Nelson's warship employing ordinary carpenters who could be easily found, pledging to cede their ironclad invention to the Confederacy without compensation or profit other than reimbursement for their material and labor expenses, and travel costs, which was approved.

---

17 FILOR vs United States. See also, Heinlein.
18 Fair, pg. 61.

Arriving at New Orleans in mid-September 1861 with brother Charles attending to Nelson's business interests at Albany after late October, the Tifts went to work on their ship, the *CSS Mississippi*, locating their shipyard – which had to be created with a sawmill, blacksmith shop, hull berths, and sheds for workers - on the Mississippi's left bank above New Orleans at Jefferson City.[19] Likely through Mallory's influence the former-US Navy paymaster Felix Senac from Key West was assigned as paymaster for both ironclads.

Nuts and bolts were purchased at Macon, Mobile and Chattanooga; iron armor-plating obtained in Atlanta. As the last months of 1861 passed, the Tifts became anxious when the Outer Banks and New Bern, North Carolina fell to the enemy – with New Orleans perhaps the next target. At the same time, Mallory had approved contracts for other ironclads to begin -- a total of five under construction between Norfolk and the Mississippi River.[20]

Also being built at New Orleans was the *CSS Louisiana* by shipbuilder E.C. Murray, the keel laid at the same time but launched in early February 1862. Aboard the *Louisiana* since late-October was Lt. William H. Ward, former Key West editor and friend of Asa, as well as William C. Whittle who was later an officer on the *CSS Chattahoochie* crewed by several "Key West Avengers." The latter was executive officer of the *Shenandoah* in 1865 when former-islander Felix Senac arranged the crew's backpay.

In mid-April, 1862 the Tifts launched their ship's hull and work continued on the deck, casemate and armament. Work proceeded quickly with expectations of completion within a month's time. An impressive warship at that point, her first commander, Capt. Arthur Sinclair, who commanded the vessel, later testified of her destruction: "She was a formidable ship, the finest of the sort I ever saw in my life; she would, in my opinion, not only have cleared the [Mississippi] river of the enemy's vessels, but have raised the blockade of every port in the South."[21]

---

19 Luraghi, pg. 120.

20 *Ibid.*, pp. 108-123.

21 *Ibid.*, pg. 132.

The Tifts' were under pressure to launch prematurely due to the imminent threat of attack, the Mississippi was burned to prevent capture as the enemy fleet ascended the river. During construction the ironclad was reported by Lt. Robert Minor to be "a very formidable affair – 3 propellers and to go 9 or 10 knots."

Fully aware that the *CSS Mississippi* was nearly complete, Capt. David Porter of the US Navy thought her "strong enough to drive off the whole Union fleet," as it was "the most splendid specimen ... the world had ever seen (a sea-going affair), and had she been finished and succeeded in getting to sea, the whole American navy would have been destroyed."[22]

The accolades were for naught as *Mississippi's* powerplant was disabled just before the enemy gained control of the Mississippi River mouth, and the enemy fleet fought past the forts guarding the city on April 24th, giving Capt. Sinclair no time to find a place of refuge for the ironclad. Setting fire to the massive craft, he watched sadly as the flames consumed his ship as the enemy passed.[23]

The Tift brothers escaped upriver to Vicksburg, where they were met by angry crowds holding them and their deficient ship responsible for the loss of New Orleans – questioning their Northern birth and possible sabotage. Only by the "timely intervention" of prewar Key West friend Felix Senac were they spirited away from the angry crowd and arresting officer, though they were held in the custody of Governor John Pettus at Jackson. While awaiting scrutiny by a Richmond naval board of inquiry at Richmond the following summer, Asa and Nelson continued their naval construction activities for the Confederacy through the efforts of Stephen Mallory.

In early 1862 while building the *CSS Mississippi* the Tifts were also under contract to convert the Glasgow-built, iron-sided steamer *Fingal* then at Savannah, into an ironclad. The Tifts contract was the same for the *Mississippi* as they were not paid for their labors but reimbursed for expenses incurred for construction, largely financed by funds raised by the ladies of Savannah. Their work proceeded quickly with the ship re-christened as the *CSS Atlanta* and armed with four

---

22   *Ibid.*, pg. 131-132.

23   Fair, pg. 62.

cannon and a spar torpedo. The Northern press expressed concern that should this fast raider escape the Savannah River, the ports of Baltimore, Philadelphia, New York and Boston could be devastated.[24]

The *CSS Atlanta* and was commissioned November 22, 1862, but did not steam out to engage the enemy until mid-June 1863. Under the command of "an impetuous young officer" she ran aground assailing two heavily-armed enemy ironclads and was immediately captured. Once again questions regarding the Tift's northern-birth arose amid accusations of sabotage, but Nelson later defended their work by admitting that the *Atlanta* was no match for ironclads with guns double in size of its own and ten-inch armor. He claimed the only possible way the *Atlanta* could have sunk one of its adversaries was through the spar torpedo, but she had already been run aground and was helpless before the enemy. Nelson further noted that the Atlanta's captors sent her immediately to Philadelphia for only minor repairs, then re-christened her the *USS Atlanta*.[25] The Tifts believed that had they more time to finish the Mississippi and had the Atlanta been guided by more experienced hands, both could have altered the war's outcome. Despite the unfortunate and misdirected criticism, Asa and Nelson were considered naval pioneers for their innovative design of ironclad vessels.

The Tifts later faced a Congressional Investigating Committee at Richmond in late August 1862 to explain the loss of the *CSS Mississippi*. During this inquiry Capt. Sinclair admitted it was he who had given the command of firing the vessel to the officer he had left in charge of the ship. Felix Senac was a key witness as he had served as paymaster for both the *Louisiana* and *Mississippi*. Testifying that he had known Asa Tift since 1847 and he considered both Asa and his brother "men of integrity in business."[26] Senac went on to explain that the *CSS Mississippi's* construction "progressed without undue delays nor undue expenditures," and, except for initial delays in funding from the CS government, "always had sufficient funds available to meet expenses," sometimes having excess funds. After testimony from officers and officials involved, the Committee in mid-September

---

24 *Ibid.*, pg. 65.
25 *Ibid.*, pg. 66. See also, Luraghi, pg. 210.
26 Rapier, pg. 101.

"found that it could attach no blame to the CS Navy for the fall of New Orleans, and that though the loss of the city was a tragedy for the South, there was no use in making anyone the scapegoat." The loss of two such important warships was a severe blow to Secretary Mallory's Department, though work would continue at individual ports and rivers requiring defense amid difficulty in finding proper materials. It was clear that future efforts would be directed at acquiring armored ships from Europe with which to break the North's blockade, and Senac was sent to assist this effort.[27]

Amos, Jr. had returned to Mystic in 1840, highly-successful in business and the community, and politically a War Democrat. His oldest son, Henry H., avoided service despite his draft age and nineteen-year-old son William Orville Tift enlisted in the 26th Connecticut Regiment in 1862 for a year's duty. On a voyage to occupation duty just above New Orleans in late December, his ship briefly visited Key West. At his Louisiana posting in early January, 1863, life was easy with little to fear from occasional Southern guerillas. Orville seemed fascinated by the African slaves he came in contact with, "probably because he had never seen any of them in Connecticut." Common to Northern soldiers was their use of the "freed" African slaves to serve them in their tents, in addition to cooking, laundering, blacking boots and polishing guns. Historian Fair wrote of the irony of William's condescension toward black people, that his black servant, "though no longer a slave, was probably held in higher regard by his former Southern master." [28]

It was apparent that despite the slaves being "freed" by the arrival of the Northern troops, "the servile condition imposed by their liberators hardly seemed much an advance from slavery." Orville was discharged in 1863 after seeing little or no combat.

Following the disappointing results from their hard work on the *Mississippi* and *Atlanta*, the rebel brothers returned to Albany where they remained with their families for the remainder of the war. Nelson remained an assistant naval paymaster while the brothers shipped supplies to the Confederate army and to the naval stations at Mobile, Savannah, Charleston and Selma. Though surrounded by an

---

27 *Ibid.*, pp. 102-103.
28 *Ibid.*, pg 70.

abundance of foodstuffs and cattle, the poor transportation network could not efficiently distribute them. When the end came in April, 1865, Nelson's entire agricultural and manufacturing operations were seized by the invader. And because of Nelson's high profile and property valued at more than $20,000, he was forced to apply to the US Government for parole, and presidential pardon – as did Asa.[29]

Their New England work ethic put Nelson and Asa on the road to recovery, albeit with new labor realities amid the Reconstruction political upheavals. In 1866 they established a factory for wool and cotton not far from the railroad station, as well as an immense storage warehouse. Nelson was pardoned the following year and by 1870 he had risen to become the region's second-wealthiest planter.[30]

Asa returned to Key West and as he had received a full pardon in July 1865, was able to recover most of the property left behind in 1861. Asa and Charles became shipping agents for the New York and Baltimore Steam Ship Lines, having fire-proof storage with a steam fire engine which required no insurance on the goods. Though William Curry was the island's wealthiest man in 1873, Asa was second with some $50,000 in assets of his own and another $84,000 held jointly with Curry, and $20,000 more with Charles. He and Charles also enjoyed more business as the island's population of 3,000 had quadrupled to 12,000 by 1870. And importantly, within his valuable real estate holdings was the high lot which was still-vacant at 907 Whitehead Street.

Despite Asa's good business fortune, his family life suffered the loss of daughter Julia in 1861 and then Annie passed away in 1869 after battling tuberculosis. Four years later son William died, he and Julia both buried at Mystic. Stephen Mallory's wife Angela wrote the grieving Asa following Annie's death, "that the only one on earth that poor Asa has to cheer his old age is now taken from him."[31]

After Annie's passing Asa concentrated on business while building what was to be a happy family home of imported Italian tile and Georgia timbers at 907 Whitehead Street. Completed in 1876, he lived a quiet

---

29 Fair, pg. 75.

30 *Ibid.,* pp. 85-86.

31 *Ibid.,* pp. 86-87.

existence within the mansion while his colored maid cooked his daily meals in her kitchen and delivered them to Asa. Some confusion exists regarding the Tift mansion's construction date but there is no record of a dwelling on the lot prior to 1876.[32]

Asa's magnificent home is described as "West Indian Creole" and possibly the work of Irish-born architect and contractor, William Kerr, who came to the island in 1872. He was known for buildings designed in varied historic vernaculars as well as the use of native-stone as a construction material. Very importantly Asa selected this lot for its high 16-foot elevation above sea level given his experience with hurricanes. Initial excavations revealed that just under the thin topsoil was a hard base limestone or shale, which was quarried to create a basement. As a last touch and to recall Asa's wartime experiences, a stone fountain in the shape of an ironclad warship was created at the home's entrance.

Asa's oldest brother Amos, Jr. came to the island in 1875 to live with Asa after financial problems at Mystic, while his energetic son Henry Harding was in the Georgia timber business near Nelson. Younger brother Charles passed at Key West in 1878 and his body taken to Connecticut for burial.[33]

When not overseeing his wharf business Asa was found at home, unless on infrequent visits to Nelson at Albany or other family at Mystic. Asa passed away on February 7th, 1889 and his body laid to final rest alongside wife Anna at Magnolia Cemetery at Charleston.

Nelson, known in Georgia as "the Colonel," lived on until November 18, 1891 and was buried at Albany's Oakwood Cemetery. Tift County, Georgia is named in honor of Nelson; the town of Tifton, Georgia was named for Nelson and Asa's nephew, Henry Harding Tift, the county seat of Tift County.

---

32 *Ibid.*, pg. 276.
33 *Ibid.*, pg. 95.

CHAPTER 7:

"To Be Away From This Detested Spot" – The Year 1863

Homesick men of the 47th Pennsylvania regiment scanned the horizon daily for ships carrying the coveted newspapers and letters from home. In January 1863 they learned of more newspaper offices broken into by Republican mobs and their editors arrested for printing anti-Lincoln editorials. The *Allentown Democrat*, protected by a 200-man defense force, reported gold selling at a premium and forecasting that "it won't be long until a gold dollar will be worth a bushel of greenbacks." The paper referred to Lincoln's "greenback," fiat money used to finance his war since the infamous "Trent Affair" of late-1861 brought on a financial panic. Backed by neither gold or silver, rampant inflation was the predictable result of the US government printed notes. Another editorial critical of the president's electoral debts and payoffs reported that "Dictator Lincoln had submitted a list of 120 politically-connected generals for the Senate to confirm."[1]

Being far from the bloody battlefields of the Western Theater and Virgina the ordinary soldiers of the Lehigh Valley sent to the island paradise must have appreciated the easy duty. But they might still complain of the tropical tedium of warm breezes, seagulls and pelicans - one soldier of the 47th Pennsylvania wrote of his longing "to be away from this detested spot."[2]

Apparently aware of Lincoln's plan to officially announce his emancipation proclamation on January 1st, Key West businessman, James Filor was already lodged at New York's Metropolitan Hotel from which he addressed a letter to Lincoln two days later. In the

---

1 Schmidt, pg. 388.
2 Ogle, pg. 63.

letter he noted his past investments in slave property were solely driven by the US Government's need for slave labor at Forts Taylor and Jefferson, and that the island had always remained under United States authority. In short, he argued that the government had strengthened slavery on the island by inducing he and others to purchase slaves with assurance that they would be constantly employed, and now the US Government was seizing his investment without due compensation. It is unknown if Mr. Filor ever received an answer, but in the meantime his slaves had melted away with previous acts of "emancipation" issued by federal officers needing unskilled labor for fortifications, personal servants or cooks.[3]

The island was shocked to hear in late January that the Department of the South commander at Hilton Head had abruptly ordered the deportation of the (white) families "of all persons who have husbands, brothers or sons in Rebel employment, and all other persons who have at any time declined to take the oath of allegiance, or who have uttered a single disloyal word, in order that they may be all placed within the Rebel lines." They were to be taken by ship first to Hilton Head, then passed through Southern lines into South Carolina. Historian Browne accurately compares this order to the ruthless "reconcentrado policy" of Spanish General Valeriano y Nicolau Weyler at Cuba some thirty years in the future. Weyler was in America during the Civil War as a young military attache' and observer of Sherman's brutal march through Georgia and the Carolinas.[4]

The deportation order was addressed to Col. Good of the 47th Pennsylvania who had relinquished command to Col. Morgan of the 90th New York when the former was earlier detached to Hilton Head. Though the 47th Pennsylvania returned to the island before Christmas there were no orders for Good to be restored to command. It therefore fell to Morgan to enforce the order and round up those fitting his superior's order, which affected some 600 island families and reportedly left both the island's military and the civilian population "seething with unrest".[5] The US Navy's local commander opposed the action, "complaining of the illegality and inhumanity" of Hunter's

---

[3] Smith, pg. 1. See also Filor vs. United States.
[4] Browne, pg. 95. See also The Spanish War, pg. 56-57.
[5] Schmidt III, pp. 423-424.

order, "which, if carried out, will deport ... whole families of law-abiding Union people, whose only offense is having disloyal relations in the rebel employment."

Included in the deportation would be former-Mayor Walter C. Maloney, Sr. and wife, whose son had earlier escaped the island to serve as an officer in Florida's Coast Guard, as well as Daniel Davis whose son also served the Confederacy. They and others faced selling their homes, possessions, packing a few belongings and sail into exile in the Low Country. Ironically, Maloney Sr. strongly opposed independence and voluntarily led the loyalist "Union Volunteer Corps" of older island men and merchants who feared losing their businesses.[6]

Morgan would be happy to expel the outspoken Maloney, Sr. who regularly sparred with the Northern military over private property appropriation, and decried Morgan's revocation of Good's previous order restoring municipal authority to publicly-elected officials.[7] Morgan anticipated that his draconian measures would eliminate any remaining public expressions of independence sentiment on the island, evident as island ladies with loved ones far away were seen in public with "secession" cockades adorning their dresses. One Northern soldier confided to his diary that: "[T]his place is altogether Secesh, it proved itself this day by their conduct.[8]

These measures were calculated to be a stern warning to "sympathizers with Rebellion" and no leniency or favor would be shown. Soon afterward orders were issued that any islanders having any male relatives in Confederate service, or who have at any time declined taking the oath to the US Government, must report to headquarters and register their names by February 17th. Doing so would surely make one a target for imprisonment in Fort Taylor or exile to the mainland.[9]

Bombarded with complaints from Union men and officers condemning the order, Hunter rescinded his deportation order, restored Col. Good to command and ordered Col. Morgan and his

---

6 Browne, pg. 96.
7 Schmidt III, pg. 403.
8 *Ibid.,* pg. 405.
9 *Ibid.,* pp. 411-414.

quartermaster to Hilton Head to face charges of disloyal practices lodged against them by former-Mayor Maloney. The local army newspaper reported on December 20th that Morgan's "actions had been severely criticized by the townspeople." Maloney continued to be a thorn in the military's side, even for many years after the war was over regarding property adjacent to the barracks owned by Maloney.[10]

All islanders were elated that the deportation order was changed, especially since it was from many of those considered "secessionists" that loyalist Key Westers and soldiers had received comfort during the yellow fever outbreaks. Most of all the island was happy to be rid of the hated Morgan, so much so that the more tolerable proconsul Col. Good was welcomed back with the gift of a "gold-hilted sword." The islanders were rewarded as Good again recognized recent military-supervised elections and directed that civil authority be restored Jan. 1, 1863. The military would still retain control over arrivals and departures from the island and the sale of spirituous liquors.[11] Despite a humiliating loss to outnumbered and outgunned South Carolina forces at Pocotaligo three-months earlier, Good was now feted as a returning hero.

Unrelenting in its resistance to Lincoln's war in 1863, the *Allentown Democrat* newspaper railed at the President's emancipation decree of January 1. It wrote:

> Democrats of the Lehigh Valley opposed the Republican administration's war. They were suspicious of the shifting justifications for it. They weren't interested in fighting to free anyone. They denounced the president's restrictions on civil liberties. And they predicted the bloodshed would lead to bigger disasters.

On February 11, 1863 the same paper wrote: "The Abolitionists in Congress have taken another step, not towards restoring the Union the way it was under the Constitution, but towards equalizing the Negro with the white man ... even to mix Negro soldiers in the same company with white soldiers." This view seemed representative of Valley soldiers expressing opposition to black soldiers occupying an

---

10   *Ibid.*, pg. 367.
11   *Ibid.*, pg. 378.

equal position to the all-white 47th Pennsylvania. The editorialist wrote that "There is no good reason why the white men of the North should expose their lives and endure all the hardships of the camp, the march and the field, for the benefit of Negroes; and they will not do it if they can avoid it. Negroes are fit subjects for an Abolition war; were it a war for restoration of the Union as it was, there would be no need to call upon Negroes to join the army."[12]

The Lehigh Valley soldiers were not unique in their condescending view of black people as the men of the 48th Pennsylvania Regiment of the Schuylkill County region, with an ethnic makeup of Scotch and German, were just as eager to have "contrabands" within their lines near New Bern, North Carolina perform the hard labor of entrenchments and fortifications. While occupying northeastern North Carolina in early 1862 their inland raids included "carrying off some 12 N****** as well as destroy the railroad." The 47th regiment did the same in their Florida raids to obtain black "soldiers."[13]

As related in a previous chapter many "Pennsylvania Dutch" migrated a century earlier into western North Carolina where they became farmers and some holding slaves. The 1842 census of Catawba county reveals that out of a total population of 8,862 there existed 21 free black persons and 1,569 slaves. The 12th North Carolina Regiment of this region included men with names such as Corpening, Hahn, Arendt, Hunsucker, Isenhower, Miller, Propst, Reinhardt and Reitzel. These men bravely fought for the South at Fredericksburg and "went into the Gettysburg fight with 1400 men and came out with 127."[14]

It should be pointed out that officers interested in advancement were especially careful to avoid racial antipathy though it often was revealed, but the letters of soldiers were more pointed. In fact, the following year a white officer of black troops sent to Key West wrote of the 47th Pennsylvania being "Dutch" and full of "copperheads," the first was a period corruption of the "Deutsche" language spoken by

---

12 Warner, pg. 1. See also Allentown Democrat online.
13 Priest, pg. 23; 50.
14 Hahn, pg. 95.

these ethnic Germans; "copperhead" was a disparaging term for anti-war, anti-Lincoln Northerners, usually Democrats.[15] Predictably, the black troops were not embraced by the white Pennsylvanians.

As the war progressed and the Radical Republicans increasingly-controlled military promotions for field grade officers, the latter had to quietly accept the change to a war of emancipation or accept rank stagnation. With the recruitment of white soldiers faltering and violent riots in response to the hated draft, Lincoln's War Department increased its use of black soldiers. The latter were paid less, were easier to obtain during inland raids of plantations, and had no representation in Congress to complain of poor treatment and low, or no pay. With Key West being within the US Army's Department of the South region headquartered at Hilton Head, the 47th regiment became increasingly utilized for interior raids to seize "contrabands" to be put into uniform (either with or without their consent.) Knowing the department would get no white reinforcements for new operations against the South, black troops became the alternative. To this end, Col. James Montgomery arrived on the island in early February to enroll or conscript any available black men for his planned 2nd South Carolina "Volunteers" regiment. This was at the same time the Pennsylvania regiment experienced a soldier's desertion, a man from Lewisburg who was found stowed away on an outbound transport ship.

Not surprisingly the 47th Pennsylvania's three-year veterans who first enlisted in a war to preserve the Union felt tricked into fighting an abolitionists' war after Lincoln's edict was announced. To this point Gen. Fitz John Porter reported that Lincoln's announcement was ridiculed in the army, provoked disgust, discontent, and expressions of disloyalty he viewed as insubordination.[16]

Their first encounter with the South's black residents found them as "contrabands," wandering into camp from burned plantations, bewildered, seeking food and shelter. While some of the soldiers may have remembered slavery in Pennsylvania and disliked it in the South, they were far from being outright "abolitionists" seeking unconditional liberty of the black man. For example, though being populated by more free blacks than any other northern city in 1860, Frederick

---

15 Schmidt III, pg. 821.

16 Marvel, pg. 180.

Douglass stated in 1862 that "There is not, perhaps anywhere to be found a city in which prejudice against color is more rampant than in Philadelphia." In George Fahnestock's letter home in June 1863 revealing how the common Pennsylvania soldier had now come to view colored men in uniform, he wrote that the use of black troops would "save the valuable lives of our white men." This realization was not only confined to Pennsylvanians as Ohio soldier Sam Evans wrote that "My doctrine is that a Negro is no better than a white man and will do as well to receive [Rebel] bullets and would be likely to save the life of some white men."[17]

After Lincoln agreed, under strong pressure from Northern governors who feared losing reelection, that contraband black men in the South could be enlisted and counted against State troop quotas, the race was on for the paid agents of each State to scour the occupied-South for black men to be enlisted in place of able-bodied Northern white men who were well-employed and had no interest in the war. True to the North's preference for racial separation, the newly-freed black men were placed in segregated regiments under white officers.

This influx of new recruits in early 1863 came when the North's manpower needs grew with vast Southern territory to be occupied and guarded. The war to date had led to uncertain progress toward conquering the South, the frightful battlefield carnage and the maimed coming home brought enlistments to a standstill, and some hundred thousand blue-clad soldiers had deserted. The War Department was also aware that many regiments would soon reach the end of their enlistment terms and return home to a booming wartime economy and wages. This reality begat outright national conscription in February 1863 with its myriad clauses for substitutes, exemptions, and commuting personal service with a cash contribution – paying $300 would buy one out of one troop levy, but if called in the next levy that draftee had to pay again.[18] Too often the paid substitute was recently released from prison or a bounty-jumper from another State.

As the US government was printing its own fiat money which the States were utilizing, astronomical sums were being offered to raise the troops needed to continue the war against the South. The aggregate

---

17 Paradis, pp. 6-7.
18 Marvel. Pg. 183.

of bounty monies paid in eastern Pennsylvania – exclusive of the US bounty – in the calls of 1863 and 1864 was just over $26 million. The bounties paid in the western division of the State totaled over $17.1 million for a grand total of over $43 million.[19]

By early September a thousand conscripts a day were arriving at Washington under heavy guard to deter desertion. It was said that "thieves seeded every lot, ready to stomp or stab anyone who resisted their pilfering." A Vermont brigade expecting two hundred conscripts lost 50 of them to desertion on the way to join the unit. The brigade NCOs either locked up or tied up the conscripts to prevent them from running off. A colonel of artillery was convinced that the men never wanted to serve and only wanted the bounty or purchase-money offered them.[20]

But back on the island, support for Southern independence was discovered in the ranks of the occupiers' officer corps. On April 11th the 47th'Lt. H.H. McClune was court-martialed for having uttered "The South is fighting only for her rights and cannot be conquered; the confiscation of property is not right; the present government is an abolition government" and the like. McClune was sentenced to be confined "during the present rebellion."

Interestingly, one soldier-diarist believed McClune was "displaced in time, and his views considered enlightened" for the period such as "women's suffrage, the waste of war, and the good that could have been done with the vast expenditures of resources dissipated in wars. The diarist thought it difficult to imagine McClune using alleged "foul and beastly" language as charged with.[21] Subsequently McClune was court-martialed and put to demeaning hard labor for his enlightened, but "treasonable" utterances.

The same diarist wrote in early April of a "reported secessionist" commencing a tirade of abuse in a literary meeting, while ridiculing the meeting of Yankee high-brows "in a low and contemptuous

---

19 Ford, pg. 67.
20 *Ibid.*, pg. 191.
21 Schmidt III, pp. 460-462. See "Miscellanea," H.H. McClune, Gazette Company, 1907.

manner." His reward for the outburst was to be beaten by nearby soldiers, and the "next morning the 'Secesh' appeared before the provost marshal to be fined $50."[22]

Also illustrating the divide between Valley men serving in the military and their home region, as well as what soldiers thought they were fighting for, the *Sunbury Gazette* of late April contained a letter from a 47th Regiment sergeant complaining of citizens [at home] not wholeheartedly supporting the war. Writing "such men are traitors and cowards, we are fighting in the same cause now as [in the beginning] ... but at home there is something wrong, and you ought not to allow it ... They tell us we are fighting for nothing but to free n****rs and that our government don't do as they ought, and the President thinks more of a n****r than of a white soldier ... There is but two sides, the one is for the Union, the other is for the rebellion ... The best thing would be to stop all newspapers, and not allow them to be sent to the army. Letters of a disturbing character should also be forbidden ..."[23]

At the same time, the 47th regiment was characterized by the *New York Tribune* as being too strongly against the Lincoln administration, or "Copperhead," according to a letter from home received by one soldier in early May. Believing the perception was based on conversations with officers the soldier noted that "Gen. Brannan entertained a dislike to Negro soldiers, and our regiment, I think, shared it."

The soldier continued: "I think they were right in so far as opposition to making the Negro soldier hold a higher position than did the white one, is concerned. It was this undue honor that for a week or two was being paid to the colored men that stirred up discontent among us. Gen. Hunter very soon discovered that he had made a mistake in exalting Negroes too much and consequently adopted a plan of explaining his altered views by speaking of them as subordinate troops. This is as it should be."[24] Penning a letter home the following month denouncing the *Allentown Democrat's* anti-war position, he called it a "traitorous sheet" and hoped it would have to suspend publishing "for want of patronage."

---

22   *Ibid.*, pg. 479.
23   *Ibid.*, pp. 486-487.
24   *Ibid.*, pp. 491-492.

Alcohol often brought the Northern soldier's racial antipathy to the surface and this occurred on Sunday, May 3rd when a New York soldier bayoneted the colored servant of the Surgeon and may have killed him.[25]

Later that month another soldier wrote home that he was not fighting to free the black man. He felt they were the same as the white man and should be free, but wanted "a place given to them where they are to stay [in the South] & a law will be [passed maybe] that they will [dare not] come north …" This letter, like many others of the regiment, referred commonly to black people as "n*****s," and there was a genuine stated fear that northern whites would lose their jobs to freed black people flooding north and work for low wages.[26]

In May 1863 former Fort Taylor paymaster and multi-lingual Felix Senac was posted to Europe as Confederate munitions purchasing agent and to assist Henry Hotze in his efforts to promote Southern interests in Europe. He was unexpectedly accompanied by exiled Ohio Democrat Clement Vallandigham and Lt. Col. Arthur Freemantle of England's Coldstream Guards.[27] Senac's relative Stephen Mallory had much to do with Felix's appointment - Senac's daughter Ruby was to marry Hotze in 1867.

Also in May Key West's popular Capt. Francis Watlington began his Confederate naval career by departing the island to be commissioned lieutenant aboard Admiral Franklin Buchanan's *CSS Tennessee* at Mobile Bay. This was the largest ironclad ram of the Confederate Navy at 209 feet long and a beam of 48 feet – perhaps its size keeping the Northern navy at bay until August 1864. From the beginning of war Capt. Watlington had likely engaged in profitable blockade running and may have been under US military surveillance.

Key West was now securely under military control and island municipal officers elected in late-May and were supervised by the military in exercising their respective duties. The crackdown against

---

25 *Ibid.*, pg. 488.
26 *Ibid.*, pp. 508-509.
27 Rapier, pg. 112.

dissent continued as the Provost Marshal was authorized to seize the private property of anyone discovered to be in the service of the Confederacy, military or civil."²⁸

The steamer *Nassau* arrived at the island from New Orleans in mid-June with a cargo of black laborers to replace white soldiers doing wharf maintenance. One Pennsylvania soldier wrote of this ship "with a lot of N***** numbering fifty-nine to be a work gang on the Wharf of this place permanently ... they are a shiftless looking set, much like the South Carolina N******." The soldier wrote shortly after of pretending to "muster" into the Quartermaster Department one of the laborers after dressing him in a uniform, and read army regulations to him while making him swear an oath with his hand upon a dictionary. These laborers were reported to be in unofficial government service but not paid for their work.²⁹

One of the colored men now unofficially mustered was assigned mess hall cook according to the Pennsylvania diarist, who complained of the black soldier's wives also drawing government rations and musing why the wives of white soldiers did not enjoy a similar privilege.³⁰

Islanders Charles Berry, Thomas Burns and John B. Sands were among the first "Key West Avengers" transferred from the infantry to sea duty with Stephen Mallory's help, and assigned to the *CSS Chattahoochie* in Georgia. A devastating boiler explosion on May 27th killed sixteen crewmen including islander Charles Berry. Seamen Burns and Sands were on board but fortunately not injured.³¹

As was evident to local US military officials for some time, Lincoln's Secretary of the Navy Gideon Wells had become suspicious of the captured blockade runners held at the island and later purchased by suspicious parties. He wrote the fort commander in late June that it was quite likely that most of the condemned steamers "sold at Key West will go into the hands of the rebels or the blockade runners unless purchased by the Government." He felt the obvious solution was to buy the captured vessels rather than auction them for gold, but

---

28 Schmidt III, pg. 503.
29 *Ibid.*, pp. 527-532.
30 *Ibid.*, pg. 575.
31 Fandom, 7th Florida Regt.

which his government sorely needed to finance the war.[32] And as the volume of British subjects violating the blockade increased so did the appeals to British Ambassador Lyons to have them released. When the master, first mate and chief engineer of the British steamer *Victor* were caught and confined to a cell at Fort Taylor in June, Crown law officers complained of them being treated as common felons.[33]

The nearly-complete ironclad *CSS Atlanta* from the Tift Brothers shipyard steamed down the Savannah River on June 17th to attack two enemy ironclads, faring poorly after running aground and being forced to surrender.[34] Aboard was the nephew and former clerk of island businessman James Filor, Lt. George Arledge. Arledge was imprisoned at Fort Lafayette until exchanged.

A sense of irony ruled the day at Key West on July 4th as the Provost Marshal's office was finely decorated and US flags were waved by noisy Unionists to celebrate American liberty, all while the island was under virtual martial law. At noontime and after the Pennsylvania regiment paraded through town a 35-gun salute boomed in recognition of each State, including those which were no longer within the Union. The 35th was for West Virginia, recently admitted to the Union as a new slaveholding State after the forced partition of Virginia.

Given the 47th's duty station so far from home in "enemy territory," a soldier wrote home of his shock to read that "Rebels were marching unmolested" through Pennsylvania's Cumberland Valley, that Gen. Hooker had allowed this to occur and of the shame that his fellow Pennsylvanians refused to "take care of themselves."[35]

It would not be until early August 1863 that the 47th's soldiers were reading July editions of Lehigh Valley newspapers which had arrived by steamer, learning of early July's Gettysburg battle as well as the subsequent anti-draft riots in New York City which involved many Irish and German workers, which was finally quelled by three regiments in blue arriving from Gettysburg. Pennsylvania also experienced its own anti-draft riots which spread from the eastern cities to the mining areas

---

32   Schmidt, pg. 540.
33   Negus, pg. 28.
34   Fair, pp. 65-66.
35   Schmidt III, pp. 563-567.

of Schuykill, Bucks and Columbia counties. Some Pennsylvania draft dissenters resorted to burning the barns and sawmills of the despised draft officers, while mine owners being pressed for the names of their workers were threatened with the destruction of their mines should they cooperate with Lincoln's men.[36]

In mid-July Key West learned of Union soldiers in Boston firing volleys into a crowd of anti-draft protestors and some noting the irony of this and the British in March, 1770. The island's occupation soldiers already knew of Detroit's early March anti-draft riot spurred on by mostly German, Dutch and Belgian immigrant workers who feared being conscripted into a war to free African slaves who might come north and take their jobs. Young Northern men were being assisted by secret societies to avoid conscription, and how to desert once taken. Wisconsin Governor Edward Salomon, a German immigrant himself, called out State militia to control immigrant mob attacks on his draft centers.[37]

Pennsylvania's Governor Curtin had not questioned Lincoln's authority to order conscription the previous year and like other governors challenged the quotas assigned to each State. It appeared that States with more Democratic voters were assigned higher quotas – and with Curtin very much owing his election to Lincoln's help he was not in a good position to argue. The governor of the new West Virginia argued that Lincoln's draft would drive as many into Southern armies as it enrolled in the Northern army. Like other governors advised Lincoln, Curtin was aware that without financial bounties to attract "volunteers," few men would step forward. Money and the promise of land was used to attract recruits from abroad, and as charged by Prague's *Die Morgen Post* in March 1863, the Homestead Act is a common lie, a way to lure Austrian subjects to America to enroll them in the Union army ..." Prussian minister Baron Grabow wrote Seward of German immigrants seeking land to cultivate were instead enlisted at Boston "under the allurement of $100 in gold" but paid in greenbacks. The minister wrote of more emigrants coming soon who he expects will face the same coercion into the US Army. And Belfast's

---

36 *Ibid.*, pg. 603.
37 Randall, pp. 412-413.

Ulster Observer chastised Lincoln for his sacrifice of Irish emigrants in battles and that he "should look elsewhere than the decimated homes of Ireland" for more victims.[38]

When Lee advanced toward Gettysburg in early July 1863 Curtin implored his heavily-Democratic State to enlist in defense of their homes but his citizens did not respond. Ironically, Lee's presence did arouse citizens to raise a cry of States' rights against Lincoln's suspension of habeas corpus, arbitrary arrests and the hated draft. Even *New York Tribune* editor Horace Greeley railed against conscription, stating "drafting in an anomaly in a free state, it must and will be reformed out of our system of political economy."[39]

In late July, the soldiers on the island received word of the $402 reenlistment bonus offered to veterans of the 47th Pennsylvania as their three-years terms were expiring, an extravagant amount when coupled with the State, county and town bounties.[40] Consider this in light of early war median income in Pennsylvania of about $500. After this was announced at Fort Jefferson where liquor was banned and no doubt to cheer the men of Company F to reenlistment, each man received a drink in the morning and another in the afternoon.

Lehigh Valley papers in early September carried advertisements from individuals and agents for paid substitutes, those willing to take the place of a drafted man. One advertisement read: "Wanted immediately, three able-bodied men to serve as substitutes for three years or the war, for which good prices will be paid. Apply at the office of the *Sunbury American*." Numerous attorneys at law hawked their services to help "properly fill out the papers" of anyone who had been drafted or had a legal claim to exemption. Additionally, the *Sunbury American* published an ad for a Pennsylvania Provost Marshal who offered a ten-dollar reward and "expenses incurred" for the apprehension of a deserter." The draft and its exemptions had created the conundrum of paid-substitutes, all too-often unscrupulous men who took the money and bounties, put on the uniform and deserted at the first opportunity.[41] Not all men who took the substitute or

---

38   Sideman & Friedman, pg. 123.
39   Hesseltine, pp. 292; 297.
40   Schmidt III, pg. 590.
41   *Ibid.*, pg. 631.

bounty money were unscrupulous. Some recent immigrants who were either near-destitute themselves, or having relatives in need, signed up for the generous inducements offered. Patriotism had little or no attraction and their goal of course was to avoid combat and return home alive to live a wealthier life with their bounties in hand.[42]

British military observer Arthur Freemantle wrote in his diary of some fifty Northern deserters in Louisiana who believed "Our government has broken faith with us. We enlisted to fight for the Union, and not to liberate the [slaves]."[43] While at New York and awaiting a ship back to England, Freemantle noted the prevalence of anti-war, anti-Negro feelings among many Northerners. His observations of three months brought him to the conclusion that the mass of respectable Northerners, though they are willing to pay [for substitutes] do not naturally feel themselves called upon to give their blood in a war of aggression, ambition and conquest. For this war is essentially a war of conquest."[44] Over 2000 Union deserters had been arrested in Illinois from the time of Lincoln's edict and the end of June, "who protested that they had enlisted to save the Union, 'not to free the n*****s.'"[45]

Northern commanders complained of the poor quality of soldiers sent to replace those killed and maimed. At Petersburg General Grant admitted in mid-1864 that the majority of them were pure mercenaries, and "many diseased, immoral or cowardly." Only two weeks later Grant was told that the War Department was receiving half as many men as were being discharged after fulfilling their enlistment terms. And volunteering has virtually ceased."[46] Desperate measures were needed which required attractive financial incentives for existing men to reenlist.

In the end it took the generous bounty monies, the month-long furlough home and an appeal to vanity with sleeve chevrons to retain many of the veterans, but not all. In Gen. Meade's Army of the

---

42   Larson, pg. 7.
43   Freemantle, pg. 89.
44   *Ibid.,* pg. 308.
45   Daniels, pg. 77.
46   Rhodes, pg. 323.

Potomac fully one-half of his veterans went home rather than face death another day. And as veterans they could not be conscripted by draft boards.[47]

In Mid-September, those "Key West Avengers" who had not yet transferred to the CS Navy engaged in fierce battle at Chickamauga, often cold and hungry. Robert Watson related how they dodged the enemy grape, cannister, shot and shell and falling trees; at night the sounds of musket volleys, falling trees and the endless groans and shrieks of the wounded made sleep impossible. Watson's company was able to surround and capture a Yankee colonel and his staff despite their being armed with Colt repeating rifles. Soon after the Confederate victory at Chickamauga - the second most-bloody and costly in human lives in the war - Watson's regiment was visited and reviewed by President Jefferson Davis.[48]

Watson's diary vividly relates the poor diet and conditions which the Southern soldier endured. Often breakfast was nothing more than "musty sour cornbread and water" or "miserable boiled beef" with molasses and a drink of whiskey a rare treat. In early November Watson made "a fine cheese" of cow hoofs boiled to a jelly, then salt, pepper and corn meal added before allowing the mixture to cool. To rid their underwear and clothing of the ever-present bed bugs and lice, frequent boiling was necessary. Sleeping in the cold rain was not uncommon and, if feeling unhealthy, a doctor might prescribe "powders and rub the breast with croton oil," the latter of which would cause the skin to blister terribly. Unless medicines were captured from overrun enemy camps or came via blockade runner, the South had to depend upon teas and boiled solutions made from bark and root. During the war and after it was common for men like Watson to suffer from intestinal maladies caused by poor diet.[49]

In the fall 1863 election a strong Democratic opponent challenged incumbent Republican Gov. Andrew Curtin. Pennsylvania Supreme Court Chief Justice George W. Woodward was a Democrat who had not only declared Lincoln's draft illegal, but also declared government "greenbacks" unconstitutional. Curtin's supporters began painting

---

47 Montgomery, pg. 96.
48 Campbell, pp. 73-76.
49 *Ibid.*, pp. 76-80.

Woodward as disloyal, anti-soldier and pro-secession since he did not condemn Southern independence. Woodward was excoriated by the Republican press for a December 1860 speech in which he advocated letting the South depart in peace, and blamed abolitionist agitation for the coming of the war.[50]

Pennsylvania's Republican "Union League" clubs organized voters across the State alleging that Woodward was being supported by secret Confederate societies intent upon thwarting free elections. Lincoln assisted by ensuring that US government clerks from Pennsylvania got to their polls via fifteen-day furloughs; Pennsylvania troops were sent home as well to vote and be at the polls to inspect voters and their ballots. Justice Woodward's supporters complained that so many soldiers were now absent from their regiments that General Lee might have captured Washington in this hour of voting fraud and military weakness. Through Lincoln's assistance, Curtin won reelection with a 15,000-vote majority.

A wise politician, Curtin ensured that Pennsylvania soldiers on the island and elsewhere were aware that Judge Woodward was as a Democrat opposed to soldiers voting in the field. The island's soldiers responded with a letter stating that they were "as a unit for the re-election of Gov. Andrew G. Curtin." This was soon followed by another with the names of officers and men of the 47th considered deserving of promotions.[51]

Finding new recruits in central Pennsylvania was very difficult with the *Allentown Democrat* reporting "that the recruiting business was all played out at this place." Fewer men volunteered to fight the South, risking death or maiming for life, plus, wages and employment opportunities had grown in the Lehigh Valley with the booming Northern war economy.[52]

Aware of the political problems of conscription and an election year soon to arrive, in late June the War Department initiated financial incentives in order to retain veterans. The strategy was to offer the veterans enough money to remain in their unit, add an immediate 30-

---

50 White, pg. 29.
51 Schmidt III, pp. 615; 644.
52 *Ibid.*, pg. 421.

day furlough home at government expense, and appeal to the soldier's patriotism and vanity with a special "Volunteer Veteran" chevron to be worn on the sleeve to exhibit his new and exalted status.

With these impressive incentives, the 47th's colonel was pressed by his superiors – while suggesting his promotion to a higher grade if successful - to exert a strong effort to re-enlist his entire regiment as their three-year term would end in October. His subsequent pitch to the regiment highlighted the $402 incentive, which included a $2 "recruiting premium," the sleeve chevron and 30-day furlough home. The $402 was paid in installments just in case the veteran thought of disappearing with his newly found wealth. Once home the "Volunteer Veteran" sought the generous town, county and State bounties and credited toward the quota Lincoln had set. Some veterans shopped area communities for the most generous bounty amounts, as those credited to a particular town meant another resident did not have to enlist. Alternately, those who did not re-enlist were required to pay their own way home.

A regimental diarist recorded the excitement of about 100 men of the regiment re-enlisting "for 3 years in the Veteran Corps, receiving the bounty & thirty days furlough home, to go home on the steamer *'Union'* now at the wharf." He noted the irresistible lure of $402 had men making hasty decisions, with some losing part or all to robbery and whiskey once home.[53]

The re-enlistment figures show at least 451 of the 47th's men re-enlisted which accounts for about 50% of regiment's average strength during the war. Something the Colonel did not disclose to his men as he encouraged re-enlistment was an official notice just received that a colored regiment was to be sent to Key West. Well-aware of the strong antipathy of his troops toward black soldiers in blue and how this would certainly curtail re-enlistments, and he instructed his subordinates that "No one outside our office needs to be informed of this. It'll be a bitter pill for our boys to live aside the n*****s, I'm afraid. We'll see."[54]

---

53 *Ibid.*, pg. 668.
54 *Ibid.*, pp. 646-655.

A true "bitter pill" for men of the 47th in mid-October was the *Sunbury American* paper which published a list of Lehigh Valley men exempted from Lincoln's draft, which stated their varied reasons, names of the substitutes and the names of those paying commutation money. Many of the central Pennsylvania papers were publishing these lists which were sure to infuriate soldiers on the island.[55] Added to this was the arrival in early December of the steamer *De Molay* from Boston carrying some 800 recruits, mostly substitutes, under armed guard and not permitted to come ashore lest they desert.[56]

As was becoming more common after the destructive raids to Florida's interior, the steamers *San Jacinto* and *Adela* arrived at Key West in late September with many mainland refugees, black and white, and prisoners to be paroled by the island's Provost Marshal.[57] Also reaching the island was one refugee named Zachariah Brown who along with six others claimed to have fled rebel tyranny.

A new US District Court Attorney for the Southern District of Florida was appointed in late-October, Ohio-native Homer G. Plantz. The former private secretary of Treasury Secretary Chase, he was selected for reasons beyond his daily responsibilities. A strategic plant of Chase to promote his presidential ambitions, Plantz would assure military officers of future promotions should they assist his efforts for the Secretary. Aware of why Plantz was appointed Lincoln secretary John Hay wrote that Plantz was there to enrich himself and channel votes toward Chase's nomination.[58]

Before November ended and the first "Volunteer Veterans" were due to return from furlough home, it was learned that men from Companies B and I from Allentown had "engaged in a bloody affray" with Irish workmen from a local foundry. They were aboard a train when "wordy warfare" broke out between the groups followed by knives, stones, cudgels and iron bars freely used for about 15 minutes. There were life-threatening injuries and the incident was blamed on ethnic differences and the effects of alcohol.[59]

---

55 LGS3, pg. 676.
56 *Ibid.*, pg. 706.
57 *Ibid.*, pg. 641.
58 Smith, GW, pg. 276.
59 Schmidt III, pg. 701.

The town was quiet by this date with any outspoken "secessionists" already driven from the island voluntarily, forcibly deported or arrested and detained in Fort Taylor and then sent northward to prison. Alexander Patterson was re-elected mayor once again during the island's military-supervised election, winning the seat with the expected large majority of votes cast.

General municipal elections were held in early December, and Mayor Alexander Patterson reelected with an expected large majority. The end of 1863 and beginning of 1864 was celebrated at a "Union Club Ball" in the courthouse, gaily decorated with the Stars and Stripes and colorful naval signal flags.[60] The venue was the very same as that of the mass meeting of islanders who elected three delegates to vote for independence two years earlier.[61]

---

60 *Ibid.*, pp. 707; 726.
61 Browne, pg. 91.

CHAPTER 8:

"THE MASSACHUSETTS IDEA"

> The early Spanish explorers saw natives as untamed, belligerent, idolatrous savages "laden with sins and vices" not accustomed to a peaceful coexistence, "nor to lay down their liberty so easily at the discretion or alien volition of other men, nor at the determination of those monks and priests" who accompanied them. [1]

Human slavery is of course as old as recorded history and of course not confined to North America, and people of all continents, countries and colors have practiced it since the dawn of civilization. Arab Muslims began enslaving black Africans in the ninth century, and until the nineteenth century the Trans-Sahara slave trade of Arabs and Berbers carried ten million Africans to North Africa and the Arabian Peninsula.[2] The enslavement of white Slavic peoples by Arab Muslims gave the practice the name we know it by, and Europeans did not enter the trade until the 1400's when Portugal established trading posts on the West African coast; and it wasn't until 1503 that the Spanish introduced slavery to the New World, followed by the British in 1562.

American Indians enslaved captives not killed outright in warfare, and also sold them to newly-arrived Europeans as forced labor. New England Puritans sold Pequot captives in the 1630s, mostly women and children, into West Indies slavery; New England's transatlantic slave trade of the mid-1700s, along with that of England, populated

---

1 Davis, pg. 60.
2 Mitcham, pg. 2.

North America with African slaves sold by their own people and not sent to the West Indies and Brazil. It is reported that human slavery covertly exists today in parts of Asia, Africa and South America.[3]

The Spanish crown authorized Ponce de Leon in 1514 to enslave Indians who refused the Catholic faith, as well as using imported African slaves to extract profits from their Cuban sugar plantations. After 1672, Spain used many black slaves and Indians for construction of the massive Castillo de San Marcos at St. Augustine.[4]

In 1702, numerous Florida Indians were enslaved by Carolina's Royal Governor James Moore when his troops destroyed the town of Ayavalla on the St. Marks River, and captured nearby settlements. The many Indian captives served as restitution for black slaves taken earlier from Moore's Carolina colony.[5] In retaliation, Spanish Governor Jose de Zuniga in 1704 encouraged fugitive slaves to escape from British plantations to the north, welcoming them as free subjects.[6]

After the cession of Florida to England in 1763, the Crown offered free land to attract permanent settlers, and more acreage for each additional person settling the land, white or black.[7] In 1767 the English brig *Augustine* brought 70 Negroes from Africa to St. Augustine for labor, with one east Florida planter having "over 100 Negroes on his plantation."[8]

After the American Revolution, many British Loyalists, or "Tories," fled to the Bahamas from Florida, Georgia and South Carolina and brought their slaves with them.

It was during this time that plantation owners in Georgia and South Carolina lost many slaves escaping to the wilds of Florida. The frequent cross-border Seminole raids on plantations often killed entire families and carried off more slaves, eventually pushing the American

---

3   Fogelman & Engerman, pg. 13.
4   Tebeau, pg. 59.
5   Brevard, pg. 71
6   Garvin, pg. 1.
7   Tebeau, pp. 75; 80.
8   Williams, pg. 95.

government toward military solutions and annexation. Interestingly, the name "Seminole" itself translates to "seceder" or "runaway" from the Creek nation, which occurred in 1750 under Chief Secoffee.

The Seminole tribe initially acquired black slaves as gifts from the British after 1763 or were purchased by them in imitation of Europeans, and held in "a type of democratic vassalage" to the tribe.[9] Though not considered the equals of the Seminole and living in separate settlements, black runaways were trained to hunt, fish and fight against white settlers who lived on Seminole land. After the tribe's defeat in 1839, many of these "black Seminoles" accompanied the tribe to resettlement in the West.[10]

Only twenty-two years later, resettled Seminoles fought bravely against Northern soldiers in the three Seminole Mounted Volunteer regiments of the Trans-Mississippi Department, led by Major John Jumper, whose Seminole name was "Hemha Micco." Seminoles also fought alongside the victorious Florida and Georgia forces at the Ocean Pond (Olustee) battle on February 20, 1864.

One Northern soldier wrote a New York friend just after the engagement:

> The most desperate enemy that we have to contend with here is the Florida Indians in roving bands of bushwhackers [who] occasionally steal upon our picket lines under cover of night ... Many Redskins are sharpshooters. During the recent battle, they took themselves to the tree-tops and picked off many of the officers of the Colored Troops. [11]

The emancipation of Africans in North America was first attempted by Virginia's Royal Governor Lord Dunmore in November 1775 after fleeing to his waiting ship as American patriots established control of the colony. His emancipation proclamation decreed all slaves free who would join his forces to suppress the colonists' independence movement. During the War of 1812 Vice Admiral Sir Alexander

---

9   Garvin, pg. 2.
10 Brevard, pg. 89.
11 Letter of Lt. French to NY, March 6, 1864.

Cochrane decreed the same to take away agricultural laborers and arm them to fight against American military forces. Lincoln's edict of January 1863 was not an original idea.

It is also important to recall the extreme violence and carnage in Saint-Domingue, now Haiti, between 1791 and 1804. The violent result of emancipation there left an indelible imprint on white Southerners who feared a similar fate should northern abolitionists prevail. The Haitian slave revolt began with some 100,000 slaves brutally massacring 4,000 white men, women and children while destroying sugar, indigo and coffee plantations. Many white survivors fled the island carrying horrific stories to the American South, which came to fear Cuba as the next island to be ruled by former slaves, then the United States if the abolitionists prevailed.

In 1845 Key West's relatively small black population was only two hundred, free and slave, many of whom came from the Bahamas. As Monroe was one of the few Florida counties without an agricultural economy, there was no need for a large labor force for planting and harvest. What increased the black population of Key West beyond some domestic servants who often "self-hired" themselves for additional income was the US Government's fort construction beginning in the mid-1840s.

The Corps of Engineer's system of slave-leasing for construction projects can be traced to the building of the navy yard at Pensacola in the 1820s, overseen by Massachusetts-born engineer William H. Chase. During his tenure as superintending that project, "the engineers quickly became the major renter of local slaves." When Forts Taylor and Jefferson began in the mid-1840s, "the army had become the federal government's principal leaser of slaves, and within the US Army, the Corps of Engineers was the major slave employer." A primary reason for this was the hot summer months when Northern skilled workers refused to come, plus the need for many unskilled workmen during the initial stages of construction. Between the decade 1840 to 1850, the army increased the black population of the island some 350 percent, with the black population growing more rapidly than the white.[12]

---

12 Smith, pp. 500-501.

To help thwart the illegal slave trade between Cuba and the US, Florida's Legislative Council in early March 1822 "fixed a fine of $300 for every Negro imported into the State from outside the United States," and every black person so imported would be declared free.[13]

The 1832 town charter granted by the Territorial Council authorized a tax on "free Negroes, mulattoes and slaves," with a subsequent town ordinance forbidding Negroes on the streets after 9:30PM. Free or slave, they were exempt from this ordinance only with written permission from city officials or their owners.[14]

Nonetheless, black people became an integral part of prewar Key West as many social gatherings on the island prominently featured Pablo Rogers, a popular colored musician. Historian Browne also mentions the Fish and Clarke clans being "fine seamstresses" who crafted the linen shirts and white duck suits worn by elegant gentlemen of that day. Key West's respected colored pilots included Peter & Samuel Welters, George Garvin and William Williams, plus "Uncle Tom" Romer who came from the Bahamas and was known to all local seamen. Other pilots were James Rubio and John Cornell, who came from St. Augustine. Sandy Cornish, or "Uncle Sandy," was well-known and respected for his fruit trees and flower garden. Arriving about 1846 were Hannah Brooks and Petronia Alvarez who became Key West's first trained nurses and were said to have treated almost every family on the island.[15]

There existed a relative racial harmony prior to the war, and many white and black residents worshiped together. At the new St. Paul's Episcopal Church in 1848, the congregation's black members sat in a reserved section, a practice which endured until 1888 when St. Peter's Episcopal was erected. Interestingly, when the island's Baptists sought membership in a Connecticut Baptist Association, they were quickly dropped when it was found that one Key West member owned slaves.[16] The Key West Baptists saw no reason to be excluded for what they understood was lawful, and especially since New Englanders had transported so many enslaved Africans to North America. This biracial

---

13 Dodd, pg. 118.
14 Browne, pp. 50-51.
15 Browne, pp. 171-172.
16 *Ibid.*, pg. 43.

worship was later noticed by a New York soldier who wrote in early February 1862 that "here the slaves are dressed almost as nicely as their masters and enjoy great privileges. They worship with the whites and then have meetings of their own three times a week."[17]

When work on Fort Taylor re-commenced in April 1845 the US Army engineers brought in their first slave laborers and two years later imported eleven more to work on Fort Jefferson at the Dry Tortugas. Northern-born engineer Captain Daniel Woodbury admitted increasing Fort Jefferson's slave labor force from forty to fifty-six in 1856 and keep them employed for longer periods for fiscal efficiency. The government policy at the time set their workday at 10 hours, usually 7 a.m. until sunset and an hour break for dinner at 12 p.m., and their treatment by the engineers was often harsh. This did not seem to change during the Civil War with Brannan constantly requesting "contrabands" to labor. Pennsylvania soldier would be relieved by the arrival of this labor force, as it would make their life easier. The forts usually relied upon skilled masons from the north. Though there were several slave mechanics and stone cutters, "almost ninety-five percent of the slaves at Fort Taylor" were unskilled.[18] After war began the Northern occupation forces 1861-1865 continued the use of black labor on fortifications, holding them to work even after emancipation. Island slaveowners who leased their bondsmen understandably wanted them protected from overwork, disease and malnutrition. Though free workers were responsible for their own health care, clothing and food, black workers were deemed more reliable and superior to white in the sultry, tropical climate.

Despite having all but destroyed piracy in the Caribbean, the US Navy had not stopped the illicit slave trade to Spanish Cuba which was peaking 1840-1860, and supported by New York City financiers. After increased US Navy patrols in the Caribbean in the late 1850s, Key West became a receiving center for the human cargoes of slavers captured and most likely destined for Brazilian or Cuban planters.[19] During the spring and summer of 1860, Key West held 1432 Africans taken from three captured slavers, all American-owned with Cuba as their destination. The US government housed them in barracks-like

---

17 Schmidt II, pg. 114.
18 Smith, pp. 7-9.
19 Williams, pg. 109.

"barracoons" for the duration of their stay. Here they received medical attention, though it is recorded that 295 died due to "afflictions of the lungs" as well as dysentery and diarrhea while awaiting transportation to Liberia. By July 19th, all had departed Key West for repatriation.[20]

One interesting example of captured slavers was the *Bogota* of New York, taken off Cuba in late May 1860 by Lt. John Newland Maffitt of the *USS Crusader* and escorted to Key West. The Africans, some 450 men, women and children, were forty-five days from the African slave-trading base at Ouidah, the Kingdom of Dahomey. Mafffit was to become a celebrated blockade runner, privateer and Confederate naval commander after 1861. *The Wilmington* (North Carolina) *Daily Journal* noted in its September 25, 1863 issue: "It is a curious fact for those who maintain that the civil war in America is founded upon the slave question, that Maffitt should be the very man who has distinguished himself actively against the slave trade."[21]

During the 1861-1865 conflict an ingenious Northern officer tagged Negroes as "contrabands" which means "booty" or "plunder." And though Lincoln's Republicans and their abolitionists allies never tired of blaming the aristocratic South for the black man's plight – they would not hold the sellers of the black man more reprehensible. It has been pointed out often that the black men, women and children arrived in "New England bottoms, and more than one fortune in Newport or New Bedford owes it origins" to slave trade profits.[22]

On the eve of war in 1860 the population of the island was 2302 white, 160 free black and 451 black slaves. More would come during the war and as early as mid-January 1861 the fort engineer was requesting that 300 "contrabands" from Virginia and South Carolina be sent to the island as fort laborers.[23] White troops unhappy with laboring on fortifications in the heat were elated in late March 1862, one writing that "we will have easy times" when the expected 500 contrabands arrive from Port Royal, South Carolina.[24] In this same month orders were issued by Fort Taylor's commander "regarding the

---

20 Malcolm, pp. 1; 8.
21 Shingleton, pp. 28-30.
22 Curtis & Thompson, pp. 241-242.
23 Schmidt III, pg. 101.
24 *Ibid.*, pg. 185.

degradation of private property," pertaining to the slaves of residents being appropriated as personal cooks and servants of the soldiers and officers. The orders read: "Negro slaves shall on no account be harbored in the quarters or encampments of the troops ..." [25] Despite the order some soldiers devised ways to employ cooks to prepare their meals and servants to run personal errands. The need for fortification laborers had become acute and the fort's commander was aware of the difficulty in men re-enlisting if they were used for hard labor. In late April 1862 Brigadier-General Brannan, promoted to district command for his part in securing Fort Taylor a year before, "reported that the need for contrabands to work on the fortifications was an "absolute and urgent necessity." As a result, hundreds of black "contrabands" were shipped to Key West from occupied Louisiana and South Carolina who would be later conscripted in February 1863.[26]

The occupation's quartermaster "emancipated" about twenty black men from their owners in mid-1862 for laborious fortification work. When owners protested the seizure the fort commander, a New Yorker, proclaimed an end to slavery on the island to clear the way for the quartermaster to confiscate any black persons.[27] In essence, the slaves were freed with military protection and put to heavy labor work which white Northern soldiers avoided.[28]

Especially noteworthy was the commandant's acquisition of a black servant himself, taken from the home of an island resident. When the officer was later transferred with the servant in tow, the town mayor had him taken off the ship and restored to his owner. Prior to the ship sailing away with the New York troops, four other black servants had been found stowed away.[29]

It was not until late January 1863 that official notice of Lincoln emancipating black slaves in the seceded States, but not slave States still in his union, arrived on the island, which caused "considerable celebration among the blacks" at Key West and at Fort Jefferson. Those in domestic service in town left their owners, but those at Fort

---

25   *Ibid.*, pg. 170.
26   *Ibid.*, pg. 205. See also Williams, pg. 19.
27   *Ibid.*, pp. 305; 315-316.
28   Davis, pp. 241-242.
29   Schmidt III, pg. 374.

Jefferson were forced to remain at their labor. Apparently unhappy with freedom under his Northern masters, a fort worker named "Henry" said that if emancipation was true, "they would like to go to one of the English islands and be "real free." [30]

At both forts the black man's value to the occupation force was as fortification labor, which white soldiers avoided, or as personal; servants. The work at the new Martello towers at Key West was advancing slowly by February 1863 with only six black workers and more requested.[31] It was at this time that emancipation-minded Col. Morgan returned to command at Key West and was welcomed by a jubilant colored population who considered him second in popularity only to Mr. Lincoln.

The North's response to Lincoln's proclamation was predictable: large numbers of blue-clad soldiers were disgusted by the proclamation after signing on to "save the Union," not emancipate African laborers. Those soldiers recently enlisted with promises of bounty money or coerced with threats of a draft, were the most chagrined and poised to desert, and paid substitutes disappeared at the first opportunity.[32]

The Sunbury (Pennsylvania) *Gazette* of May 2, 1863 published the letter of occupation soldier Sgt. Christian Beard complaining of the anti-war views prevalent at home and advocating censorship:

> They tell us we are fighting for nothing but to free n*****s, and that our government don't do as they ought, and the President thinks more of a n****r than of a white soldier ... There is but two sides, the one is for the administration and the Union, the other is for the rebellion ... The best thing would be to stop all newspapers, and not allow them to be sent to the army. Letters of a disturbing character should also be forbidden ...[33]

---

30   Schmidt II, pg. 401.
31   *Ibid.*, pg. 406.
32   Hesseltine, pg. 290.
33   Schmidt III, pp. 486-487.

The black man's increasing value as a soldier in blue can be traced to August 1861 when the three-month volunteer's hitch ended, and after the carnage of First Manassas and resoluteness of the South's desire for independence was realized. Lincoln desperately demanded troops to continue his war though Northern governors replied that volunteers came forward slowly and eventually only generous bounty money would attract enlistments. In October 1861, Lincoln's secretary of war suggested the use of captured slaves as laborers and even soldiers on the coast of occupied South Carolina, as the contrabands consumed government rations and lay idle all day. This early proposal to utilize black men was well-received by governors having difficulty attracting white men for their regiments, though at the time Lincoln opposed it.[34]

Since the first year of the war the black soldier was a novel experiment at occupied Hilton Head, South Carolina as displaced "contrabands" fell within Union lines. The later invasion at Jacksonville and raids on the Florida coast in 1862 intentionally carried off black men to be enrolled and dressed in blue. The object of the Jacksonville invasion was according to Saxton to occupy the town "and make it the base of operations for arming the Negroes and securing in this way possession of the entire State of Florida" – in other words, inciting servile insurrection." At occupied Pensacola in the fall of 1862 the ruthless Hungarian-born Gen. Asboth organized "several companies of Negro troops for his "Corps d'Afrique" to augment his force; colored troops were used to pillage and burn Eucheanna and Marianna, two villages in western Florida.[35]

The North's decision to use colored troops was due to the white Northerner's reluctance to enlist through outright evasion and substitutes, and if the white Northerner did enlist it was costly to the local, State and federal government in bounties paid. Black troops proved inexpensive and Lincoln's War Department organized its Bureau of Colored Troops in early 1863.[36] The slaves taken from ruined South Carolina, Georgia and Florida plantations diminished the need for white northerners drafted. In addition, they could

---

34 Hesseltine, pp. 286-287.
35 Davis, pp. 224; 228.
36 Ogle, pg. 76.

not vote and had no government representatives to complain to of mistreatment, hard labor duty and low – if any pay. Lincoln's War Department later issued General Order 215 on June 22, 1864, which required that black troops be paid the same as Northern white troops, with the exception of bounty money. The black recruit was restricted to a maximum $100 bounty. If the black recruit was a free man prior to the war, he was to receive the same as the white recruit. The slaves taken from plantations and enlisted in Florida had no legal standing as free men regarding the bounties, though State recruiters actively sought them to count against their own State quotas and thus relieve as many white men from the hated draft. There were many instances of the bounty monies due black recruits stuck to the hands of the rapacious State agents.[37]

In early 1862, Gov. John Andrew of Massachusetts met with Secretary of War Stanton to solve the dilemma of few enlistments "for the war [Andrew] had so sedulously promoted."[38] Both being Radical Republicans and intent upon defeating the South at any cost, it was agreed that Massachusetts could raise regiments of black men counted toward the State quota of troops assigned. With so few black men within Massachusetts, Andrew sent agents to scour other States for enlistees, which produced a sufficient number to form the Fifty-fourth Massachusetts regiment although only 13% were actually residents of that State. The Fifty-fifth Massachusetts regiment was composed of black men from twenty-five States as well as Canada and Africa.[39]

Other Northern governors followed the "Massachusetts Idea" with Iowa's governor seeing the practicality of the matter, viewing black men as "a means to an end, and if one more Negro went another white man could stay at home."[40]

The above was underscored by the North's War Department not conducting any large-scale operations through 1863 in order to conserve both land and sea resources. General Halleck let his commanders know that small-theater offensives like North Carolina, Georgia and Florida would not receive additional troops, and grumbled that "every

---

37 Ford, pp. 24-25.
38 Hesseltine, pg. 287.
39 Daniels, pg. 95.
40 Hesseltine, pp. 288-289.

general is pressing for more troops as though we had a cornucopia of men from which to supply their wants." Therefore, more coastal and interior raids from Hilton Head became necessary to bring forth more black men to fill the blue ranks decimated by expiring enlistments and fewer white enlistees.[41]

Perhaps the greatest irony of the War was the black population of the South attaching themselves to the invader sweeping down from the North. Especially in the case of Massachusetts and its desire to use black men in place of able-bodied white men who would rather remain at home, this was the State which first codified a slave code for Africans as well as being preeminent in the transatlantic slave trade, along with Rhode Island. Without Britain's and New England's slave trade, there would have been no Africans in the South to emancipate.

The decision to enlist black troops was not well-received in Northern ranks. In central Pennsylvania, the *Allentown Democrat* on February 11, 1863, criticized the Republicans for equalizing the races and suggesting that black and white soldiers be mixed within the same military company. The Allentown paper continued: "There is no good reason why the white men of the North should expose their lives and endure all the hardships of the camp, the march and the field, for the benefit of Negroes; and they will not do it if they can avoid it. Negroes are fit subjects for an Abolition war; were it a war for restoration of the Union as it was, there would be no need to call upon Negroes to join the army."

Many 47th Pennsylvania regiment soldiers remained convinced they were fighting to "save the Union" and not to free anyone, but their views were undergoing change with rather easy duty and steady pay far from the front, having black men stop bullets was preferential.

"They tell us in the north," one soldier wrote in a letter home, "that the negroes are ignorant and incapable of taking care of themselves. Now this is utterly false." The black folks at Key West worked hard, saved their money, and behaved as well as any white person would. A private in the 47th wrote in a letter home that he had no interest in sharing the north with freedmen and hoped they would be prevented from leaving the South, "that they dare not come north."[42]

---

41 Newsome, pg. 16.
42 Ogle, pp. 69-70.

It proved often difficult to enlist black men with homes on burned plantations as many feared leaving their families helpless in the midst of the devastation. Northern States like Pennsylvania still had had to endure Lincoln's draft though paid-substitutes and very generous enlistment bounties attracted white soldiers. To fill the ranks, the Northern Congress passed a "mercenary bill" of nearly three-quarters of a billion dollars to attract enlistees.[43]

Contrary to the common belief that black troops were sought only by the North, on April 28th, 1865, the commanding general of Confederate troops in Florida, directed ten prominent Floridians "to proceed at once to raise a company of Negroes to be mustered into the service of the Confederate States for the War." This was a result of the Confederate Congress authorizing on March 3, 1865 that 300,000 black troops be enlisted to augment existing Southern armies.[44]

The Department of the South's commander in January 1863 was Gen. David Hunter who authorized Col. Thomas Higginson's First South Carolina Colored Regiment to embark on a plundering raid up the St. Mary's River near Fernandina. After the unit had desolated farms and plantations, the colored regiment returned to Hilton Head with railroad iron, pine lumber, rice, bricks and a flock of stolen sheep. Hunter purposely separated his operations for black troops and believed they "could not consistently with the interests of the service be advantageously employed to act with our [white] forces." As anti-draft riots plagued the North and white men avoided military service, black soldiers could be obtained – very often against their will - by raiding the isolated plantations of South Carolina, Georgia and Florida. On the raids, the colored troops carried additional rifles and uniforms for black men spirited away from the ruined plantations and their families abandoned. As only one of five nominal black regiments on Hilton Head had ever reached authorized strength, more plantation raids deeper into the South Carolina and Florida coasts were planned to carry off slaves.[45]

---

43 Randall, pg. 430.
44 Davis, pp. 227-228.
45 Daniels, pg. 85.

To better avoid additional conscription of Northern white men, Lincoln in early December 1863 boasted that a "full one hundred thousand [colored men] are now in the ranks who take the place of white men." Additionally, New England textile mill owners lobbied Congress to increase black enlistments "in order to reduce the draft of their white employees" and urged equal pay for black men to better entice them into the blue ranks.[46]

In early February 1863 notorious Kansas Jayhawker Col. James Montgomery arrived at Key West, officially-authorized a month earlier to enroll free and refugee black men into a new regiment, called the "2nd South Carolina Volunteers." This veteran of the mid-1850s Kansas internecine conflict was known for his bloody, destructive raids on non-combatants; historian Albert Casteel described Montgomery, a past associate of John Brown, as "a sincere, if unscrupulous, antislavery zealot."

Montgomery spent ten days scouring the island for black men to enroll – forcibly if necessary – if they were not already in US government employ. As the army's need for labor was acute, many were protected by military authorities to continue as fortification labor, especially for the new Martello towers. Montgomery's notice clearly left unprotected black men no choice as they were "HEREBY ORDERED" to report to the Courthouse:

> In compliance with instructions received from Headquarters, Dept. of the South, every male person of African descent, between the ages of fifteen (15,) and fifty (50,) who have not already enrolled themselves, are hereby ordered to report in person forthwith to Col. Montgomery, at the Court House, Key West, there to undergo a medical examination, preparatory to embarking for Hilton Head, S.C." By Command of Jos. S. Morgan, Col., 90th N.Y. Vols, Commanding Post.

In this manner 124 black men on the island who listed their birthplaces as Alabama, Virginia, Georgia, South Carolina, Ohio, Nassau and elsewhere in Florida, were conscripted into US military

---

46 Daniels, pg. 86.

service and taken to Port Royal Island, South Carolina on February 23rd. Many if not all of these men were the "contrabands" requested earlier by Brannan.

The *New York Tribune* wrote of Montgomery's visit to Key West on March 7, 1863:

> Quite a sturdy battalion of black soldiers was raised in this town, and a short time ago sent up to Hilton Head, SC. Slavery seems extinct in the key, and nearly all the colored people remaining here are the women, children and old men. [47]

At Hilton Head, the Ohio-born Montgomery dressed his new troops in blue uniforms while rigorously drilling them in the rudiments of military order, marching and stern discipline. They would soon become familiar with Montgomery's tactic of swift raids along the South Carolina and Georgia coasts, plus give them ample opportunity to bring the grim and deadly realities of war home to American civilians in the South. Officially, these military expeditions were intended to simply disrupt cattle operations and salt-making facilities, but under Montgomery devolved into the burning of farms, mansion or slave cabin, destroying rice and corn crops, and carrying off black men to deprive Southern farms of agricultural workers. The latter were often reluctant to leave their wives and families alone with little to eat and at the mercy of roving bands of refugees. Northern recruiters of black men like James T. Ayers, who admitted more success when assisted by armed black soldiers, "found surprising the initial reluctance and the lack of enthusiasm by the slaves or ex-slaves to join the US Colored Troops," and "offered all manner of excuses not to enlist." Some "recruiters" were arrested by Northern provosts for kidnapping Negroes who refused to enlist in blue. This helps explain the relatively low number of black men taken from Florida – 1,044 out of a total black male population of 32,000, free and slave. Their regimental leadership consisted entirely of white officers - usually avid abolitionists - as black officers were not allowed in Northern regiments.[48]

---

47 Schmidt III, pg. 438.

48 Franklin, pp. xvi-xvii; 45-46.

By the middle of March, 1863 the "2nd" – with little training other than donning uniforms – accompanied Higginson's regiment on the destructive Jacksonville raid. Higginson sent his second in command, Col. Montgomery of the "2nd," up the Broad River to establish rendezvous points for black men taken from nearby plantations, and if trustworthy, armed and uniformed. Montgomery's 120 newly-minted soldiers reportedly "plundered everything in sight" and the steamer returning them to Jacksonville heavily burdened with stolen valuables and forage. On the 29th of March the "2nd" departed Jacksonville with its soldiers mesmerized by the sight and roar of the flames they ignited as fire consumed the town.[49]

During one of their most notorious raids, and despite no Southern troops in the area, the "2nd" participated in the destruction of Darien, Georgia in mid-June 1863. Montgomery's fellow officer, Col. Robert Shaw of the 54th Massachusetts Regiment, condemned the frenzy of looting, destruction and arson, and "in a private letter wrote that his understanding of Montgomery's reason for pillaging and burning the undefended town as "Southerners must be made to feel that this was a real war, and that they were to be swept away by the hand of God, like the Jews of old." Montgomery said to Shaw, "We are outlawed, and therefore not bound by the rules of regular warfare." [50]

Part of Montgomery's force were black men brought from Key West who ironically assisted in destroying the birthplace of former Key West mayor and staunch Unionist Walter C. Maloney, Sr.

The devastation wrought by the "brigand habits" of Montgomery's troops upon civilians elated Radical Republicans, but it also brought condemnation from others like Col. Robert Shaw who saw these outrages bringing dishonor to Negro troops. Montgomery's fellow officer, Col. Thomas Higginson, wrote: "This indiscriminate burning and pillaging is savage warfare ... demoralizes the soldiers – and must produce a reaction [among white Northerners] against arming the Negroes." Even the *Boston Commonwealth* editorialized that

---

49 Smith, pg. 266.
50 Rose, pg. 252.

the South's long-held fear of mass emancipation would result in the "horrors of servile war" had been given "the colors of truth" by Montgomery's colored troops.[51]

After a very brief training period at Hilton Head the 2nd was assigned to an expedition to occupy Jacksonville, Florida in early March, and conduct raids up the St. John's River to Palatka, "collecting Negro recruits, stealing and plundering. "Hogs, horses, and beeves were stolen or slaughtered; smoke-houses and corn cribs, stripped ... Household furniture broken up. Trunks and chests were rifled. Women were insulted and abused. The torch was applied to out-houses and barns."[52]

After some skirmishing with Florida forces, the 2nd evacuated Jacksonville at the end of March. The *Cotton States* of April 14, 1863, reported: "Captain J.J. Dickison engaged the transport *Mary Benton* on March 27th, having on board 500 Negro troops of ... Montgomery's command," resulting in the death or wounding about twenty-five black soldiers. "The Yankees left in great haste, and did not stop until they reached Jacksonville, which city was evacuated the next day."[53]

Returning to Beaufort where the "2nd" remained through July, the unit was involved in raids up the Combahee River as well as to James Island on feints for a future attack on Fort Wagner. At James Island the invading forces suffered 30 killed and lost 14 as prisoners, some Key West men possibly among that number. Two of the Key West men reportedly were awarded the Bronze Medal for bravery at Morris Island. After the failed assault on Fort Wagner in mid-July which shattered the Northern attackers, South Carolina forces abandoned the fort on September 7th after withdrawing the garrison and all artillery.

The 2nd remained near Charleston on picket duty through January 1864, when it returned to Hilton Head, then assigned to Jacksonville in early Feb 1864, when it became the 34th US Colored Troops. The "new" 34th was part of a failed operation of six colored regiments along with white New York and Ohio units led by Gen. John Hatch, November 30, 1864, known as the battle of Honey Hill in South Carolina, near

---

51   *Ibid.*, pg. 253.

52   Davis, pg. 232.

53   Dickison, pg. 178.

Pocotaligo. The veteran Southern forces of mostly Georgia infantry regiments and South Carolina cavalry, reinforced with Georgia Militia and Reserve forces, suffered but 50 casualties and only 8 killed; Northern forces lost 755, with 88 killed and 44 being captured.

Of the black men conscripted at Key West in February 1863, eighteen died during the war. Six were killed and two wounded in action - the remaining ten died from non-combat-related causes such as disease. Several were listed as deserters.[54]

---

54 *FKSHJ*, Vol. 23, No. 4, Summer 2013.

CHAPTER 9:

"CROSSING THE LINES INTO REBELDOM" - 1864-1865

> In order to create a Union sentiment at the South, we must satisfy the people of that section that we are stronger than they, and thoroughly earnest in our purpose of preserving the soil of the United States undivided. We must show them that if they persevere in rebellion they cannot escape hunger and misery, that they will be outcasts without property rights of any kind; that it is a mere question of time how soon they will be hunted down.
>
> *Harper's Weekly*, June 14, 1862

Since the occupation began many islanders left for the mainland to become refugees and provide intelligence to Florida authorities regarding the forts and numbers of soldiers. Departures - forced or voluntary - had been accelerated by the fort's commander complaining of islanders' "disunionism" since May of 1861 and directing the mayor to draw up a list of residents and "extra mouths" who might have to be fed by the US government. With the island blockaded and under martial law he issued an ominous directive to rid the island of extraneous people.[1]

Thirty people left the island in early June 1861 for Cedar Keys and the interior rather than submit to the forced oath of allegiance. A month later a Northern soldier estimated that despite the latest departure of Key Westers a third of the remaining residents "were secretly

---
1 Schmidt III, pp. 45-46.

secessionist and were kept peaceful only because of the fort's cannons." In the continuing quest to suppress thoughts of independence among islanders the port's naval commander decreed in August 1861 that the crew of all ships departing Key West's harbor must take the government oath. Many took it with no intention of observing it.[2]

In mid-September 1863 the *Philadelphia Inquirer* reported a large number of families with household goods boarding for Tampa which it called "a poor, unimportant town in the bay – already replete with half-starved Rebels from Key West." A government official observed that the Key Westers he considered "the most violent" had already left though their baneful influence remained over the island's predominant "Conch" population who were to be monitored closely.[3]

The military deportations of families as well as voluntary removals from Key West resulted in a substantial Key Westers-in-exile community formed at Tampa and Clearwater by March of 1862. The "Key West Avengers" serving nearby were welcomed into their homes for food and entertainment until they departed for Tennessee. Life here for civilians was precarious as Northern troops from Key West would land to ransack homes, kill livestock, burn clothing and buildings before returning to their boats. The only defense for civilians was to move further inland as the raids became more frequent.[4]

The possibility of attack from mainland Florida forces initially worried the island's military officials who took preemptive measures for this and other reasons. Northern invasions near Jacksonville in October 1862 gained little militarily but their increasing use of colored troops for destructive raids on civilians developed into a continuing strategy. To thwart the raiding parties intention to carry off black men needed for Florida's agricultural production, plantation owners withdrew to the State's interior with roving cavalry units protecting them.

After the fall of Vicksburg in mid-1863 the cattle herds of central and north Florida increasingly fed Southern armies in the field, and Northern forces began concentrating their efforts on disrupting cattle-

---

2   *Ibid.*, pp. 59; 65; 73.
3   *Ibid.*, pg. 75.
4   Campbell, pp. 28-29.

raising areas of Florida as well as the coastal salt works which helped preserve the meat supply. Northern raids came inland from Fernandina and Jacksonville while military expeditions from Key West to Cedar Keys and Tampa threatened interior cattle areas.

This Northern strategy not only terrorized Florida civilians on the coasts and interior, but also encouraged and supplied deserter bands from both sides living in the swamps. These deserters raided isolated farms and plantations, driving off cattle, hogs, and armed refugee blacks who raided small Florida communities on their own.[5] The raids to Florida's interior were also designed to attract and enlist Southern deserters into the 47th Pennsylvania which sometimes occurred. More often than not these were hungry, desperate men looking for food, a clean bed and especially Yankee greenbacks. They would just as often desert at he first opportunity.

One perplexed Pennsylvania soldier at Key West mused in a letter home just what induced these men to apparently forsake the Southern army, enlist in his army, then desert again at the first opportunity with a full stomach, money, clothing and new musket. A case in point was the 47th enlisting two young fishermen in June 1863, Joseph and Edgar Baker. After only a month in the Pennsylvania regiment and eating their share of government rations both deserted, likely heading for the mainland with new muskets to rejoin their Florida comrades.[6]

The already-mentioned refugee Zachariah Brown who allegedly fled to Key West in October with seven others "to escape rebel tyranny" related to his new friends how they were compelled to live in the woods to avoid capture by the "rebels." Believed to be truthful most were immediately enlisted in the 47th Pennsylvania regiment and counted toward Lehigh Valley's troop quotas which relieved some Pennsylvania men from the hated draft. The soldier-diarist of this account was soon aware that once these men were enlisted, fed, uniformed and paid they would desert at the first opportunity.[7]

---

5   Davis, pg. 260.
6   Schmidt III, pg. 527.
7   *Ibid.*, pg. 654.

Another guileless mainland refugee was Enoch Daniels who came to Key West from Charlotte Harbor in December 1863. Enoch's plan was to captain 100 refugee volunteers raised on the island, armed and equipped by the US military, and then sent to conquer the country between Charlotte Harbor and Tampa Bay where he claimed large herds roamed.[8] He also claimed that as many as 800 "rebel" deserters and others were hiding in the woods of central Florida to avoid Confederate conscription and would join Northern forces if given the opportunity.

Undeterred by past experiences with mainland refugees, the 47th Pennsylvania mustered twenty-nine refugees as the "Florida Rangers" led by "Captain" Enoch Daniels. The new "Lt." Zachariah Brown would be assigned to Fort Taylor. With this new force on hand a mainland incursion from Key West was scheduled for mid-December, supervised by an officer of the 47th Pennsylvania.[9]

Additionally a small post was established below Charlotte Harbor on the Caloosahatchee River with a company 47th Pennsylvania soldiers. After landing and joining more refugee soldiers, all marched inland and captured a fort and its three occupants. The detachment searched the area and found no cattle to rustle but did seize four barrels of turpentine. They returned to their boats to find that the six refugee soldiers left to guard them were gone, having returned to their previous loyalty.[10]

Within a month's time after departing for the mainland Lt. Zach Brown had deserted with three of his refugee soldiers, all intimately apprised of the expedition's intent. Now back on the mainland Brown related his observations at Key West regarding fort defenses, armament, troop strength and warships in the harbor.[11] It was finally recognized by the Northern commander that Zach Brown's and others "treachery" of feigning desertion from the Confederacy, taking the oath and enlisting in the 47th had all been designed to lure US troops into mainland ambushes. But due to the ongoing devastation of the interior by Northern raids the stream of refugees and alleged deserters came

---

8   *Ibid.*, pg. 705.
9   *Ibid.*, pg. 712.
10 Schmidt II, pg. 401.
11 Schmidt III, pp. 709-712.

to Key West in search of food, shelter and work. The wary soldiers now viewed all with suspicion even after taking the government oath and requesting enlistment.[12]

Nonetheless, additional soldiers were needed for mainland cattle-disrupting operations and more recruiting began for mounted refugee soldiers to help search the mainland for disaffected rebels who might take the oath and enlist. Though Northern expectations of Floridians' war-weariness was high and few men came forward to enlist, the "Second Florida Cavalry" was finally activated with 40 men at the end of March.[13] This initiative was not without problems as one-third of the refugee enlistees had gone over to Florida forces after reaching the mainland. After this further "treachery" the commander at Key West wisely forbade shipping arms and ammunition to mainland groups claiming loyalty and "Unionism."[14]

As the year 1864 closed all work on fortifications, especially the Martello towers, continued unabated with skilled white masons from the north – "whose character left something to be desired" utilized where needed. Two of them attacked a man and his two black employees, stoned his house and threatened his servants. The troublesome masons were arrested the next day and imprisoned at Fort Jefferson for six months, which of course depleted the ranks of skilled brick masons.[15]

The 47th Pennsylvania was notified of its transfer as part of the Red River campaign, a major Northern offensive in the Trans-Mississippi theater. The Pennsylvanians would join the 30,000-man offensive operation opposed by 10,000 hastily-assembled Southern troops and perhaps have an opportunity to salvage their reputation after Pocotaligo.

The soldiers of this regiment received good news that the borough of Easton "taxed" its residents to give a $300 bonus to veterans who already reenlisted and the same to those reenlisting before the draft took place. There was a caveat of each man being credited to Easton's

---

12 *Ibid.*, pg. 776.
13 Schmidt II, pp. 812-819.
14 *Ibid.*, pg. 832.
15 Schmidt II, pg. 409.

draft quota no matter where the man was from, and in essence a reenlistment allowed an Easton man to avoid the draft. Allentown and other area towns offered only $75 reenlistment bonus if credited to themselves; men from Northumberland County complained that they received nothing – but soon received news that they would receive $150 each for reenlisting and being credited to that county.[16]

The *Allentown Democrat* of February 17th reported that sixty Easton County men had reenlisted and credited themselves to Key West which meant no bounty money. The paper wrote of the men doing this "so some of their friends back home would have the opportunity to see what army life was all about."[17]

The "Key West Avengers" at the same time were also reenlisting as Sergeant Robert Watson's regiment assembled to unanimously approve continuing their service while expressing confidence in their military leadership and President Jefferson Davis.[18] They were more motivated by patriotism and the defense of their homes rather than bounties paid, which would have been worth but little. A valuable "bounty" for the "Avengers" would be the hoped-for transfer to service afloat with regular meals and a dry place to sleep.

At Key West the regiment replacing the 47th Pennsylvania disembarked from the steamer *Charles Thomas* on Washington's Birthday 1864. This was the 800-man, 2nd US Colored Troops regiment from the Washington area, with about one-fifth from Maryland and the rest from Virginia and elsewhere. Their arrival brought the total of Northern troops on the island, Fort Jefferson and Cedar Keys to 2,786.

Captain Wilder, a white officer of the 2nd USCT wrote soon after arriving that the people of Key West "held Southern-sentiment and most were dedicated Confederates." He added his feeling that residents, including the Unionist mayor, would have preferred that the *Charles Thomas* "was sunk with all persons on board lost." Another officer wrote that the 47th Pennsylvania regiment his unit was relieving "were also very much opposed to us. They used every sort of epithet against me, as did also the citizens. There, as elsewhere, the courteous received us civilly.

---

16 Schmidt III, pg. 739.
17 Schmidt II, pg. 425.
18 Campbell, pp. 92-93.

We lived under the cold shadow of displeasure of others, which in a hot climate was not very comfortable, after all."[19] The captain derisively referred to the Pennsylvanians as "Dutch" and "Copperheads," referring to their Lehigh Valley political predilection as Democrats.

Despite being a newcomer to the island and without a closer understanding of Key Westers, Wilder wrote derisively of islanders being "not pre-eminently distinguished for intellectual activity," and if the town were wrecked by a tornado, "the arts would not be lost." He viewed the island's "Conchs" as ignorant with peculiar customs and manners, and "rebel almost to a man."[20]

The *Philadelphia Inquirer* reported in March that the Conchs were greatly upset by the colored soldiers who patrol the town, though the white soldiers in blue were admittedly uncomfortable with serving with colored soldiers. The paper continued that the secession element was "greatly in the majority and dormant for the time being."[21]

One member perhaps representative of the 2nd USCT regiment was Private James T. Taylor, a free black shoemaker in Charlottesville, Virginia. He remained there until 1862 when he moved to Washington to allegedly escape Southern conscription, but was caught there by Northern conscription. While serving on the island he married a Key West lady in mid-April 1865 and subsequently returned to Virginia after mustering out in January 1866.[22]

The colored regiment's white chaplain left an interesting account of his observations after arrival and not being well-received by either the citizenry or US Navy personnel. He thought that many lazy and worthless men had found lucrative positions in the US Navy and inhabit the island's hotels – and that a naval officer "seems to be more a gentleman of leisure than a military officer." Of island life under military occupation he wrote: "Every man's hand is against his brother, socially, and scandal is unlimited."[23]

---

19 Schmidt III, pg. 783.
20 *Ibid.*, pg. 780.
21 *Ibid.*, pg. 812.
22 BlackVirginiansinBlue.
23 Schmidt III, pg. 818.

Welcome news finally reached Key Wester Robert Watson and 17 other "Avengers" on the 3rd of March as they received their assignments to the Confederate Navy where they felt they could contribute the most as seamen. Many including Watson went to the ironclad *CSS Savannah* at that city, ironically where Asa and Nelson Tift's shipyard had converted the blockade runner Fingal into the *CSS Atlanta*.[24]

The darker side of the North's conscripted and paid-substitute soldiers was being felt in their regiments as 280 prisoners from the Army of the Potomac arrived aboard a steamer in early May. With military prisons at the North overflowing these men – described as a motley, sorry-looking lot - were being sent to Fort Jefferson which already held some of the worst offenders.[25]

Military operations against the mainland continued from the island in early May as "Headquarters District of Key West and Tortugas" commander, Gen. Daniel Woodbury, was himself to lead an expedition to capture Tampa with the recently-arrived 2nd USCT regiment. The beef supply of central Florida continued to be an important target of Northern forces at Key West, and the use of colored troops might attract black Florida men into blue uniforms.

Once on the mainland Woodbury's troops burned barns and looted homes while searching for cattle herds, and fought several sharp skirmishes in July and August against Florida militia and its famed "Cow Cavalry." The latter was officially known as the First Florida Special Cavalry led by Major Charles J. Munnerlyn, a South Carolinian appointed by President Davis. The force was the brainchild of Seminole War veteran Capt. James McKay of Tampa who recalled its highly-efficient "cracker cavalry" and an effective way to deter cattle raids. As Florida was barren of military age men, many Florida veterans in the Florida-beef dependent Army of Tennessee were detached for this service.[26] After several brief skirmishes and captured beeves, Woodbury's raiders returned to Tampa and their boats to take

---

24 Campbell, pg. 97.
25 Schmidt III, pg. 842.
26 *Ibid.*, pg. 842; 885.

them back to Key West. In a case of extreme irony, many of the cattle taken by the raiders had been destined for Union prisoners suffering at south Georgia's Andersonville stockade.[27]

The 2nd USCT was being decimated by a yellow fever epidemic during May and June which ultimately took half the unit's officers but somehow did not affect enlisted men. One company of the 110th New York lost a third of its men and several officers while ships carrying necessary supplies avoided the island as the disease raged.[28] The epidemic reached the point where the island became an immense hospital amid an intense heat wave with temperatures above 100. The fever would also claim the life of the district's commanding officer, Gen. Woodbury, who lingered until mid-August. He was soon succeeded by Gen. John Newton who came from the Western Theater to Key West.

The 47th Pennsylvania's combat experience in the ill-fated Red River campaign under General Banks ended in late May, 1864. Here the unit sustained heavy casualties and men captured at the Sabine Cross Roads battle, then were routed at the Pleasant Hill engagement. They would not return to Key West and instead were sent to the Shenandoah Valley as Washington was being threatened by Gen. Jubal Early's forces in July 1864.

After Early retreated down the Valley the 47th's camp was prepped for the upcoming 1864 presidential election pitting incumbent Lincoln against Democrat Gen. George McClellan. If the soldiers obtained Lehigh Valley newspapers, which may have been easy to smuggle in, both the *Allentown Democrat* and *Der Republikaner* endorsed Gen. McClellan for the presidency over Lincoln. The electoral losses suffered by Republicans in late 1862 resulted in their embracing of soldiers voting in their camps wherever located, tactfully arguing that this was the highest privilege proof of citizenship and having one's voice heard, but very aware of the potential of controlling those votes. The *Republican National Standard* of Salem, New Jersey editorialized in mid-1864 that denying soldiers the vote would "denigrate them to the level of the negro, so far as political rights are involved."[29]

---

27   Taylor, pp. 198;208.
28   Schmidt III, pg. 861.
29   White, pp. 18-21.

This argument was paralleled with an ongoing purge of Democrat-leaning army officers, the highest profile one being Gen. George McClellan who was targeted for removal by the Radicals. If politically-appointed officers oversaw the distribution of Republican ballots – or unfortunate loss of Democratic ballots – Republican victory was assured. Viewing their party as "the federal government" itself which, in times of trouble, could justifiably mobilize the powerful voting bloc it had in its army and when necessary, use it as a tool to control any opposition at the polls.

In August 1864 former Key West editor and now-Lt. William H. Ward served as executive officer aboard the Confederate raider *Tallahassee*. During its successful career of capturing or destroying enemy merchant ships, the raider not only caused panic along the New England coast but New York merchants found few if any willing to insure the cargoes of their ships.[30]

Defending Mobile Bay, Alabama against attack in early August was Key West's Lt. Francis Watlington aboard the impressive ironclad ram *CSS Tennessee*. As the battle raged his ship was surrounded by several Northern warships firing point-blank broadsides which battered it into surrender. Watlington escaped capture and eventually was paroled at Nanna Hubba Bluff, Alabama on May 10, 1865.[31]

Though Lincoln was often portrayed as a story-telling bumpkin he made shrewd political appointments and used whatever political advantage available to him, seen or unseen. And he was certainly aware of Assistant Secretary of War Charles A. Dana being put to work using "all the power and influence of the War Department" to secure Lincoln's reelection, which included furloughing some 200,000 soldiers in November 1864 to proceed home to vote, and afterward patrol the polls.[32] Dana was an early confidante of Lincoln who earlier sent him to the West to spy on the unknown US Grant who had achieved some victories over his opponents.

---

30 Luraghi, pp. 310-311.
31 Luraghi, pg. 327.
32 Daniels, pg. 105.

Another aspect of controlling the military was control of the US mail, especially to and from a remote island like Key West. The letters of the 47th Pennsylvania, both incoming and outgoing, were almost certainly censored to eliminate any information considered improper or sensitive. This would have been done by cutting or crossing out the offending passage. Any soldier expressing doubts regarding the war or his officers' abilities would have his letters censored and also face investigation – while a soldier expressing support for the war and Republican party would have his letters approved. Without a doubt Allentown's German-language papers and *Allentown Democrat* editorials echoed typical Northern Democrat party anti-war positions, desire for peaceful compromise, quick restoration of the Union as it was prior to secession, and absolute opposition to an "abolition war." The papers could well have been denied mail access in 1863-1865 as the Radical Republican control of the war effort exerted a tighter grip on the army.

The presidential election of 1864 was close and without the soldiers' vote in six crucial States, Lincoln would have lost the election to McClellan. The Keystone State helped Lincon win reelection with all of its electoral votes obtained with a slim 20,000 vote margin. Despite Lincoln's advantages and War Department assistance the Lehigh Valley voted for McClellan, winning 64 percent of the vote in Lehigh and Northampton counties. Lincoln won the State and it was remarked that "Pennsylvania went to Lincoln, but the Lehigh Valley said no to Lincoln's war."[33]

Assigned to another privateering mission in late October 1864, former *Key of the Gulf* editor Lt. William H. Ward was elevated to command of the re-christened *Tallahassee* – now the *Olustee* and honoring the Southern victory in Florida. On this voyage the privateer captured or destroyed six merchantmen off the Cape of Delaware and fought off five enemy warships before passing under the protection of Fort Fisher's guns near Wilmington.[34]

---

33 Warner, pg. 9.
34 Luraghi, pg.

Key West's federal authorities were concerned about significant "loyalty issues" still remaining on the island as a US military board was convened to investigate the eligibility of destitute islanders receiving government food rations and ensuring that recipients had taken the government oath of loyalty to ascertain eligibility.

At Tampa, Key West Lt. Walter C. Maloney, Jr. resigned his commission in the Seventh Florida regiment in late October to join the Washington Siege Artillery guarding the Edisto River at Adams Run, South Carolina against enemy incursions. Sherman's army was nearing Savannah in late 1864 and expected to threaten approaches to Charleston from the south.

In island judicial matters, the 2nd USCT regiment's Provost Court of November 28th was presided over by its Lt. Col. John A. Wilder, which was investigating possible frauds discovered between islanders who purchased US Government property from people "not authorized to sell," possibly military officers.[35] Shortly after Wilder stated that he was also tracking some $17,500 of Government funds allegedly swindled on the island.[36] And in mid-December, Private Darius Stokes of the 2nd USCT was sentenced to be hung for the murder of his company sergeant while in Mississippi, and was carried out on land adjacent to Fort Taylor and south of the causeway. It is said he was buried in the "African Cemetery" on White Street.[37]

Ships arriving in late December brought news of the capture of Savannah after the withdrawal of Gen. William J. Hardee's forces from the city's defenses to Charleston - Hardee's departmental command included Florida. Key Westers Robert Watson, Alfred Lowe, George Curry, Frank Diaz, Samuel Morgan, Joseph Morgan and John B. Sands were all serving aboard the ironclad ram *CSS Savannah* at this time and scuttled her to prevent capture when the city was abandoned. They made their way to Charleston, then on to Fort Fisher below Wilmington in early January, serving with the naval brigade at Battery Buchanan which protected the Cape Fear River's New Inlet. This was a high and elliptically-shaped earthen mound containing two

---

35   *Ibid.*, pg. 922.
36   *Ibid.*, pg. 961.
37   *Ibid.*, pg. 927.

11-inch Brooke smoothbores and two 10-inch Columbiads.[38] Watson and others served both here and at the sea-face Battery Lamb, the 43-foot high "Mound Battery" during the heat of battle.

On January 15th a massive Northern fleet arrived off Fort Fisher for a second attack, the first of which failed. This fleet contained more cannon on its flagship than the fort itself contained, raining shot and shell upon the defenders who huddled in bombproofs to survive. Also at Fort Fisher was Lt. William Ward who had been transferred from the *CSS Olustee* to command of the raider *CSS Chickamauga* on the Cape Fear River. His new ship's path to the sea blocked by the enemy, Ward detached men to serve the fort's guns and made frequent ammunition runs to the city. The *Chickamauga* bravely lobbed shells from behind the fort toward the enemy though his most deadly fire was directed at the enemy landing parties. Lt. Ward kept up his fire until forced to sail the 18 miles upriver to the safety of Wilmington.[39]

The outgunned main Fort Fisher garrison capitulated after a bloody defense and 20,000 projectiles – 1.5 million pounds of iron - had rained down upon them. Watson and his comrades escaped capture by quickly crossing to Battery Lamb near Smithville on the mainland, then marched toward the city. Along the way they paid a black resident $30 for cornbread and meat; a little further Watson traded a pair of trousers to another black man for rice and bacon to cook.[40]

On January 18th they reached Battery Campbell, one of four located three miles below the city. It was perched on a high, sandy bluff and armed with five cannon which included a 30-pounder Parrott rifle and 6.4-inch 32-pounder gun. After improving the battery's defenses with the help of local black men, the Key Westers fought off several attacks and cold, rainy weather with little shelter or food before being ordered march around the city in the dark just after midnight on February 21st to evacuate the city. A further march of some 27 miles was needed to reach railcars to take them to Greensboro and eventually Richmond and Drewry's Bluff where they joined the Naval Battalion at Drewry's Bluff.[41]

---

38 Fonvielle, pg. 45.
39 Hairr, pg. 78.
40 Campbell, pg. 150.
41 *Ibid.*, pp. 155-156. See also: Fonvielle, pg. 389.

Forced upriver to Wilmington Lt. Ward anchored in the harbor to determine how to escape. He found the only way to avoid the *Chickamauga's* capture and future use by the enemy was to steam up the Cape Fear River's northwest branch which was swollen with recent heavy rains. Before its final grounding, the ocean-going raider had made it some 17 miles to Indian Wells near today's East Arcadia. There he ordered the ship scuttled and burned, afterward marching to the railroad and likely naval duty at Drewry's Bluff. The cannon had been removed as magnetometer tests of the wreck in the 1970s revealed no evidence of large metal objects.[42]

The first month of 1865 was quiet on the island as district commander Gen. Newton planned a strong thrust to the State's panhandle and possible capture of Tallahassee, the last Southern capital not in Northern hands. At the same time Capt. McKay at Tampa began planning his assault on Fort Myers, a center of enemy activity since the previous summer. The Confederate cavalry attack took place in mid-February with nearly 300 cavalry. They swept past stunned Northern pickets, but after the capture of some enemy troops and realizing the fort too strong for a cavalry assault, a retreat was ordered.[43]

On February 24th Newton's 1,000-man expedition of white and colored troops - the 2nd Florida cavalry of refugees (which records indicate was never mounted), the 2nd USCT and 99th USCT -sailed from Key West in steamers bound for St. Mark's, with three companies of colored troops diverted to Punta Rassa near Fort Myers.[44] As the main force moved inland from St. Mark's in early March it was confronted at Natural Bridge by Gen. Sam Jones' makeshift band of about 700 defenders - local invalids, older men, and students from the West Florida Seminary - what would eventually become Florida State University. After three futile assaults and taking 150 casualties – 21 killed, 89 wounded and 38 captured, Newton retreated in haste to his boats while the Florida defenders suffered only 3 killed and 23 wounded.

By this time news of Charleston's evacuation in February would have reached Key West as well as the looting and burning of Columbia by Sherman's bummers by the month's end. Southern forces were now

---

42 Hairr, pg. 89-93.

43 Taylor, pg. 211-212.

44 Schmidt, pg. 974.

marching northward ahead of Sherman's army into North Carolina and toward a final clash at Bentonville. Gen. Newton's ill-fated expedition returned to the island after a second setback for US forces against lesser-armed and equipped Florida units. One year earlier a well-armed and equipped Union force was badly routed at Ocean Pond.

Despite these victories in Florida the war was in its final days in March as Gen. Lee's defenses at Richmond and Petersburg were nearly broken and the battle at Bentonville, North Carolina resulted in a stand-off between Generals Joe Johnston and Sherman. Lee's starving and depleted army was forced out of Richmond and Petersburg in early April with Robert Watson and his Key West comrades from the Naval Battalion at Drewry's Bluff following, the latter captured likely near Saylor's Creek. Lee was forced to capitulate on April 9th at Appomattox; Johnston negotiated surrender terms on April 26, 1865, at Durham Station in North Carolina.

Learning quickly of Richmond's capture by Grant's massive army, Fort Taylor fired a 30-gun salute on April 10th. Ten days later the island learned of Lee's surrender to Grant at Appomattox causing a two-hundred-gun salute from the fort's cannon. It was reported that a procession took place in town to observe the war's end, followed by an evening "illumination." Emily Holder of Fort Jefferson recorded that "even the secessionists" who were in evidence lit candles and flew the Northern flag.[45]

With the war coming to an end Gen. Newton began negotiations with Confederate Lt. Gen. Sam Jones for a formal exchange of prisoners held in Florida. Newton claimed to have few Confederate prisoners as his custom was to send them to New Orleans prison camps. Gen. Jones would not surrender his Department of Florida and South Georgia troops until May 10, 1865.[46]

The shooting war was over and the task of forcibly reuniting a defeated people whose homes, land, and towns were laid waste to by their late enemies would now begin in earnest.

---

45 Schmidt, pp.988-990.
46 *Ibid.*, pp. 986-987.

A few occupation soldiers who had rented or owned property on the island saw opportunities for a healthy return on investment and perhaps saw the future of Key West as a travel destination. The 2nd USCT's Lt. Col. Wilder wrote home in late April for "speculation" money to purchase property owned by soldiers being reassigned and willing to sell cheaply. One was the island home of a captain claimed to be worth $7,000 that Wilder could obtain for only $4,500 – and he had the inside track. The intention was to sell the home later in the year for $6,000, or rent it, a tidy profit in both cases.[47] The Florida land boom had begun.

On April 22nd the *Ella Morse* arrived at Key West in the late afternoon with news that Lincoln was dead. On board were more Northern prisoners destined for Fort Jefferson, three of whom were "slung up for rejoicing over" the assassination and the others stating that it should have occurred four years earlier. They were quickly cast into a fort casemate on a diet of bread and water. Others were bound with hands behind and drawn up just off the floor; some of the guards wanted to shoot or hang them but their officers intervened.[48]

As General Lee was evacuating Richmond the Confederate Government removed itself and its records to Danville, Virginia as the new capital. As Lee capitulated to Grant, it was moved to Greensboro, North Carolina near Gen. Joe Johnston's army, then to Charlotte once he surrendered. With Lincoln out of the way, the Radicals in Congress could now focus their full retaliatory energy on the Southern leaders who they wanted captured, tried like the unfortunate Mrs. Surrat and summarily hung. The leaders must be caught.

The Department of the South commander at Hilton Head, which in turn commanded the Key West and Tortugas District, was informed in late April by Gen. Sherman of the possible routes that the fugitive President Jefferson Davis may take to escape the country, perhaps to Cuba, or the Bahamas.[49]

---

47 *Ibid.*, pg. 995.
48 *Ibid.*, pg. 992.
49 *Ibid.*, pg. 994.

A few days later an aide to Sherman arrived on the island with word that President Davis, his Cabinet and much treasure in Confederate gold would try to escape the country from one of Florida's coasts – east or west. The naval squadron was alerted to watch for suspicious activity and the following day Gen. Newton departed the island for Cedar Keys to alert vessels there of Confederate officials trying to escape. In addition, ships from Key West were dispatched to Key Biscayne to tightly guard passages and inlets to prevent possible escape attempts there. This continued until word came that Davis and his entourage had been captured in Georgia, however the Cabinet members were still at large and had to be captured.[50]

Looking to obtain a first-hand view of postwar conditions in mid-May was Secretary of the Treasury Salmon Chase, who visited Key West on May 24th, 1865. Chase undoubtedly met with US District Attorney Homer Plantz – his former private secretary and political appointee – as well as local military commanders before departing for Havana that evening.[51] Returning less than a week later for a brief stay, he then departed for Apalachicola.

The district commander at Key West received information on May 24th that Cape Sable picket boats had captured a boat containing 8 people, all armed, and appearing to be persons of importance – Southern General and Secretary of War John C. Breckinridge was thought to be with them. Sailing down the Florida coast at night they hid themselves during the day with Havana as their destination. Two were believed named in the trial of Lincoln's assassins, others were thought to have been involved in plots to torch Northern cities in retaliation for burning Southern towns and homes.[52]

The *Philadelphia Inquirer* had established a reporter on the island early in the war who had come to know the island and its people well by 1865. Writing in late May regarding the return of Unionist sentiment at Key West the reporter observed that residents who initially were "secessionists and sympathizers" in 1861 continue to remain "bitter in their feelings."[53]

---

50   *Ibid.*, pp. 995-998.
51   *Ibid.*, pg. 1004.
52   *Ibid.*, pp. 1003-1004.
53   *Ibid.*, pg. 1006.

Former Fort Taylor paymaster Felix Senac was still in Europe as the war ended, his time consumed with final payments to Confederate officers and officials leaving for the US or elsewhere. He was instructed to take residence in England to await Capt. James I. Waddell and his *CSS Shenandoah* after its extended cruise of raiding US shipping in the Pacific and Atlantic. Mallory had issued Capt. Waddell his sailing instructions and probably told Senac of the itinerary. The ship and crew arrived at Liverpool on November 6, 1865, and shortly afterward Senac issued them their wages due from Confederate accounts in Europe.[54]

The end of the war made all anxious to depart for home and in mid-June the naval squadron at Key West was preparing for a reduction of its warship strength. Fort Jefferson remained garrisoned for the time being as some 522 prisoners, mostly imprisoned for political reasons, were still incarcerated, some in ball and chain. On July 23rd the steamer *Florida* arrived at Key West for coaling before continuing to Fort Jefferson with the Lincoln assassination conspirators aboard.[55] Nearly a month later and the war over, Fort Jefferson's resident 110th New York regiment boarded the steamer *Tonawanda* to transport them northward. The ship stopped at Key West to coal while the soldiers visited local bars.[56] Soldiers who were to remain on occupation duty were those of the 2nd USCT at Fort Zachary Taylor, not mustered out until January 5, 1866.

There were still several Confederate officials the Key West District commander was advised to be on watch for since the evacuation of Richmond and the capture of President Davis. Attorney General George Davis resigned his office at Charlotte and was thought to be fleeing the country. At the last Cabinet meeting at Abbeville, South Carolina, both Secretary of State Judah Benjamin and Secretary of War John C. Breckinridge resigned and were thought to be fleeing the country as well.

Key Wester and Secretary of the Navy Stephen Mallory accompanied President Davis to Washington, Georgia, submitting his own resignation to Davis as "he could no longer be useful."[57] From there

---

54 Rapier, pg. 194.
55 Schmidt, pp. 1017-1018.
56 *Ibid.*, pg. 1023.
57 Durkin, pg. 342.

Mallory set off for La Grange, near Atlanta where his wife Angela and their children resided, and where he was arrested a few days later. On the way for Fort Lafayette via carriage he was joined by Benjamin Hill and Gen. Howell Cobb and treated with "great civility" by his guards.[58] They reached their destination and cells on June 4th. Though Mallory believed he would not be held long, the Radicals wanted him tried and executed for "setting on foot piratical expeditions against the US" and treason. He was released on partial parole March 10, 1866, thanks in great part to the man he served as law clerk under at Key West, William Marvin, who interceded on his behalf.[59]

Breckinridge made his way south into Florida with assistance from Capt. J.J. Dickison's cavalry. After boarding a waiting ship and enduring a harrowing escape from pirates and US Navy steamers, he reached Cadenas, Cuba and exile on June 11.[60] Judah Benjamin did much the same in his journey down the west coast of Florida by boat, then to Knight Key on July 7th and landing at Bimini three days later.[61] Former Attorney General, George Davis, first arrived at a cousin's home near Lake City, then to sparsely-settled Sumter County where he hid for three months as Dickison's troopers found an appropriate boat and captain near Smyrna in mid-September to escape to Nassau. After a month of attempts at crossing the Gulf Stream in a leaky, poorly rigged boat and learning that the Northern government had released other Cabinet members, he turned the boat toward Key West. Intending to sail to Washington to surrender himself to authorities, he was arrested on the island in mid-October while awaiting a northbound steamer to be imprisoned at Fort Hamilton until his release on January 2, 1866.[62]

The end of the war did not end the hostility and enmity that emerged between Floridians, and the island was no different though it escaped the worst of the "stored up malice and short-shrift and bloodshed" existing in the rest of the State. Prior to the war Floridians differed with each other over seeking independence and once war

---

58 *Ibid.*, pg. 344.
59 *Ibid.*, pg.381.
60 Davis, pg. 340.
61 Meade, pg. 322.
62 Ashe, pg. 1.

commenced Florida's government sequestered the property of "Union" men. Those "Union" men had led plundering raids during the war to destroy the property of their neighbors who wanted independence, and this of course led to retaliation. When the war ended, the Northern government was the "Union" and guardian of the "Union" man as well as the black man.

The one-time "Union-man" was now a "scalawag" Republican who saw his alliance with the carpetbagger as an opportunity for bettering his condition, which very often added to the hostility neighbors already harbored toward him.[63]

---

63 Davis, pg. 591.

CHAPTER 10:

KEY WEST'S BIRD OF PASSAGE – HOMER G. PLANTZ

"Birds of passage" refers to Northern opportunists who came into the Florida seeking political office or favors from the federal government. Some were Treasury officials who confiscated land for alleged non-payment of taxes and helped themselves to the proceeds, others were purely political appointees who saw an opportunity for personal gain and graft.[1]

In late-October 1863 Secretary of the Treasury Salmon P. Chase appointed a new US District Attorney for the Southern District of Florida at Key West, a very lucrative position for the trusted person chosen. Chase's selected his own loyal, private secretary, Ohio-native Homer G. Plantz, to this office of trust for special political reasons. In addition to official duties, the new District Attorney was to use his influence to promote Chase's thinly-veiled 1864 presidential candidacy while directing reconstruction and political activities such as pro-Union rallies around Florida.

Plantz's appointment followed the Secretary's meeting with Lyman D. Stickney, a Vermont-born political opportunist who somehow convinced Chase he was a native-born Florida Unionist dedicated to the political reconstruction of "his" State. Stickney lavished the Secretary with optimistic reports of Union sentiment among "loyal" Floridians, leading him to believe "his campaign would benefit greatly"

---

1   Davis, pg. 476.

by appointing his own men to key government positions.[2] Had Plantz been a man of honor and probity prior to meeting Stickney, those qualities quickly evaporated as he became enmeshed in his accomplice's political and financial machinations.

Revealing where his true loyalty lay in December 1863, Plantz wrote Chase a glowing endorsement of Stickney's integrity after the Secretary asked him for an opinion, reassuring him that Stickney "was universally respected and trusted by our best men here; and as heartily denounced by copperheads and ex-secessionists."[3]

Lincoln's secretary John Hay said Homer Plantz "went [to Florida] with but two ideas, to steal money for himself and votes for Salmon P. Chase" and to become Lyman Stickney's useful adjutant.

Chase, who had the presidential bug since 1860 when his candidacy was proposed but Lincoln was chosen as Republican nominee, now saw a golden opportunity as part of the party's Radical element that wanted Lincoln replaced in 1864. Encouraged by fellow Radicals, in late 1863 Chase began laying his campaign's groundwork and using the Treasury Department to his advantage. He would appoint Treasury agents in occupied areas of Florida to extract oaths of allegiance from residents to establish "reconstructed" voters, who would then elect new representatives, usually Northern opportunists, to support him. If successful, these delegates of "reconstructed" Florida would nominate Chase at the Republican Convention. In this he was greatly-encouraged by Stickney and Plantz, who stood to benefit themselves.

The Treasury Secretary's plan was to benefit from the Confiscation Acts passed by Congress in late 1861 which made all property used to support the Confederacy liable to seizure by the US Government. The second Confiscation Act targeted the property of all Confederate officials, with a provision that gave the Southern people sixty days to abandon their new government or face property seizure. Another threat was added to this in mid-1862 with the Direct Tax Set, "which, once Union troops occupied rebel territory made homes, lands, farms and plantations" subject to seizure and sale by the US government if newly-assessed taxes were not paid.

---

2   Blue, pp. 218-219.
3   Smith II, pg. 277.

The intention of the acts was to deny the "rebels" materials and wealth used to continue resistance, with the proceeds used to finance the North's military costs; they might also enable unscrupulous Northerners to transfer this wealth to themselves while destroying the South militarily and politically. As Treasury Secretary, Chase oversaw the apparatus to implement and enforce these acts.[4]

Florida at that time was largely open areas of sparsely-occupied areas, except for Northern-held Key West and Jacksonville, the latter destined for occupation by Northern troops four times. Northern troops often raided the interior to destroy farms and plantations, carry off the black men who worked them and the cattle herds that Southern armies depended upon for beef. For Salmon Chase – or Lincoln – to find voters in sufficient numbers to "reconstruct" the State would be difficult if not impossible. By 1864, Floridians of any loyalty were tired of the raids and oaths of allegiance, and simply wanted to be left alone.

Lincoln's plan dictated that when citizens numbering a tenth of Florida's 1860 population recited the loyalty oath they could vote for a "reconstructed" State government he would recognize.[5]

For the State to hold a nominating convention for president in 1864 it had to be "reconstructed" according to Lincoln's ten-percent of 1860 registered voters plan as well as occupying as much Florida territory as possible. Those citizens had to also be willing to swear an oath to the US government and both Lincoln and Chase sent their men to Florida to accomplish this task.

Originally a Vermont lawyer and New Harmony Transcendentalist, Stickney had been in Florida early in the war as the partner of a Virginian who was rumored to have established a base for illegally importing slaves. He was also involved in an early war scheme to found two new townships near Fort Myers which was approved by the Florida legislature but failed from lack of funding. Described as a "shifty manipulator", Stickney acquired an old sloop with which to operate between Key West and the mainland, selling wood pilings to US officials at Key West while contracting with Florida Confederate officials on the mainland. While at Key West, he posed as "an ardent

---

4   Clarke, pg. 262.
5   Daniels, pg. 90.

unionist, agitated political questions" and failed in his attempt have delegates to the US Congress elected, himself no doubt included, from that Union-controlled outpost.[6]

After suspicious federal authorities embargoed the sloop, Stickney took up residence in a Key West hotel to agitate for an election to send a delegate, himself, to Congress. Soon disappearing, he left an unpaid hotel bill and was in Washington by June 1861. Here Stickney cultivated the friendship of other Florida "refugee loyalists" looking for a place on the government payroll while authoring an article prophesying the riches coming from increased agricultural production by thrifty farmers from the North, and published by the Department of Agriculture. Stickney gained an audience with Secretary Chase posing as an old Florida resident, and landed a position as a member of the "newly created Direct Tax Commission" of June 7, 1862, which began confiscating the land of Southern property owners. As property could be seized by commissioners without court action, these men need only follow the conquering armies to proceed with their work of confiscation.[7]

Also at work at this time was the New England Emigrant Aid Company of Eli Thayer who envisioned the immigration of twenty to fifty thousand Northern immigrants to areas "which had not yet responded to the influence of Yankee civilization," as had been attempted in Kansas nearly ten years earlier. Encouraged by Lincoln in late 1861, Thayer's plan was to place confiscated lands of Florida's rebels into the hands of loyal men, who would use "confiscated Negroes" as apprentices. As Lincoln had already broached the subject of black colonization to the Caribbean, Thayer added that "should the time ever come when it might be found necessary or expedient to remove the Negro population from the country, his company would "execute a suitable plan for the purpose."[8] Not surprisingly, Stickney, by virtue of his unpaid Key West hotel bill and work in landing illegal Africans early in the war claimed to be a Florida native and citizen, was a supporter and advocate of Thayer's colonization scheme.

---

6   Smith I, pg. 111.
7   *Ibid.,* pg. 112.
8   *Ibid.,* pg. 115.

Stickney visited Gen. David Hunter at Hilton Head in January 1863 and was impressed with the plundering raids of his colored troops, envisioning their use to invade and occupy large parts of Florida for reconstruction political purposes, and his personal benefit. Also at Hilton Head was Gen. Rufus Saxton, a protégé of Salmon P. Chase, who desired Florida "cleared of the enemy" and the State made into an asylum for freedmen.[9]

Thayer's scheme and enthusiasm was cooled by serious Northern military reverses of 1862 as Lincoln feared Lee and Jackson's armies marching into Washington, but schemes of Florida's colonization continued unimpeded. In early January 1863, a group representing some 5,000 German-Americans asked Lincoln to give them confiscated Florida land to farm. This plan addressed the common Northern fear of freedmen migrating northward and taking the jobs of white labor; Thayer reasoned that the newly-arrived and "just employers" from the North would help keep them in the South. One of the most vocal in this regard was Gen. William T. Sherman, who wrote his brother, an Ohio Senator, in late April, 1863: "I don't oppose Negro-arming further than I have no confidence in them and don't want them mixed up with our white soldiers. I would rather see them armed and & colonized in Florida & North Arkansas ..." [10]

Lyman D. Stickney was now employed and well-positioned to plot his rise to prominence. Though assigned to Florida, his time was now more profitably-spent at South Carolina's Sea Islands making patriotic speeches to freedmen and ingratiating himself with such officers as Gen. Quincy Gilmore, Gen. Rufus Saxton and soon-to-be "Prince of Carpetbaggers" Gen. Milton Littlefield at Hilton Head. All three officers were fellow-opportunists who anticipated promotions, glory and possibly high-political office in the postwar if they cooperated with Stickney and helped sell his plan to their superiors.

While there Stickney observed many ex-slaves being taught basic military drills, something he would report to Lincoln. Massachusetts preacher-soldier Col. Thomas Higginson appreciated Lyman's interest in colored soldiers at an emancipation celebration, writing that Stickney "added something" to the event." Lyman sensed the

---

9   Smith II, pg. 264.
10 Smith I, pp. 124-125.

Hilton Head officers' desire for personal glory, promotions and future political careers and wanted to use them and their colored troops to invade Florida and help him "reconstruct" the State - and his own political future.

Stickney accompanied Col. Higginson's First South Carolina Regiment of colored troops on their plundering raid at Jacksonville in March 1863, with the newly-formed Second South Carolina Regiment of Col. James Montgomery joining the force. Most of the latter had been conscripted at Key West earlier that month. As the invading force departed Jacksonville at the end of the month, the fires they set engulfed the town and Stickney left with only thoughts of using the same forces to overrun additional Florida territory. Stickney returned to Washington in April to report to, and flatter Secretary Chase, then ask his to request from the War Department gunboats, infantry, cavalry plus "six Columbiads" with which to assist he and the other Direct Tax Commissioners in Florida. He assured Chase that as long as the federal taxation and trade regulation statutes were "vigorously enforced," then Florida would become a loyal and free State before the next Congress met.[11]

In June 1863 Stickney was in New York City assisting in the sale of seized railroad iron from the Florida Railroad Company by Florida provost marshal James Latta, one of Stickney's "Ring" members. New York buyer Calvin Robinson was yet another "Ring" member looking to profit from the war. Meanwhile, in Florida, Stickney's fellow Tax Commissioners were auctioning "unredeemed" property in Fernandina, and spending $2200 to advertise the tax sale in the Stickney-owned *Peninsula* newspaper. The two personally bought up two blocks each of town property, one buying a lot for each of his two sons for taxes owed.[12]

Protected by Northern soldiers throughout the occupied South, federal treasury agents scoured the countryside in search of anything of value, especially cotton bales, to seize. In Florida alone, some 5,460 bales were seized from owners in the name of the government, and many more illicitly taken by military officers and Treasury agents, as "many of the newly-appointed civil officials of the US Government in

---

11 Smith II, pg. 267.
12 Smith II, pg. 270.

Florida proved to be shameless grafters. The thievery practiced by them – Treasury Agents and US Marshals – became so notorious that it was openly condemned by their more honest or financially-unsuccessful brother officials. Too often the treasury agents and marshals seized property for non-payments of taxes, and then sold it to themselves at prices they wished to pay."[13]

When he came to Washington to lobby for his Florida project in September 1863, Lincoln undoubtedly knew of Stickney's relationship with Chase.[14] Lyman presented Lincoln with a petition from the "loyal citizens of Florida," requesting a large military force to defeat "Confederate rule." He knew that Lincoln was aware that such a reconstructed State would send a representative to Congress as well as elect delegates to the Republican National Convention to nominate someone for the office of president.[15] It is about this time that historian and author Smith surmises that Chase began to seriously consider himself a serious rival to Lincoln for the presidency. As Florida was a relatively easy possibility for "reconstruction" – few organized Southern troops to resist invasion, Jacksonville in hand and Key West secured – both Lincoln and Chase coveted its presidential nomination delegates.

After Stickney visited Chase to report on Direct Tax Commission matters, the Secretary confided to his diary on September 6: "Stickney had just arrived from Florida, and lastly from Morris Island. He says that it is easy now to take possession of Florida; that five-thousand men can accomplish it. General Saxton desires the command, and General Gilmore approves the expedition, and is willing to spare one or two regiments to aid it. If the business can be promptly taken hold of, and pushed vigorously, Mr. Stickney is confident that Florida can be restored as a Free State by the first of December."

Chase was further enmeshed in the project by Stickney-ally, the Reverend Mansfield French, who provided "stirring Biblical assurance that a colored army marching into Florida would create such a panic among the secessionists there 'as when the Syrians fled, through fear, from Samaria."[16]

---

13 Davis, pg. 331.
14 Daniels, pg. 89.
15 Smith II, pg. 269.
16 Smith II, pg. 276.

With Key West being the strongest Northern-held position in Florida, Chase needed a trustworthy ally to advance his presidential candidacy and thus appointed his admiring private secretary Homer Plantz as the new US District Attorney at Key West. Plantz was to become an integral part of Stickney's political "Ring."

Key West in the latter-half of 1863 was under complete control of the Northern military and any outspoken islanders either deported or imprisoned. The municipal elections were supervised by the military with Unionist Mayor Alexander Patterson celebrating re-election victory by another large majority.[17] The year closed with the island's Union Club Ball held at the courthouse on New Year's Eve, and decorated by the Stars and Stripes and naval signal flags.[18] Key West had become a quiet, military-occupied and "loyal Unionist" island.

Once Plantz settled into his official position at Key West, met fellow federal officials and military officers as well as assorted local leaders professing "Unionism," he gained a sense of the island's often-submerged political sentiments. Writing to Secretary Chase on December 1st he expressed his frustration at discovering "what everybody wants is to be let alone; not to be required to take sides on any questions; and, better and chiefly, not to have any questions to take sides about."[19] As Plantz came increasingly under Stickney's influence, he likely learned that for the sake of continued profitable employment and personal financial success to convince the Secretary of ascendant Unionism in Florida, however inaccurate.

On December 19th District Attorney Plantz sailed to St. Augustine to take part in a staged-Unionist meeting to encourage Floridians to accept Lincoln's recent ten-percent plan of reconstruction and ultimate recognition of a "loyal" government. This required 10% of eligible voters to take the oath of allegiance to his government before framing a new constitution acceptable to Lincoln – though this hardly represented the majority of voters in the State. Critical to Stickney and Plantz was Lincoln's requirement that oath-taking citizens had to reside in Northern-occupied areas of their States which explains Stickney's more than casual interest in the colored troops at Hilton Head.

---

17 Schmidt III, pg. 707.

18 *Ibid.*, pg. 726.

19 Plantz letter to Chase, 12.1.1863.

In addition to Plantz were other Stickney "Ring" members who were announced and given authority to call a convention of Florida "delegates."[20] Another one involved in Stickney's circle at this juncture was Col. Milton S. Littlefield who General Gillmore named to enroll Florida's black recruits with the title of General Superintendent for recruiting colored regiments. He had the authority to select the white officers for new colored regiments and importantly, oversee the new US and State enlistment bounties paid to black recruits. Interestingly, he would make the determination which Northern State's quota the Southern black men would be accredited to, which would be one less white citizen to be drafted.[21] After the Northern fiasco at the Ocean Pond (Olustee) battle Littlefield found few black men willing to be killed in the place of white soldiers, though he tried to keep up with the demand for them. Many of the colored troops received little if any bounty money owed – or if the recruit existed at all. A postwar investigation into fraudulent bounties paid found that Littlefield certified to the mustering in of a large number of colored men who only existed on paper though $300 bounty was paid by the US government. Littlefield's associates in New York apparently arranged for town, county and State bounties to be paid for the colored soldiers "on paper."[22] General Littlefield's name was often heard during Florida's railroad speculation and frauds during reconstruction.

Additional pro-Union meetings of red, white and blue bunting, bands and federal appointees were held at Key West and St. Augustine on New Year's Day, 1864, both calculated to create the impression of "strong Unionist sentiment on display." The "Ring" ensured that Secretary Chase was made aware of the "cheering crowds" to increase the Secretary's hopes for the State's reconstruction and electoral votes for his presidential candidacy.[23]

On New Year's Day 1864 at Key West's then-predominantly black Baptist church both US District Judge Thomas J. Boynton and new US District Attorney Plantz spoke to the assembled congregation on

---

20   Smith II, pg. 277.
21   Daniels, pg. 91.
22   Daniels, 101-102.
23   Coles, pg. 26.

the anniversary of Lincoln's proclamation, though many of Key West's black residents were free prior to the war. Also speaking that day were Postmaster Henry Albury and others holding federal offices.[24]

It was Plantz's responsibility to locate and encourage pro-Union sentiment among Key West's population, and second to groom pro-Salmon P. Chase delegates from Monroe County to an upcoming Florida convention. That event was scheduled for the following March 1 at St. Augustine in an attempt to organize a parallel State government "loyal" to Lincoln. Another federal appointee, Postmaster Henry Albury was sent to the mainland "to give the weight of his influence towards a Union movement" and encourage residents, and often those imported, to take the oath.[25]

Back on the island, Plantz helped organize an "unconditional Unionists" meeting at the Baptist church in late January to explain Lincoln's amnesty and reconstruction scheme, advocate for the convention, as well as promote the presidential candidacy of Salmon P. Chase. The event drew an overflow crowd. Joining Plantz was US Navy Admiral Theodorus Bailey, Postmaster Albury and North Florida District Judge Philip Fraser from occupied Jacksonville. The latter explained to the audience that as the owner was no longer responsible for the bondsman's food, shelter and medical attention, "the emancipation of the slave would benefit the poor white man of the South, taking labor into view."[26] Judge Fraser was a Pennsylvanian and viewed labor as a Northerner.

Lincoln was well-aware of his treasury secretary's presidential ambitions and using patronage power to appoint his own people to key positions. Lincoln's secretary John Hay wrote that Lincoln would allow Chase his own way in political machinations "rather than getting into a snarl with him" by confronting him. Nonetheless, Lincoln sent Hay, with a presidential appointment and rank as a major, to Jacksonville in January to oversee the amnesty registration of Floridians who took the oath, while at the same time keeping close tabs on Plantz and Stickney.

---

24 Schmidt III, pg. 733.
25 *Ibid.*, pg. 746.
26 *Ibid.*, pg. 754.

Continuing his personal assessment of Union-loyalty existing in Florida, Hay went on to Key West in early March while sketching "pen-pictures of the sea and reefs and human derelicts." Being aware of District Attorney Plantz's loyalty to Chase, he likely met briefly to only exchange courtesies. Writing of his brief visit to the island and meeting "some of the queer inhabitants of the town ... [Hay thought them] "a race of thieves and a degeneration of vipers."[27]

In mid-March the Stickney-controlled executive committee of Florida's nascent Republican party not-surprisingly appointed Homer Plantz, Judge Phillip Fraser and Stickney himself as Florida delegates to the Republican national convention to be held in early June at Baltimore.[28] Shortly after, Plantz sent Chase a lengthy analysis of the political situation in Key West, explaining that at least one-third of the population "were Union-men, more than enough to effect reconstruction" of the State under Lincoln's ten-percent plan. Plantz had little real evidence of actual pro-Union sentiment as residents simply attending a staged-rally provided no real assurance, but both he and Stickney reported "their successful efforts to organize Union meetings."[29]

Buoyed by this report and with an eye toward improving his Radical-credentials, Chase instructed supporters that the "unionist-Florida" movement would now include suffrage for freedmen who served in the US military or could read and write. This meant black men captured or enticed away from their homes during raids and placed in blue uniforms, would be eligible to vote as Florida citizens. Still, the total number of Florida's black men serving in US forces barely exceeded 1000 for the entire war, and both Plantz and Stickney urged immediate military pressure to bring more of Florida under Union occupation. They envisioned black troops from Hilton Head landed at Jacksonville, marching unopposed into Florida's interior while conquering large swaths of territory, and producing the necessary ten-percent voters who would support Chase for President.

---

27 Thayer, pp. 165-166.
28 Smith II, pg. 291.
29 Blue, pg. 219.

Unfortunately for Chase his top co-conspirators in Florida badly misled him by making "little effort to consult the people" at St. Augustine and Key West "and enroll the numbers necessary." When Hay was at Jacksonville during Gen. Gilmore's invasion and accompanied by Stickney, it was clear to Lincon's secretary that less than ten-percent of the residents were willing to recite the oath of loyalty to Lincoln's government.[30]

The new District Attorney wisely held a ball at his residence on February 4th to better introduce himself to the island's military and civilian leaders, which gave him the opportunity to carefully look for those who might be supportive of Secretary Chase. *LGS3, pg. 764).* Knowing his sponsor's Radical leanings, Plantz would be suspicious of and report on West Pointers who would likely support Gen. George McClellan's presidential ticket. Those he found supportive of Chase would be assured of military or political career advancement should the Secretary gain the presidency.

With Chase, Stickney and Plantz all optimistic of Florida's possible reconstruction, despite the poor groundwork of the latter two, this political-military operation of 5,500 troops was launched in early February to bring a large swath of northern Florida under Northern control.

This expedition led by Brigadier-General Truman Seymour arrived at Jacksonville the afternoon of February 7, 1864, and that evening began his thrust inland which immediately netted 100 prisoners. Encountering little organized opposition, within four days his force had penetrated to within a few miles of Lake City and over halfway across the peninsula to Tallahassee.

The previous December General Quincy Gilmore, Seymour's superior, had suggested to General-in-Chief Halleck that an invasion from Jacksonville could recover the northern portion of the State for the Union, capture the South's beef supply and carry off more black men who could be put into blue uniforms. Though aware of the political benefits of the expedition to his friend Stickney as well as Secretary Chase, the general made no mention of this.

---

30 Blue, pg. 219.

Gilmore had not authorized Seymour to advance to the Florida interior, and was shocked to hear of the latter's intention to penetrate without supplies to the Suwannee River – 100 miles inland of Jacksonville. Seymour's reasoning – later admitted to Gilmore – was his expectation that "the people of this State, kindly treated by us, will soon be ready to return to the Union; they are heartily tired of the war." Seymour himself may have been taken in by the unsubstantiated reports of Florida's "unionism" propagated by Stickney, Plantz and company.[31]

The battle of Ocean Pond (or Olustee) took place on February 20th which thoroughly routed Seymour's well-equipped force, a combination of New York, Massachusetts, Connecticut, Rhode Island, New Hampshire and US Colored Troops, including artillery and cavalry. The battle proper did not begin until 3PM when the intense musket and artillery fire of Florida and Georgia troops under Gen. Joseph Finegan began, causing the Northern front line to flee to the rear in disorder, which hampered the effective deployment of artillery. By 5PM two more colored units arrived on the field but were routed by a determined Southern advance. Notably, one of the colored units involved was Col. Montgomery's "Second" which had secured most of its men from Key West earlier that month. The Union casualties numbered 1861 – 203 killed, 1152 wounded and 506 captured - the second bloodiest battle of the entire war for the Northern army. One Northern unit lost is colors – regimental flag – possibly the 7th New Hampshire or Second South Carolina Volunteers, and the routed Northern force left behind 1,600 rifles and 130,000 rounds of ammunition. Seymour wrote in a post-battle report that "the misfortune arose from the 7th New Hampshire regiment having lately been filled with conscripts and substitutes, of a very inferior class." [32]

The victor's loss was 93 men killed, 847 wounded and 6 missing, and this force gained six captured field cannon and 39 horses. Despite the Northerners being armed with 7-shot Spencer repeating rifles with which a unit could release a hailstorm of bullets at an opponent, the musket-equipped Southern force triumphed.[33]

---

31 Nulty, pg. 303.
32 Schmidt II, pg. xiv.
33 Bornet, pg. 251.

As news of Seymour's defeat quickly made its way to Northern newspapers – it was not suppressed - those of the Democratic fold charged Lincoln with sacrificing Northern soldiers for political gain and that Hay's mission was merely a "political trick to gain delegates" at the 1864 Republican-Union party convention. The *New York Herald* opined that Lincoln had expressly directed the expedition "for political objectives." [34]

The reversal also derailed the efforts of Stickney, Plantz, et al, thus ending any possibility of Florida's quick "reconstruction" under Lincoln's new amnesty and ten-percent plan, and usefulness for Lincoln or Chase. The latter saw his hopes for the presidency dim and perhaps finding himself a victim of overly optimistic encouragement by his Florida agents who had expected to profit through his presidential candidacy.[35] Stickney and Plantz both believed that "no power on earth" could prevent Lincoln's renomination but Stickney- always flattering his targets - informed Chase of seeing a "strong tide" rising for him at the Republican convention's opening session. He might need Chase in the future.[36] The Ocean Pond disaster also meant that US District Attorney Homer Plantz could now concentrate more fully on his duties at Key West and not be distracted by Stickney's larger targets of opportunity which continued unabated.

As the "reconstruction" and Ocean Pond debacles faded into memory, Plantz's former boss and sponsor paid a visit to Key West on May 24th and discussed pressing Treasury concerns and tax seizures – and possibly Stickney's activities which might net them both an income. Chase also met with top military officers during the afternoon, and departed for Havana that evening.[37] After a patronage dispute with Lincoln the following month, Chase resigned his Treasury position. To keep Chase's presidential hopes at bay, Lincoln appointed Chase Chief Justice of the Supreme Court on December 15, 1865.

---

34 Smith II, pg. 290.
35 Blue, pg. 219.
36 Smith II, pg. 293.
37 Schmidt III, pg. 1004.

Homer Plantz continued in his position as Southern Florida US District Attorney until 1868, after his wife Elizabeth passed away at Key West the previous year. In 1868 Plantz was appointed Judge of the First Judicial District of the Florida Supreme Court, possibly through his former boss and now Chief Justice Chase.

Stickney had of course made enemies along the way, including fellow Tax Commission agent Harrison Reed who advised Lincoln of Stickney's early war relations with Florida's "secession" legislature. In addition, a congressional document in the form of a committee report made public "the tawdry details of Stickney's Florida "ring" which an investigation had uncovered the previous spring." After this Stickney's name was seldom heard in Florida's postwar world of "Reconstruction."[38]

A fitting commentary on "Reconstruction" was offered by black Charleston editor Richard Harvey Cain who wrote that when it concluded, "the Negroes had gained nothing, Southern whites have nothing left and the Northern jackals have taken all the booty."[39]

---

38 Smith II, pg. 293.
39 Curtis & Thompson, pg. 249.

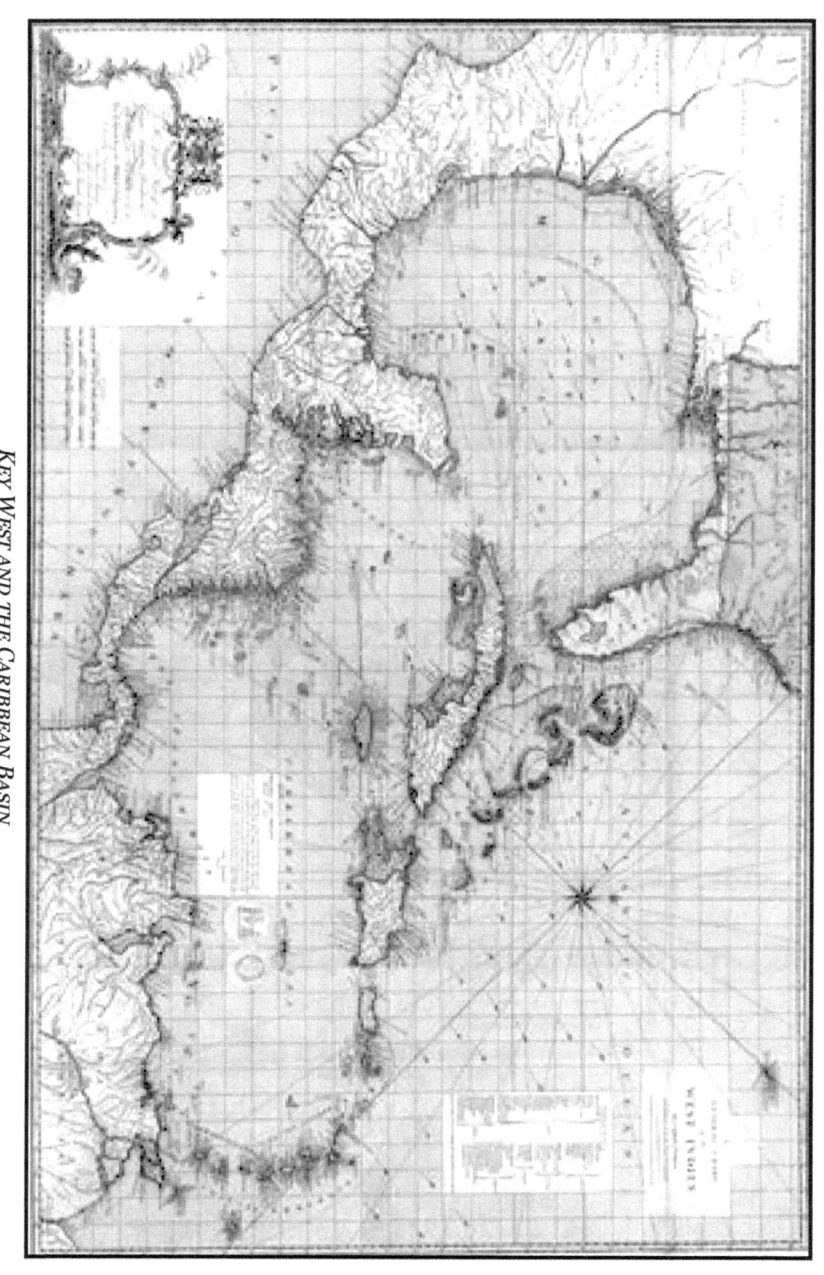

Key West and the Caribbean Basin

CHAPTER 11:

"Key to the Florida Pass" Caribbean Geopolitics

The art of fortification is as old as man's instinctive quest for security.[1]

The strategic importance of Key West's unique position with a natural, protected, deep-water harbor, was early recognized by visiting naval officers as it guarded "The Pass" through which shipping would travel in and out of the Gulf of Mexico. The coming of the Civil War accelerated completion and occupation of the two masonry fortresses — Fort Zachary Taylor on Key West itself and Fort Jefferson on Garden Key some 70 miles westward – as well as the addition of two Martello Towers on the island to thwart possible enemy landings and attacks on Fort Taylor.

In late March 1822, US Navy Lt. Matthew Perry arrived with orders to survey the coast and harbor of Key West, dubbing it "Thompson's Island", after Secretary of the Navy Smith Thompson. By the end of that year Key West had become a naval depot to protect US commerce from, and clear the seas of, troublesome Caribbean pirates. Perry reported:

> The island's advantages in time of war with any European power having West Indian possessions, are still more important, both as it respects the protection of our own commerce and the annoyance of our enemy. A superior enemy naval force occupying the island could intercept

---

1   Williams, pg. 3.

the whole trade between those parts of our country lying north and east of it, and those to the west, and seal up all our ports within the Gulf of Mexico.[2]

Another naval visitor, Commodore John Rogers wrote in a letter dated November 24, 1823:

> Nature made it an advanced post from which to watch and guard our commerce passing to the Mississippi and back. At the same time its peculiar position and excellence of its harbor make it the a key to the commerce of Havana, to the entire Gulf of Mexico, and the returning trade of Jamaica. I venture to predict, that the first important naval contest in which this country shall be engaged will be in the neighborhood of this very island. [3]

Naval strategists during Andrew Jackson's presidency studied the Caribbean while marking their maps to show Britain's West Indian bases and referring to the Dry Tortugas as the "Key to the Mexican Gulf." They considered Key West the logical spot for the bottom link in the chain of coastal forts from Maine to the Mississippi.

Further, future Confederate naval officer Lt. Josiah Tattnall, who in 1829 surveyed the keys in the sloop *USS Florida*, wrote these words at the time:

> A naval force, designed to control the navigation of the Gulf, could desire no better position than Key West. I have no doubt that an adversary in possessing a large naval means such as Great Britain would make these harbors its habitual resort. Tatnall continued that the defense of the harbors could be achieved by an inferior navy and commerce with points of refuge, He pointed out that the US had to fortify the islands to keep them out

---

2   Browne, pg. 9.

3   Browne, pg. 71.

of enemy hands as their location was ideal for an enemy wanting to cut the lifeline between the Mississippi and the Atlantic seaboard.[4]

Ironically enough, during the great blockade of the Confederacy, Tortugas was useful to the Union just for that reason.

"Anaconda Plan" author General Winfield Scott added his opinion that "The fortification at Tortuga was of national concern and of far greater value even to the most distant parts of the Atlantic coast and to the people on the upper waters of the upper Missouri, Mississippi and Ohio rivers than to the State of Florida." The two forts – Taylor and Jefferson - were to be a partial answer to problems recognized in the Monroe Doctrine as military strategists looked with mixed feelings toward the melting pot of Latin-American independence. "The unsettled condition of the governments of the former [Spanish] provinces on the Gulf of Mexico," wrote the Secretary of the Navy, "requires that our trade with the interior of that Gulf should be protected by a suitable naval force." The US was powerless to enforce its doctrine against European intervention in Central and South America if it lacked the enforcement power.

The then-independent Texas Republic was an additional concern as it was increasingly impatient with US scruples against annexation, plus it was negotiating with European powers for recognition and protection. Even the far West entered the strategic picture, for the dream of a Central American railway, soon to be realized, showed the Gulf to be an important link in communication with the Oregon Territory.[5] Lastly, after the Mexican cession of 1848 and the discovery of gold in California, "communication between the eastern United States and the West by ship dictated that sea lanes in the Caribbean be secure."[6]

The War Department conceived a masonry "American Gibraltar" at Garden Key, a six-sided, super fortification three tiers high with 250 cannons. Key West's Fort Zachary Taylor was commenced in July 1845 with the majority of artisans and mechanics being new Irish and German immigrants, recruited by a New York agency. The construction

---

4   Manucy, pg. 304.

5   *Ibid.*, Manucy, pg. 305.

6   Cortada, pg. 43.

of the forts themselves greatly increased the use of African slaves on labor gangs, usually "two dozen or more" and hired out by their island owners. Both forts were severely damaged by the 1846 hurricane and restarted the following year, but by 1856 only foundations were complete and walls barely visible above the water.

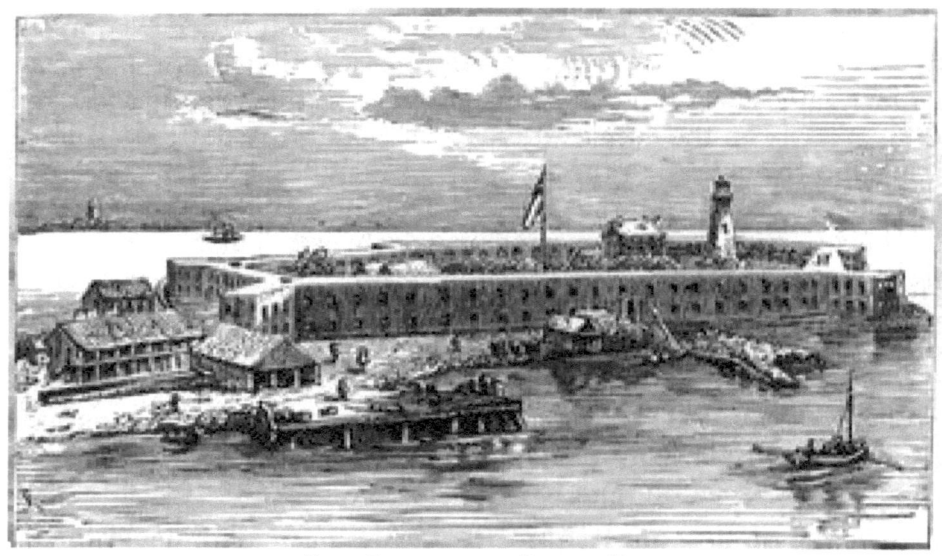

FORT JEFFERSON AT GARDEN KEY

Beginning in the fall of 1847, the engineers, African and Irish labor toiled at Garden Key using New York cement and New England granite, and overseeing the labor laying the intricate brickwork was Capt. Daniel P. Woodbury of New Hampshire. This fort was officially named "Fort Jefferson" in early November, 1850."[7]

Just after Florida's decision for independence in mid-January, 1861, a Confederate privateer arrived at Fort Jefferson to demand its surrender to the State. This demand was rebuffed and the ship warned off with threats of cannon fire. Additionally, the surrender of Fort Taylor was also demanded by Irish immigrant and former US Army artilleryman-turned Key West-merchant, Henry Mulrennan, who was instructed to leave the island or face indefinite imprisonment within the fort's casemates.

---

7   Manucy, pp. 307-308.

In early April, 1861, Fort Taylor's commander was notified that "further defenses, outside Fort Taylor, were under consideration" and instructions forwarded on August 14th. Plans issued called for two identical masonry "Martello" towers of Corsican inspiration though square rather than round, built simultaneously, one "east" (near today's airport), and one "west" (at today's Higgs Beach). They would be 56-feet square, 36-feet high and with sea face walls over eight-feet thick to resist cannon fire from attacking ships. Retrospectively, the towers as well as Forts Taylor and Jefferson, were obsolete by the time of their completion. The "Martello" design dates back to 1794-1810 and resistance to cannon projectile technology of that era.[8]

Given the April 1861 timing of instructions to begin work on the Martello towers, Lincoln's War Department could have been responding to the real possibility of European recognition of the American Confederacy as well as military intervention and strengthening their position at Key West. And at this time, Ferdinand Maximilian of the House of Habsburg had already been invited to accept the Mexican crown and military establishment.

Despite the April, 1861 timing, it would take time to install foundations and obtain sufficient brick to construct these smaller fortresses. Also, as the war began and weapons technology improved with cannon-barrel rifling, military experts were well-aware of their destructive power against thick masonry walls as would be soon demonstrated against Fort Pulaski near Savannah.[9]

Understanding the international dimensions of Key West's unique position at the edge of the Caribbean greatly illuminates why the Northern government was reluctant to lose the fortifications at Key West, as well as at Pensacola, Florida. Both allowed the United States to project political and commercial influence backed by strong seagoing military force, and both helped enforce the Monroe Doctrine. New York speculators cooperated with West African and Cuban interests who speculated in slave importation, with many New York ships involved.[10]

---

8   Williams, pg. 17.

9   Manucy, pg. 312.

10   Harris, pg. 79.

The Caribbean basin was an active center of intrigue well before 1860 with Cuban annexation plans afoot and called for by the Southern Commercial Convention in 1855, as well as invasion plans by American mercenaries and William Walker's filibustering in Nicaragua. Notably, in 1849 the US government arranged a treaty with Nicaragua for exclusive rights to build and fortify a canal to the Pacific.

At the same time, the British and French hoped to contain American expansion into central and South America after the Mexican War. The British had a colony in Belize, and a protectorate over the Mosquito Coast on the eastern shore of today's Nicaragua and Honduras. The British also enjoyed good relations with the governments of Costa Rica and Guatemala, and their consul Frederick Chatfield, "was especially active in trying to prevent American inroads." In response, the American commissioner to the region, Ephraim George Squier, was busy thwarting British resistance.[11] Both the British and US expansionists were eying the narrow Isthmus for a canal to link the great oceans.

The friction between the US and Britain culminated in the Clayton-Bulwer Treaty of 1850, aimed at preventing possible war over territorial interests and claims, especially concerning a future canal. It stipulated that neither signatory would ever "occupy, or fortify, or colonize, or assume or exercise any dominion over Nicaragua, Costa Rica, the Mosquito Coast or any part of Central America," nor make use of any protectorate or alliance, present or future, to such ends.[12]

Early in the secession crisis, the British watched with interest as it witnessed the breakup of the North American Union, which many continental monarchists concluded was the predictable result of what they viewed as "mob rule." Later in the war, Northern-friendly Russian Minister in Washington, Baron de Stoeckl, wrote his government in early December, 1864 of the "rule of the mob" in America and viewing the war as "the result of democracy", would serve as a warning to Europe.[13]

On January 1, 1861 Baron de Brunow, Russian Ambassador at London, wrote his government that the British heartily approved of the separation of North America into two republics, "which will watch

---

11 May, pg. 87.
12 Humphreys, pg. 178.
13 Adams, note pg. 593.

each other jealously and counterbalance one against the other." The British, since the War of 1812, had watched the growing strength of the United States and its often-stated desire to annex Canada. Observing this breakup and believing it permanent, the *London Economist* wrote in February 1861 that should the United States lose its southern half, "Great Britain would willingly permit the North to secure compensation for loss of territory by annexing Canada – provided the Canadians themselves desired it."[14]

Even in April 1865, the *London Quarterly Review* asserted that even yet "the mass of educated men in England retain the sympathy for the South which they have nourished ever since the conflict assumed a decided shape." America was plainly headed for a military despotism and her example should warn England from moving in the same direction. The classes which govern this country "are in a minority" and the British must beware of majority rule.[15]

The assassination of Lincoln provided not only an opportunity for an outpouring of expressions of sympathy, but it also gave the Radicals a chance to exalt Lincoln's leadership in democracy.[16] In truth the North sought Southern land and resources as Seward suggested to a foreign diplomat when asked why the South could not be free to depart in peace, replying that they could leave the country but must forfeit their property.

Revealing the extensive commercial underpinnings of the North's war against the South, *New York Tribune* correspondent James S. Pike wrote on January 11, 1861, of the European commerce "pouring through the Gulf of Mexico, and the possession of the Florida forts necessary for its protection were," he thought, 'in themselves of sufficient importance to create and justify a war" upon the Southern Confederacy." His concern, shared by Northern commercial interests that a Southern Union would benefit from the Gulf's maritime traffic rather than the North.

---

14   *Ibid.*, pp. 48-50.
15   *Ibid.*, pg. 586.
16   *Ibid.*, pg. 587.

The value of Northern merchandise, specie and tonnage" passing through the "Pass" in 1856 was $450,000,000, and should it and the forts pass into the control of a Southern Confederacy, "so too would pass over control of commerce in the Gulf." *New York Times* publisher Henry J. Raymond warned William Yancey of Alabama that should Southern independence succeed, the North would be "surrendering to a foreign and hostile power ... the whole Gulf." Raymond worried that the extensive wreck and salvage cases now under federal jurisdiction would fall into the hands of a "secession judge" who would be "antagonistic to Northern commercial interests." The most worried person was Secretary of the Treasury John A. Dix, who foresaw economic disaster for the North if Southern ports and their tariff revenue were lost to the new Confederacy and its low tariff.[17]

By 1860 the South, through import and export tariffs collected at its ports, was responsible for nearly 87% of the total US Treasury's coffers and its departure could not be tolerated.

By March of 1861, the *London Times* came out in favor of the justice of American South's struggle for independence, writing that "No treachery has been at work to produce the disruption, and the principles [of a free and independent government] avowed are such as to command the sympathies of every free and enlightened people ... but mankind will ultimately judge ... the two Republics ... by the conduct they pursue and the position they maintain among the Powers of the earth." Their internal institutions are their own affair; their financial and political arrangements are emphatically ours. Brazil is a slave-holding Empire, but by its good faith and conduct it has contrived to establish for itself a place in the hierarchy of nations far superior to that of many Powers which are free from this domestic contamination.

"If the Northern Confederacy of America evinces a determination to act in a narrow, exclusive and unsocial spirit, while its Southern competitor extends the hand of good fellowship to all mankind, with the exception of its own bondsmen, we must not be surprised to see the North, in spite of the goodness of its cause and the great negative merit of its absence of slavery, sink into a secondary position, and lose the sympathy and regard of mankind."

---

17 Smith, pp. 104-106.

On May 13, 1861, Queen Victoria issued a declaration of neutrality which recognized the American South's belligerency, an internationally understood status which provided Confederate States ships the same privileges in foreign ports as US ships, to include fuel, supplies and repairs, but excluding military equipment. This belligerent status also allowed the Confederate government to contract with British companies as well as purchase vessels for a navy.[18]

The proclamation also prohibited British subjects from joining either side's military, breaking the North's blockade or equipping ships of war for either side. The primary Northern concern at this point was that belligerent status was merely a prelude to full diplomatic recognition of the Confederacy in the family of nations. Through the summer of 1861 both Britain and France watched the armed conflict unfold, with the Confederacy's stunning victory at First Manassas on July 21st reinforcing British opinion that Southern independence was inevitable.

In August, John Slidell of Louisiana and James Mason of Virginia, both experienced in foreign affairs, were selected as diplomats to Britain and France and departed Charleston aboard the *Theodora* on October 14th, eventually transferring to the *RMS Trent* at Cuba, thence to England. They were intercepted by a Northern warship, seized, and carried into captivity at Boston while the Northern press applauded the incident. Lincoln was enthused about the capture and very reluctant to release his two captives, but soon realized that his government had done just what the United States had accused the British Navy of doing in 1812 and which led to war.

It is important to note again that Lincoln had absolutely no experience with international diplomacy and against best advice was refusing to release his prisoners. William Seward had traveled extensively abroad prior to becoming Secretary of State and understood the dire consequences of insulting the flag of England. Compared to his predecessor James Buchanan, who served as Secretary of State (1845-1849) as well as US Minister to England under President Franklin Pierce, Lincoln was an international affairs novice. His Secretary of State, William Seward, at least had spent seven months in Europe in 1859 and met many foreign leaders – he was the only member of Lincoln's cabinet with any geopolitical perspective. The

---

18 Mahin, pg. 48.

British government remained wary of Seward who was noted for being both belligerent in expression and indiscreet with sensitive information. At the same time the *London Times* viewed Seward as the evil genius of the warlike policy toward England, convinced that the unlettered Lincoln was incapable of any international maneuvers.[19]

A British diplomat Lincoln initially met with on December 4th wrote his government that despite Lincoln's simple assurance of no desire for trouble with England, he could not ignore the strong impression that the policy of the US government "is so subject to popular impulse that no assurance can or ought to be relied on under present circumstances."[20] Lincoln, in his next annual message to Congress avoided mention the "Trent Affair," but relying upon Secretary Cameron's estimate of quickly enlisting 3 million men, boasted of showing the world that he could easily quell disturbances at home while protecting ourselves from foreign threats."[21]

Despite Northern braggadocio, Lincoln's rickety financing of its war and knowing New York banks were about to suspend specie payments, the Trent affair contributed greatly to the virtual collapse of war finance, which depended on public confidence. By mid-January 1862, Lincoln was forced to issue greenback fiat currency as his government was simply out of money.[22] By the end of the war the North had become burdened with rampant inflation, the constant manipulation of gold prices by speculators, a morass of different bond issues and four major forms of currency – national bank notes, specie, greenbacks and individual State bank notes. The last were simply taxed out of existence.[23]

In mid-December 1861 Lincoln and his cabinet discussed the serious ramifications of war with England: their breaking of the Southern blockade and a British blockade of Northern ports. He was distressed as well by the new French monarchy in Mexico and perhaps spreading to Latin America as well, and French diplomatic recognition of the Confederacy. And should the Confederacy achieve

---

19 Adams, pg. 125.
20 Mahin, pg. 64.
21 Warren, pg. 170.
22 Mitchell, pg. 322.
23 Mongomery, pg 342.

its independence, Northern capitalists feared widespread smuggling of British goods from the Confederacy into the North and thereby crippling American manufacturing. It could not have been lost on Lincoln and his cabinet that the American republic would not have existed without French intervention in 1781 which clearly made the difference between the American colonists' success or failure.[24]

In the meantime, Britain was reinforcing Canada with troops, planning invasions of the North from British Columbia and Canada West (Ontario) while US troops were occupied in the American South. Additionally, British ships would cripple Northern shipping by its blockade and preying on American merchantmen, and not necessarily in cooperation with the Southern navy. Additionally, the modern "Laird Rams" being built in England posed a very serious threat as their submerged iron prows could wreak havoc with the North's wooden ship blockading fleet.[25] Though the Northern fleet was growing by late 1861, the newer ships were "improvised merchantmen" for blockade duty as opposed to steam and sail warships.[26]

The British military sent provisional orders during the first two weeks of the Trent crisis to quickly establish an offensive base at Bermuda from which to attack the North's blockading force. Another fleet located at Havana under Commodore Dunlop would neutralize the Northern ships at Pensacola Bay while Key West and Fort Jefferson would be left to the powerful British West Indies Squadron.[27]

In retrospect the two Key West forts and new Martello Towers were built of thick, masonry construction designed with past wars with smoothbore cannon in mind, the new rifled projectiles of the British Navy would have reduced them quickly. Should the island be isolated by British blockade with food and water dwindling, surrender would have been the only option. If in full possession of both forts and Key West harbor the British would have controlled the Caribbean as Gibraltar did the Mediterranean, and very improbable that all would be relinquished at the end of hostilities.

---

24 Shy, pg. 131.
25 Adams, pg. 415.
26 Bourne, pg. 624.
27 *Ibid.*, pg. 628.

Sober minds in the Northern government soon realized that it needed saltpeter from British-controlled India, and its military would be dependent upon European rifled-muskets until 1863.[28] News that Britain was arming quickly for war and rumors of a vast fleet assembling to blockade the North exerted great pressure on the indecisive Lincoln. He finally defused the international incident in January 1862 by agreeing to free the Southern diplomats, allow them to continue to their posts and issue an apology stating the US naval officer acted without orders.

An occupation soldier wrote in February 1862 of the island being garrisoned with a large number of troops and officers commenting that anticipated attacks would come from a substantial sea power, confirming that fears of British attack had trickled down to the common soldier. During the "Trent Affair" in particular troops were trained with heavy coast artillery and busy improving the fortifications especially along the island's southern coast.[29]

By March of 1862, work on Key West's two Martello towers, the western-most begun first, had not advanced as quickly as expected. Orders now came from the War Department to accelerate and occupy these new fortifications, most likely over concerns of foreign intervention and control of the Gulf of Mexico.[30] As of March, the excavations for the West Tower had been completed, masonry work began and the central tower to be completed by end of the month. Two additional towers were contemplated for Fleming Key north of the harbor, and on adjacent Stock Island to the east of Key West. Neither of these went beyond strategic contemplation as international complications did not justify their construction.

As fortification strengthening continued on the island two batteries of mobile field artillery were landed in March of 1862 and new uniforms issued to their crews. These were fitted with brass shoulder plates to protect the artillerymen from cavalry attack and saber slashes, as possible enemy landings were contemplated.[31] As the island was cleared of vegetation to facilitate its defense one soldier wrote that the "trees are

---

28 Chandler, Jr. pp. 142-145.
29 Schmidt, pg. 124.
30 Williams, pg. 20.
31 Schmidt I, pg. 123.

all being cut down and wide artillery roads were run across the island." He added that the white soldiers were hard at work on this but 500 "contrabands" were coming from Port Royal, South Carolina and this meant that he and his fellow soldiers "will have easy times."[32]

Early in the war, England's ambassador to the US, Lord Richard Lyon, warned his government that Secretary of State William Seward might incite war with England in an attempt at reuniting North and South. With US diplomacy unable to stop what they deemed British covert aid to the South with ships and shipbuilding, England again steeled for war in April 1863. Seward's popularity had waned after Northern battlefield defeats, Southern blockade running success and strong resistance to Lincoln's Conscription Act. Lord Lyons wrote his government that with the South apparently lost by the Republican party, "the best mode to conceal the discomfiture of the [Republican] party and of the nation would be to go to war with England and attribute the loss of the South to English interference."[33]

Caribbean Colonization

A little-known component of Lincoln's emancipation edict developed in mid-1862 was the colonization of freedmen to the Caribbean. He was aware that few in the North would fight and die to free anyone after enlisting "to save the union" – nor did they want freedmen coming northward in search of work to depress wages and/or take their jobs. As the armies moved South, overran plantations and displaced slaves, the simplest solution was to proclaim them "free" in a Northern wage-labor understanding of liberty, working for themselves for whatever wage they could obtain. It was further clear that if freedmen could be kept in the South or colonized elsewhere, this was consistent with the Republican party's goal of new States and Territories populated with free, white immigrants.

When the US Congress met in mid-December 1862 the war had not gone well for the North so far and the horror of Fredericksburg was to come soon. Lincoln's intention to emancipate by decree through constitutional amendments dominated the discussion with several

---

32 Schmidt III, pg. 185.
33 Adams, pg. 429.

pointing out that it would be seen as an act of desperation. The colonization scheme would be better received by the North with Lincoln wanting owners compensated for their financial loss as the British had done – but failed to gain support within his party.[34]

Author Michael J. Douma has written extensively of Lincoln's colonization plans and noting that "Historians have long known that in the summer of 1862 Lincoln announced his intention to negotiate with foreign powers concerning the colonization of freedmen abroad." For the next two years federally-funded initiatives arose to settle freedmen in Chiriqui [Panama] and Haiti – in addition to the British Honduras, Guiana and Dutch Surinam. The talks were very serious and continued even after the war and anticipating the transport of freedmen to these islands desperately in need of laborers.[35]

The Danes also expressed interest in colonizing unwanted contrabands to work their plantations on St. Croix, now the US Virgin Islands. In 1862 Seward signed an agreement with the Danes to take all Africans captured aboard slave ships in the Atlantic to St. Croix to work as plantation labor despite Danish acknowledgement that workers on the island would not find conditions much different from previous slavery, but they would be technically "free." To facilitate the process of removal the US would authorize Danish ships to sail down the US Atlantic and Gulf coast to recruit freedmen in areas under US or Confederate control. Danish Minister Waldemar Raasloff especially viewed South Carolina as a fertile recruiting ground which was seconded by Secretary of State Seward.[36] Also fascinated with taking the "contrabands" within Northern lines was the Dutch government which sought them as labor for their colony of Suriname on South America's northeast coast.

Lincoln and Seward were not the only proponents of colonization as they were ably supported by leading Republicans Charles Sumner, Francis Blair, Preston King and Benjamin Wade.

---

34 Gallman, pg. 50.
35 Douma, pg. 2.
36 *Ibid.*, pg. 4.

Given heightened interest in Caribbean geopolitics and Seward's increasingly imperial expansionism, he approached the Danes in early 1864 regarding his government's interest in St. Thomas as a naval station. He understood the Danes labor difficulties and possible interest in ending its far-off colonial experiment while he sought to further control southern access to the Gulf of Mexico. Key West already controlled the northern access.[37]

Mexican and US relations, when former diplomat James Buchanan became president in March, 1857, were "unfriendly and almost hostile," with the former being in a state of near-constant revolution since its independence from Spanish rule. Buchanan in vain urged Congress to protect American interests in Mexico in late 1859, complaining that both parties were fully occupied with the slavery question. Buchanan raised the question once again in December, 1860 in his annual message but with no better effect than before.[38]

Another with colonization designs on Central America and Mexico was Napoleon III, who well-knew that this may necessarily embroil the US and France in war over the Monroe Doctrine. In early January 1860 Buchanan submitted to Congress a treaty with Mexico to protect American interests; it was sent to committee to become a dead letter. Subsequently, Mexico was left to its fate to become the dominion of the House of Habsburg.

Senior US Gen. Winfield Scott wrote of North-South difficulties which was published in mid-January 1861. It was his opinion that after the secession of the South "there would be no hope of reuniting the fragments except by laceration and despotism of the sword," and the result of this would make the internal upheavals of Mexico, "in comparison with ours, sink into mere child's play."[39]

Emperor Franz Joseph of Austria's young brother, Ferdinand Maximilian, was two years younger than he, and called "Max" by his intimates. Franz Joseph was scion of one of the oldest monarchies of Europe, and "regarded the American republic as an iconoclast conspiracy against the world he represented by the grace of God"

---

37 *Ibid.*, pg. 21.
38 Buchanan, pg. 267.
39 *Ibid.*, pg. 287.

himself.[40] He was determined to restore the monarchical system to North America, and succeed where Britain failed in 1781. He cared little for the Confederacy, but Mexico had been one of the "brightest jewels in the crown" of his ancestor Charles V. And it was also stressed that both Spain and the conquered Aztec Empire were once ruled by the House of Habsburg.

In early January 1861 Lincoln agreed to Lord Palmerston's demands after the "Trent Affair" and ignored the invasion of Mexico by France, Spain and England. When the three governments pressured the Mexican government to settle its debts after suspending foreign debt repayment, only the British and Spain withdrew, with French Emperor Napoleon III demanding that Mexico establish a pro-French monarchy led by Maximilian.[41]

The foreign intrigue for a Mexican monarchy was not new to the American government as Maximilian was first approached in 1859 by Mexican monarchists, and again in late 1861. He was certainly encouraged by French intervention and formally accepted the Imperial Crown in October 1863. As the forts at Key West held the "Key to the Florida Pass" and especially to Mexican Gulf ports, the strategic import is quite obvious if the US was to make serious its alleged "Monroe Doctrine."

Maximilian's forces never defeated the Republican Mexican armies and the end of the Civil War in 1865 saw the US government providing more explicit aid to President Juarez's forces and threatened to intervene militarily. Once Maximilian's French forces were withdrawn to deal with matters in Europe, his dreams of empire collapsed. He was captured and executed in 1867.

Lincoln's government suffered a despondent July through September 1863 as the Gettysburg battle carnage brought more "dead rolls" northward and his army sat in trenches rather than reengage Lee's forces. Also several Northern regiments were rushed to New York City in mid-July to quell the destructive anti-draft riots which killed 120 people, mostly black, and the Colored Orphan Asylum was burned to the ground. This was followed by the military reverse at

---

40   Tyrner-Tyrauer, pg. 64.

41   *Ibid.*, pg. 67.

Chickamauga in mid-September, a bloody repulse of Lincoln's forces which cost some 16,000 casualties. Lincoln was known to keep defeats as this from the Northern public.

It should be kept in mind that Lincoln had no foreign ally or friend other than Bismarck of Germany, who encouraged the purchase of American war bonds and applauded a strong centralized government apparatus backed by military might suppressing popular revolt.

The Imperial Russian Navy ended any practical foreign intervention on the side of the Confederacy on September 4, 1863 when its flagship the fifty-one-gun steam frigate *Alexander Nevski*, and the *Peresvet*, a forty-eight-gun frigate, sailed into New York Harbor. They were joined two days later by the sloop-of-war *Variag* and the similar *Vitiaz*. Within three weeks the Russian presence would grow with the addition of the steam frigates *Almaz* and *Osliaba*, all under the command of Rear-Admiral Lisovski. As war clouds loomed over another conflict with England and France, the Russians did not want their fleet bottled up in the Baltic as occurred in the Crimean War.

Russian Czar Alexander II had made his support for Lincoln's government clear in light of the South's "revolt," and the European press quickly noted what seemed to be an unofficial alliance between the two countries.

In late October 1862 Lincoln received a communique from Russia's Prince Gorchakov stating the obvious, that American had few friends among the Powers and noted that "Russia alone has stood by you from the very first, and will continue to stand by you." Russia of course was an autocracy rather than a constitutional republic.[42] Despite the deteriorating relations between Russia, France and England and imminent war over Poland's independence, sailing Russian fleets to the high seas for wartime action, along with Lincoln's extravagant welcome of the fleets, it was said that the arrival of the fleet's was coincidental.

On October 12, the Czar's Far East Fleet under Rear-Admiral Popov sailed into San Francisco Harbor, consisting of the sail and steam corvettes *Bogatir, Kalevala, Rinda* and *Norvik*, plus the clippers *Abrek* and *Gaidamak* – all bristling with cannon.

---

42 Woldman, pg. 131.

This was Lincoln's deliverance at a dark time, and Navy Secretary Gideon Welles writing in his diary: "Thank God for the Russians!" and writing the Russian minister in Washington that "the presence in our waters of a squadron belonging to His Imperial Majesty's navy cannot but be a source of pleasure and happiness to our countrymen. The Russian officers and crews in both harbors received enthusiastic welcomes, and were feted with banquets, parades and grand toasts to the Czar.[43]

The Russians fleets remained in the harbors for seven months and were available to Lincoln should war commence after a French and British recognition of the Confederacy. *Harper's Weekly* wrote at the time that "The Russian vessels now at large, with such aid as we can give, in precise accordance with the course of the English government toward us, could render the commerce of England insecure." With no American warships in San Francisco Harbor at the time and the *CSS Shenandoah* somewhere at sea, worried government officials there happily welcomed the Russian Far East Fleet as saviors.[44]

British press noted at the time that Czar Alexander II had recently emancipated his lowly serfs while crushing a Polish bid for independence. And now Lincoln was emancipating African's while crushing the American South's bid for independence. Beyond the Czar desiring his fleets on the high seas if war came, he knew Lincoln would welcome the "alliance" to deter European recognition and intervention in his war upon the South.

The new administration at Washington which held political power only since March of 1861 was in the process of constructing a powerful military establishment and would not countenance Southern dominion over the two fortresses which so strategically-controlled naval access to the Caribbean and Mexico. The following year witnessed a steadily-growing fleet of Northern warships strangling Southern ports as well as an army growing toward its eventual strength of 2 million men under arms. The Republican administration was not only in firm political and military control of the North and determined to do the same to the South. Under the expansionist eye of Secretary Seward the North was becoming increasingly imperial-minded as it eyed

---

43   *Ibid.*, pg. 141.
44   *Ibid.*, pg. 146.

invasions of both Canada and Mexico to expel the hated British who were supplying the Confederacy with arms and munitions as well as constructing powerful warships for it. The Caribbean was included in the expansionism with Key West being the "Key to the Florida Pass."

By 1880, the US Army's chief engineer reported on the Forts obsolescence, noting that they were designed "long before the introduction of 800 to 2,000 pounder rifled guns into modern warfare," and that "we can make but a feeble defense against the powerful fleets now prepared and rapidly increasing which will sooner or later be brought against us by some of the most powerful maritime nations on the earth, or by others nearer at hand whose offensive naval means exceed our own, and whose powers are not to be despised." [45]

Regardless of one's perspective on the Civil War, the Southern defeat eliminated any remaining impediment to American expansion and consolidation into a continental superstate of agriculture, trade and industry. By the 1880's Americans believed their horizons were infinite.[46]

> What an immense step America has just taken! Between the presidency of Mr. Buchanan and that of Mr. Lincoln, there is the distance of social revolution. The sons of Puritans are slow to move; but once set in motion, they go forward and nothing stops them.
>
> —Count Agenor de Gasparin[47]

---

45 Manucy, pg. 326.
46 McDougall, pg. 97.
47 Sideman & Friedman, pg. 13.

EPILOGUE

"The South Broken on the Wheel"

> I thought of my dear old home with all its comforts and my mother, how it would make her heart bleed to see me standing in the rain a prisoner, hungry, tired and worn out. But it's no use fretting about such things now, too late. [1]

Key Wester Robert Watson recorded this in his diary on April 9, 1865 some forty-four months after he leaving the island as one of several stowaways aboard the schooner *Lady Bannerman* anxious to join the Southern war effort. Two weeks later he added:

> Here we were, Alfred Lowe and I among strangers and enemies, not a cent to save our lives, no clothes except what we had on, nothing to eat, and a military prison staring us in the face. All this we could avoid by taking the Oath, we would not.[2]

Refusing to take a forced oath of allegiance in exchange for transportation to Key West, Watson and Lowe instead obtained passes to New York City where a friend lived - warned that wearing any "Rebel clothing" would land them in jail. They located several friends not seen in years who loaned them enough for food, clothing and transportation to Havana.

Sadly, veteran "Key West Avengers" like Watson and Lowe who returned to Key West were not welcomed by large crowds waving flags while bands played, nor did they have "Veteran Volunteer" sleeve chevrons and bonus payments which made the island's Pennsylvania

---

1 Campbell, pg. 161.
2 *Ibid.,* pg. 163.

occupiers relatively wealthy at war's end. Florida soldiers came home with little beyond worthless Confederate money and dependent upon the charity of friends and family to survive. Few returned without intestinal disorders caused by four years of malnutrition and often near-starvation; those maimed, crippled or with broken health may not have had much longer to live.

Though Watson's diary ends on April 25th, he and Lowe likely reached the island by June 1865 and found it still-occupied by Northern troops. Key West residents wanted a return to normal life though those not anxious to see the Northern troops depart were merchants who practiced dual-loyalty as did river barge owner Sim Carstairs in the film, *"The Outlaw Josie Wales."*

The last remaining Southern war materiel agent in Europe, Felix Senac was at Liverpool when Capt. Waddell and crew docked the commerce raider *Shenandoah* in early November, 1865. The ship had sailed virtually non-stop to attack Northern maritime commerce in the Indian Ocean, Cape of Good Hope, and lastly to decimate New England's profitable whaling fleet in the northern Pacific. Considering the *Shenandoah's* success against Pacific whaling ships which helped stop the slaughter of grey whale populations then, Capt. Waddell and crew might be considered for a posthumous Greenpeace award today. Former Fort Taylor paymaster Senac never returned to the island and passed away at Wiesbaden in January 1866.

Rebuilding his life with carpentry work on the island, Watson married Caroline Elizabeth Kemp three years later and in 1869 he began construction of their new home at 522 Simonton Street - still standing - where they raised their eight children. Caroline passed away in 1908; Robert in 1911. Together for eternity, they are buried alongside each other in Key West Cemetery.

As Key West was quickly occupied in 1861 by Northern troops it suffered no wartime desolation or destruction as did the rest of the State. It was to a great extent defoliated to create artillery and cavalry roads as well as "clear fields of fire" for cannon in case an attempt was made to liberate the island. And business boomed for town's merchants' savvy enough to sense increased profit margins from the blue-clad soldiers. Town life began to normalize when the US Colored Troops were mustered out in January 1866 and local government was no longer under the suspicious eye of the occupier. In 1866 the familiar and friendly Judge William Marvin, trusted by the US military, was elected mayor. He was followed in 1867 by E.O. Gwynn, a Bahamian-native, "Conch" and early island cigar maker; then voters returned Tory Alexander Patterson to the position for his sixth term. After Mayor Patterson the voters interestingly began electing several former "secessionists" who returned home.

Elated by the return of one of Key West's most popular merchants, voters elected the "witty, rollick-some, boisterous" Henry Mulrennan as mayor in 1868, and again in 1870. Henry's second term was immediately followed by Jefferson B. Browne, William D. Cash and Winer Bethel; and later Lt. Walter C. Maloney, Jr. occupied the mayoral office. Peter Crusoe returned to the island and immediately regained his prewar position as Clerk of Monroe County Circuit and Sheriff Court, which he held for three years.

Prewar-Mayor and "Tory" Walter C. Maloney, Sr. soon reconciled with son and "Key West Avenger" Lt. Walter C., Jr. upon the latter's return. In 1867 they combined to publish the *"Key West Dispatch"* newspaper until 1872. Young Maloney later served as Monroe County's collector of revenue from 1879-1881, mayor 1889-1891, and in 1894 was instrumental in organizing the island's first street railway.

Monroe County's January 1861 "independence" delegate Winer Bethel returned to the island after Northern imprisonment for his actions. In 1875 he was appointed US District Judge and served until his death two years later. His son Livingston was appointed the vacant seat.

William D. Cash also returned after imprisonment for his role in seeking independence for Florida. He became partner in Cash & Curry Auctioneers at Front and Duval Streets and in 1871 purchased the salt works on the eastern end of the island, today's airport area. Elected mayor of the city in 1872 for one term, he was an avid promoter of island business interests and was first president of the Key West "Commercial Club," later the Chamber of Commerce. His first wife Elizabeth Bartlum Cash died in 1878; second wife Josephine Lowe Cash lived until 1936. Willam passed away at his home at Duval and Eaton Streets on November 30, 1923.

Pro-independence *Key of the Gulf* editor and CS Navy privateer William H. Ward did not return to wife Emeline Francis Watlington and daughter after the end of the war. The reason remains a mystery as Ward apparently survived the war and a grave marker at a Columbia, South Carolina appears to be his.

Stephen Mallory languished in a Northern prison for his role as Secretary of the Navy and not released until early 1866. After gaining his freedom he resided with wife Angela at Pensacola until his death, November 12, 1873. Mallory was an extremely intelligent and accomplished man despite the lack of a formal education. While a US Senator and chairman of the Naval Affairs Committee, he urged adoption of new ironclad ship construction against strong disinterest. In his position as Secretary of the CS Navy and recognizing its lack of warships, he advanced not only ironclad gunboat harbor defenses but also high-seas privateering to destroy enemy commerce which devastated the US merchant marine. Mallory was fond of stating after discussing the future outcome of an issue, "nous verrons" – French for "we will see."

Mallory's appointment of Pensacola-native and relative Felix Senac as Confederate naval agent in Europe was prescient. The multilingual Senac assisted in the South's acquisition of munitions, arms and ships, and remained in Europe well after Appomattox. His last instructions were to await the arrival of Capt. James I. Waddell's commerce raider *Shenandoah* when it made port at England. The ship docked at Liverpool in the fall of 1865, was turned over to British authorities and its crew received their final payroll from Senac. The last remaining Southern agent in Europe, Senac never returned home and passed away at Wiesbaden in late January 1866.

Asa Tift returned to the island in mid-1865 and immediately began recovering many of his prewar properties, resuming the warehousing and shipping business with brother Charles. Asa still owned extensive property in Georgia with Nelson and by 1873 was considered to be the wealthiest Key Wester with the exception of William Curry. Despite continuing family tragedies, in 1875 Asa began construction of his magnificent "West Indian Creole" home at 907 Whitehead Street, crowned with an ironclad-shaped stone fountain near the entry as a reminder of the *CSS Louisiana*. Here he lived out his last years alone, passing in 1889. His unique home was sold to writer Ernest

Hemingway and wife Pauline in 1931, and where the books Death in the Afternoon, Green Hills of Africa, The Snows of Kilimanjaro and For Whom the Bell Tolls were written.[3]

Attorney William Marvin was nearly-appointed a Monroe County delegate in December 1860 but it was felt his official position as US Attorney would pose a conflict. He then agreed with independence but believed Florida should await the decision of the Border States. Marvin continued to the end of the war deciding blockade runner Prize cases, returned to New York for a year, was then appointed as Florida's first reconstruction governor. Despite having stated in December 1860 that he supported Florida's independence if the Border States did as well, in 1866 he claimed that he would have voted against independence had he been sent to Tallahassee. Marvin was elected United States senator from Florida for a term which would expire March 3, 1867, but this was nullified by Congress and he never took his seat. Marvin returned to his native New York.

Homer Plantz retained his US District Attorney position at Key West after the war ended. His old boss Salmon Chase was now Chief Justice of the Supreme Court, appointed by Lincoln to end Chase's presidential aspirations which Plantz played an integral part in. Plantz held his position at Key West until 1868 when he was appointed Judge of the First Judicial District of the Florida Supreme Court, most likely due to Chase's lingering influence. As Lincoln secretary John Hay wrote of Homer Plantz's appointment as US District Attorney at Key West, it was for the purpose of "stealing money for himself and votes for Chase."

Perhaps the most unfortunate effect of Key West's military occupation was the deterioration of relations between black & white islanders, in many cases turning them against one another. Historian Browne wrote of Northern officers encouraging residents to report disloyal speech or behavior among the white townspeople and ferret out who they deemed to be "secessionists." Those suspected of being so would be imprisoned in one of Fort Taylor's cells, deported to the mainland, or sent north to prison for this crime. Those seeking the favor from the occupation troops and perhaps retribution against past adversaries caused many problems. This may have been the case when black drayman Noah Lewis of Wall & Company "was induced

---

3   Fair, pg. 277-278.

to report" in mid-1862 that his superior William D. Cash "made treasonable utterances against the US government, wishing every Union officer and soldier would die of yellow fever."[4] This wartime atmosphere pitting neighbor against neighbor also affected places of worship as white members of the Baptist congregation drifted to other churches as Northern-agitated black Baptists became predominant.[5]

Virginia-born island merchant Jefferson Beverly Browne, historian Browne's father, was among those supportive of Florida's independence in December 1860. He continued into the postwar as a successful island merchant and served as mayor 1870-1871 after Henry Mulrennan's second mayoral term. When the island was visited by former President Jefferson Davis and wife Varina in December 1867 they were the guests in the elder-Browne's home. The dinner table was said to have been ornamented with an arrangement of flowers and fruits from the garden of former-mayor Walter C. Maloney, Sr. Though the latter had been a dedicated "Tory" during the war he nonetheless considered Davis the city's guest and "entitled to all consideration."[6] In 1880 the island was also visited by former-President US Grant on his return from a world tour, and accompanied by General Philip Sheridan. It was reported that stores were closed on this day in a holiday atmosphere.[7]

Not necessarily a "Key West Avenger" but well-worthy of mention is Dr. Jeptha Vining Harris, born at Abbeville, South Carolina in 1839. Receiving his medical education at the University of Mississippi he graduated in 1859 and afterward served as an assistant surgeon in both the Confederate States Army and Navy during the war. Dr. Harris did not arrive on the island until 1885 when he was appointed Collector of Customs, a position he held while also resuming his medical practice. Deeply interested in improving public education he was subsequently appointed Key West school superintendent and a new high school in 1909 bore his name. Dr. Harris married Mary Perkins of Mississippi

---

4   Browne, pg. 94.

5   *Ibid.*, pg. 44.

6   *Ibid.*, pg. 17.

7   *Ibid.*, pg. 19.

on March 5, 1861 and their union produced three children: Jeptha V. Harris, Jr., Louis and Martha. Dr. Harris passed away on November 21, 1914 and is buried in Key West Cemetery.

Dr. Harris's son Jeptha, Jr. was an attorney who in 1897 built the southernmost house in Key West; his wife Florida Euphemia the youngest daughter of island millionaire William Curry. Their island home was the first with electricity as Florida was acquainted with Thomas Edison. They were both early investors in Henry Flagler's railroad venture to the island.

Well-ahead of Mr. Flagler's plan for a railroad to the island was former-Confederate General John B. Gordon who in 1883 received a franchise from the Florida Legislature to construct a rail line to Key West. A veritable visionary, he envisioned this as part of future steamship lines and telegraph cables across the Caribbean, plus agricultural investments in Central America. His plan may well have been influenced by Lincoln administration colonization schemes and emerging naval dominance in the Caribbean. Gen. Gordon expected Florida to become a great trading center allied with Cuba, Mexico and South America.[8] There were attempts prior to Gen. Gordon's but his was the first serious effort to traverse the islands, completing some 60 miles of rail before abandoning the project.[9]

The same year former-Confederate Lt. Walter C. Maloney, Jr. was elected mayor of the city, 1889, the United Confederate Veterans (UCV) was formed as a benevolent, historical, social and literary association. Its mission was to care for widows and orphans, disabled veterans, preserve relics and records of members, and arrange fraternal gatherings. The organization ultimately numbered over 160,000 veterans who were organized into 1,885 "Camps," with Key West's Franklin Buchanan Camp chartered on December 16, 1899 as #1214 and appropriately named in honor of a CS Navy admiral.[10] The known island "Key West Avengers" who were or could have been members at that time include Joseph S. Bartlum, Joseph Curry, Frank Diaz, Alfred Lowe, William E. Lowe, Samuel Morgan, John Pent, J.M.

---

8   Eckert, pg. 248.
9   Willing, pp. 288-289.
10 Cunningham, pg. 18.

Phipps, John W. Russell, John B. Sands and Robert Watson. "Avenger" Joseph Fagan found a new home at Tampa and was a member of the Gen. W.W. Loring Camp, UCV, #1126.

Historian Browne referred to his list of island veterans as a "Roll of Honor" and "Too much praise cannot be given to that band of noble men who left Key West ... to fight for their Southland."[11] When Historian Browne published his "Key West: The Old and the New" in 1912 many veterans had gone to their final reward and only two remained: Alfred P. and William E. Lowe who passed away in 1921 and 1926, respectively.

The ladies of Key West's strived to preserve the deeds, memory and patriotism of their men through their Stephen R. Mallory Chapter 1562 of the United Daughters of the Confederacy (UDC). The Chapter's 1917 membership totaled nineteen which included Mrs. A.D. Cleare, President and Hattie W. Collins, Vice-President. Board members were Florida B. Fosberg, Mrs. F.G. Curry, Mrs. C.W. Hattrick, Mrs. M.L. Huston and Sarah B. Pinder. Margaret Archer served as Chapter historian. (Minutes of the 24th Annual Convention of the UDC, November 1917, Appendix, page 30).

Before the last island veterans passed away the Chapter began fundraising for the Bayview Park Pavilion which would serve as a permanent remembrance of the patriotism and sacrifice of the South's soldiers. This was not unlike other communities across the South where scarce money was donated from the heart, from the many who had lost fathers, sons, brothers, cousins and uncles in the conflict. The classically-inspired monument was formally dedicated "To the Soldiers and Sailors of the Confederacy" on January 19, 1924, the birthdate of Gen. Robert E. Lee.

Mary Elizabeth Dickison, wife and biographer of Florida's "Swamp Fox" Capt. J.J. Dickison, wrote of stone and marble remembrances:

> Their friends and people, to their future praise,
>
> A marble tomb and monument shall raise,
>
> And lasting honors to their ashes give;

---

11 Browne, pg. 97.

Their fame, 'tis all the dead can have, shall live![12]

The island would never return to its relative isolation and close resident cohesion as the war caused social, racial and political rifts which did not end with peace in 1865. The Northern occupation did bring new investment and prosperity with a Northern business mindset which continued postwar, causing historian Browne to remark: "The noblesse oblige of Old Key West has been supplanted by the *sauve qui peut* of the new." (*every man for himself*)" [13]

---

12 Dickison, pg. 36.
13 Browne, pg. 198.

THE LAST WORD

The history of island "Conchs" dates back to Florida's acquisition from Spain and the requirement that shipwrecks in the Keys be adjudicated at Key West's District Court. Then came the Bahamian wreckers who saw financial advantages in operating out of Key West. Many of these Bahamians were the descendants of American Tories known for their allegiance to the British king and unwillingness to live under the rule of American "secessionists." The sea mollusk which provided their daily diet gave them the name "Conch."

Truth be told, Washington and his cohorts were not originally "secessionists" but became so after it became clear that Parliament would not respond to their complaints. These "traitors" in the eyes of the Loyalists came close to stretching hemp were it not for French intervention, which, had Napoleon III done the same for the American Confederacy, would have perhaps altered the outcome of the 1861-1865 war.

Those known as "Tories" could be said to have been as true to their king in 1776 as Floridians were to the Constitution in 1861. The latter, including Conchs, would readily withdraw from political union with those who would not live by the agreement they had ratified in 1845. In January 1861 they joined what they saw as a more perfect union than what existed.

The island's Conch element was apparently strong by mid-decade as evidenced by diarist William Hackley's October 1855 entry noting a "foreign element" dominating the island politically while estimating that perhaps 200 of the population were not native-born Americans. This would be the dominant group supporting John C. Breckinridge for president in Monroe County's 1860 voting. The Pennsylvania and New York occupation troops had little good to say about the Conchs they encountered and sensed throughout the war that the "secession" sentiment had only been suppressed and lay dormant, ready to reassert itself once the hand of the distant government was removed.

The "Conch Republic" publicity stunt of April 1982 recalled those early Bahamian immigrants and gave the imaginary republic its name. Though farcical then and in response to what was considered an oppressive government policy, then-mayor Dennis Wardlow announced that "if we are going to be treated like a foreign country then we will become a foreign country." The islanders of 1982, still well-seasoned with independent-minded native Conchs to provide leadership, reached back into history for an example to follow. This "secession" is celebrated annually on the island.

Though the original Conch bloodlines have been diluted since the 1840s, the close family ties and interdependence of island neighbors were a hallmark of the isolated island community. This was highlighted by late "freshwater" Conch Merili McCoy in 2008 as she reminisced of growing up as a young island girl after arriving in 1939 and being aware of the sense of community then.

The island itself remains today with a far different population but a rich history of people, places and events which are an important element of Florida history. This volume recalls an era long past but still remembered by those who see past as prologue and ponder if mankind can learn from its mistakes.

In the words of the accomplished islander Stephen Mallory,

"nous verrons."

ABOUT THE AUTHOR

John Bernhard Thuersam is native to the Niagara Falls area who has lived in the southeastern US most of his life. He holds undergraduate degrees from Villa Maria College and SUNY, Buffalo, and graduate study at the University of Georgia. Now retired from his architectural design practice of thirty years, he and wife Song reside in southeastern North Carolina.

BIBLIOGRAPHY

Books:

Adams, Ephram D. *Great Britain and the Civil War*. Alpha Books, 2018 (original 1924).

Armor, William C. *Lives of the Governors of Pennsylvania, 1609-1873*. T.H. Davis Co., 1874

Blue, Frederick J. *Salmon P. Chase: A Life in Politics*. Kent State University Press. 1987.

Brevard, Caroline Mays. *A History of Florida*. American Book Company, 1904.

Brands, H.W. *The Man Who Saved the Union: US Grant*, Random House, 2012.

Brodie, Fawn M. *Thaddeus Stevens: Scourge of the South*. Norton, 1959.

Browne, Jefferson B. *Key West: The Old and the New*. Arcadia Publishing, 1912.

Buchanan, James. *On the Eve of Secession, the Buchanan Administration*. D. Appleton, 1866.

Burke, J. Wills. *The Streets of Key West*. Pineapple Press, 2004.

Burlingame, M.; Ettinger, J. *Inside Lincoln's White House: Civil War Diary of John Hay*. Southern Illinois University Press, 1999.

Campbell, R. Thomas, editor, *Southern Service on Land & Sea*. University of Tennessee Press, 2002.

Carr, Dawson. *Gray Phantoms of the Cape Fear: Running the Civil War Blockade*. John F. Blair, Publisher. 1998.

Condit, Uzal W. *The History of Easton, Pennsylvania, 1739-1885*. Geo. W. West Publisher. 1885.

Cotterill, R.S. *The Old South*. Arthur Clarks Company. 1939.

Cotto, Joseph F. *Runaway Masters: True Story of Slavery, Freedom, Triumph & Tragedy, Beyond 1619 and 1776*. Fourth Estate, 2021

Coulter, E. Merton. *The Confederate States of America, 1861-1865, Vol. VII*. LSU Press, 1950.

Courtemanche, Regis. *No Need for Glory: The British Navy in American Waters, 1860-1864*. Naval Institute Press, 1977.

Craven, Avery. *The Repressible Conflict, 1830-1861*. LSU Press, 1939.

Curtis, III, George; Thompson, Jr., James: editors. *The Southern Essays of Richard M. Weaver*. Liberty Press, 1987.

Daniels, Jonathan. *Prince of Carpetbaggers*. J.B. Lippincott Company, 1958.

Davis, Jefferson. *The Rise and Fall of the Confederate Government*. D. Appleton & Company, 1881.

Davis, Jr., Horace G. *Florida Journalism During the Civil War*. MA thesis, University of Florida, 1952.

Davis, William C. *Breckinridge: Statesman, Soldier, Symbol*. LSU Press, 1974.

Davis, William W. *The Civil War & Reconstruction in Florida*. Columbia, 1913.

Dennett, Tyler. *Lincoln and the Civil War: Diaries of John Hay*. Dodd Meade Company. 1939.

DeRosa, Marshall, editor. *The Politics of Dissolution: Quest for a National Identity & the American Civil War*. Transaction, 1998.

DiLorenzo, Thomas. *The Real Lincoln*. Forum Books, 2002.

Dickison, Mary E. *Dickison and His Men*. Courier-Journal Printing, 1890.

Dumond, Dwight. *The Secession Movement 1860-1861*. MacMillan Company, 1931.

Durkin, Joseph T. *Stephen R. Mallory, Confederate Navy Chief*. UNC Press, 1954.

Eaton, Clement. *Growth of Southern Civilization*. Harper Books, 1961.

Eckert, Ralph Lowell. *John Brown Gordon: Soldier, Southerner, American*. LSU Press, 1989.

Hahn, George W. *The Catawba Soldier of the Civil War*. Clay Publishing Company, 1911.

Fair, John D. *The Tifts of Georgia: Connecticut Yankees in King Cotton's Court*. Mercer Univ. Press. 2010.

Fogelman, Engerman. *Time on the Cross*. WW Norton & Company. 1974.

Fonvielle, Jr., Chris E. *Last Rays of Departing Hope: The Wilmington Campaign*. Savas Publishing, 1997.

Foster, Charles. *Conchtown, Boca Raton*. Florida Atlantic University Press, 1991.

Franklin, J. H. *Diary of James T. Ayers, Civil War Recruiter*. LSU Press, 1947.

Freemantle, Arthur J.L. *Three Month in the Southern States*. University of Nebraska Press, 1991.

Gallman, J. Matthew. *The North Fights the Civil War: The Home Front*. Ivan R. Dee, 1994.

Hairr, John. *CSS Chickamauga: The South's Forgotten Cruiser*. The Averasboro Press, John Hairr, 1997.

Harris, John. *The Last Slave Ships: New York and the Slave Trade*. Yale University Press, 2020.

Hesseltine, William P. ed., *Three Against Lincoln*. LSU Press, 1960.

Hesseltine, William P. *Lincoln and the War Governors*. Alfred A. Knopf, 1955.

Higginson, Thomas W. *Army Life in a Black Regiment*. Beacon Press. 1962.

Holder, Emily. *At the Dry Tortugas During the War*. 1892.

Holt, Michael F. *The Rise and Fall of the American Whig Party*. Oxford University Press, 1999.

Huse, Caleb. *Supplies for the Confederacy*. Ninety-Nine Cent Publishing, 1904.

Kennedy, James & Ronald. *Driving Dixie Down: Why Not Freedom?* Pelican Publishing. 1995.

Kennedy, James & Ronald. *Was Jefferson Davis Right?* Pelican Publishing, 1998.

Langley, Joan and Wright. *Key West: Images of the Past*. Belland & Swift Publishers, 1982

Langley, Wright & Windhorn, Stan. *Yesterday's Florida Keys*. E.A. Seamann Publishing, 1974.

Larsen, Bruce L. *Lindbergh of Minnesota: A Political Biography*. Harcourt, Brace Jovanovich, 1973.

Luraghi, Raimondo. *History of the Confederate Navy*. Naval Institute Press, 1996.

Maloney, Walter C. *Sketch of the History of Key West*. Advertiser Printing House, 1876.

Mahin, Dean B. *One War at a Time: The International Dimensions of the Civil War*. Brassy's, 1999.

Marvel, William. *Lincoln's Mercenaries: Economic Motivation Among Union Soldiers in the Civil War*. LSU Press, 2018.

May, Robert E. *The Southern Dream of a Caribbean Empire: 1854-1861*. LSU Press, 1973.

McClune, H.H. *Miscellanea*. The Gazette Company, 1907.

McKay, Ernest A. *The Civil War and New York City*. Syracuse University Press, 1990.

Meade, Robert Douthat. *Judah P. Benjamin, Confederate Statesman*. Oxford University Press, 1943.

Mitcham, Jr. Samuel. *It Wasn't About Slavery*. Regnery, 2020.

Montgomery, David. *Beyond Equality: Labor and the Radical Republicans, 1862-1872*. University of Illinois Press, 1981.

O'Conner, Thomas H. *Civil War Boston*. Northeastern University Press, 1997

O'Toole, G.J.A. *The Spanish War: An American Epic*. 1898. Norton, 1984.

Ogle, Maureen. *Key West, History of an Island of Dreams*. 2003, University Press of Florida, 2003.

Paradis, James M. *Strike the Blow for Freedom*. White Mane Books, 1998

Perkins, Howard C., ed., *Northern Editorials on Secession, Vol. II*. Reprint Services, 1942.

Potter, David M. *Lincoln and His Party in the Secession Crisis*. Yale University Press, 1942.

Priest, John Michael. *Capt. James Wren's Civil War Diary*. Berkley Books, 1990

Randall, James G. *The Civil War and Reconstruction*. DC Heath & Company, 1937.

Rapier, Regina. *The Saga of Felix Senac*. self-published, 1972.

Rhodes, James Ford. *The History of the Civil War: 1861-1865*. Dover, 1999.

Riley, Sandra. *Homeward Bound: History of the Bahama Islands to 1850*. Venture Press, 1989.

Rogers, J. S. *Caleb Huse: The Supplies for the Confederate Army*. Ninety-Nine Cent Publishing, 2021

Rose, Willie L. *A Rehearsal for Reconstruction: The Port Royal Experiment*. Vintage Books, 1964.

Saunders, Gail. *Bahamian Loyalists and their Slaves*. MacMillan Education. 1983.

Schmidt, Lewis G. *Civil War History of the 47th Pennsylvania Volunteers*. Self-published. 1989 (Schmidt I)

Schmidt, Lewis G. *Civil War in Florida, A Military History. Vol. III, Florida Keys & Fevers.* Self-published.1992. (Schmidt III)

Schmidt, Lewis G. The *Battle of Olustee: The Civil War in Florida, A Military History, Vol. II.* Self-published 1989. (Schmidt II)

Shingleton, Royce. *High Seas Confederate: Life & Times of John N. Maffitt.* USC Press, 1994.

Shy, John. *A People Numerous and Armed: Reflection on the Military Struggle for American Independence.* Univ. of Michigan, 1990.

Sideman, B.; Friedman, L., editors. *Europe Looks at the Civil War.* Orion Press, 1960.

Silbey, Joel H. *A Respectable Minority: The Democratic Party in the Civil War.* WW Norton, 1977

Sitterson, J. Carlyle. *The Secession Movement in North Carolina.* University of North Carolina Press, 1939.

Smiley, Nora & White, Louise. *History of Key West.* Great Outdoors Publishing, 1959.

Smith, Derek. *Civil War Savannah.* Frederic C. Biel Publisher. 1997.

Stebbins, Consuelo. *City of Intrigue, Nest of Revolution.* University Press of Florida. 2007.

Tebeau, Charlton W. *A History of Florida.* University of Miami Press, 1971.

de Toqueville, Alexis. *Democracy in America.* Vintage Classics, 1990.

Thayer, William R. The Life of John Hay, Vol. I. Houghton-Mifflin Company, 1908.

Turner-Tyrnauer, A.R. Lincoln and the Emperors. Harcourt Brace & World, Inc. 1962.

UDC 24th Annual Convention Minutes, Chattanooga, TN, Nov. 14-17, 1917. Richmond Press, Inc., Printers, 1918)

Warner, Ezra J. *Generals in Grey.* LSU Press, 1959.

Wooster, Ralph A. *The Secession Conventions of the South.* Princeton University Press. 1962.

Viele, John. *The Florida Keys, Vol. 3, Wreckers.* Pineapple Press, 2011.

Voegeli, V. J. *Free But Not Equal: The Midwest & the Negro During the Civil War.* Univ. of Chicago, 1967.

Warren, Robert Penn. *The Legacy of the Civil War.* University of Nebraska Press, 1998.

Warren, Gordon H. *Fountain of Discontent: The Trent Affair and Freedom of the Seas.* Northeastern University Press, 1981.

Weaver, Richard. *In Defense of Tradition.*

White, Jonathan W. *Emancipation, the Union Army and the Reelection of Lincoln.* LSU Press, 2014.

Whittle, Jr. William C. *The Voyage of the Shenandoah: A Memorable Cruise.* University of Alabama Press, 2005.

Wilson, Clyde N. *Carolina Cavalier: The Life and Mind of James Johnston Pettigrew.* Chronicles Press, 2002.

Wilson, Minnie Moore. *The Seminoles of Florida.* Moffat, Yard and Company, 1910.

Woldman, Albert A. *Lincoln and the Russians.* World Publishing Company, 1952.

ARTICLES:

Ashe, Samuel A'Court. "George Davis: Confederate Attorney General. Address to NC Supreme Court," October 19, 1915.

Bornet, Vaughn D. "A Connecticut Yankee Fights at Olustee. *Florida Historical Quarterly*, Vol. XXVII, No. 2," October 1948.

Bourne, Kenneth. "British Preparations for War with the North," *English Historical Review*, Vol. 76, No. 301, Oct. 1961.

Camp, Jr., Vaughan. "Captain Brannan's Dilemma at Key West, 1861." *Tequesta*, No. XX, 1960.

Chandler, Jr. Alfred D. "DuPont, Dahlgren and the Civil War Nitre Shortage." *Military Affairs*, Vol. 13, No. 3, 1949.

Clarke, Robert L. "Northern Plans for Economic Invasion of Florida, 1862-1865." *Florida Historical Quarterly*, Vol. XXVIII, No. 4. April 1950.

Coles, David James. "Far from Fields of Glory: Military Operations in Florida During the Civil War." Dissertation. Fall 1996.

Cortada, James W. "Florida's Relations with Cuba During the Civil War." *Florida Historical Quarterly*, Vol. LVI, No. 1, July 1980.

Cunningham, S.S. "New SCV Camps." *Confederate Veteran Magazine*, January 1900, page 18.

Denham & Huneycutt. "Letters of Corrina Brown Aldrich, Key West, 1849-50." *Florida Historical Quarterly*, Vol. LXXIX, No. 4, Spring 2001.

Dodd, Dorothy. "The Schooner Emperor." *Florida Historical Quarterly*, Vol. XXIII, No. 3, January 1935.

Doherty, Jr., Herbert J. "The Whigs of Florida." University of Florida Press *Monographs*, No. 1, Winter 1959.

Douma & Rasmussen, A. "The Danish St. Croix Project: Revisiting the Lincoln Colonization." *American 19th Century History*, 2014.

Florida Keys Sea Heritage Journal (FKSHJ). Vol. 23, No. 4, Summer 2013.

French, Frederick F. "Letter to Thomas F. Kelly," Glen Falls, NY, March 6, 1864.

Futch, Ovid L. "Salmon P. Chase and Civil War Politics." *Florida Historical Quarterly*, Vol. XXXIII, No. 3., Jan. 1954.

Garvin, Russell. "Free Negro in Florida Before 1860." *Florida Historical Quarterly*, Vol. XLVI, No. 1, July 1967

Hambright, Tom. "Forgotten Soldiers," *Florida Keys Sea Heritage Journal*, Vol 23, No. 4, Summer 2013.

Heinlein, Carston A. "Key West's Search for Fresh Water." *Florida Keys Sea Heritage Journal*, Winter 98/99, Vol. 9, No. 2.

Humphreys, Robert Arthur. *Transactions of the Royal Historical Society, 1968*. Pp. 174-128.

Hunt, Freeman, editor. *Hunt's Merchants' Magazine*, New York, Volume 26, Jan. 1852.

Kearney, William. "Autobiography of William Marvin." *Florida Historical Quarterly*, Vol. XXXVI, No. 3, Jan. 1959.

Kushlan, James A. "The Holders of the Dry Tortugas." *Tequesta* LXXX, 2020, notes.

Langley, Wright. *Diary of an Unidentified Land Official*, 1855. Tequesta, Volume XXLIII, No. 1, July 1984.

Malcolm, Corey. "Evidence for African Cemetery." *Florida Keys Sea Heritage Journal*, Vol. 13, No. 1. Fall 2002.

McKay, Jr. James. "Reminiscences of Capt. James McKay, Jr." *University of South Florida*, Volume 17, Article 16, 1991.

Manucy, Albert. "Gibraltar of the Gulf of Mexico." *Florida Historical Quarterly*, Vol. XXI, No. 4. April 1943.

Mitchell, R. "The Suspension of Specie Payments, December 1861." *Journal of Political Economy*, Vol. 7, No. 3. June 1893.

Nulty, William H. "The Seymour Decision: Appraisal of the Olustee Campaign." *Florida Historical Quarterly*, Vol. LXV, No. 3. Jan. 1987.

Palen, M. "Civil War's Forgotten Transatlantic Tariff Debate." *Journal of the Civil War Era*, UNC Press, Vol. 3, No. 1, March 2013.

Rogers, William W. "Florida on the Eve of the Civil War." *Florida Historical Quarterly*, Vol. XXXIX, No. 2, Oct. 1960.

Smith, George W. "Carpetbag Imperialism in Florida, 1862-1868." *Florida Historical Quarterly*, Vol. XXVII, No. 2. Oct. 1948 (1).

Smith, George W. "Carpetbag Imperialism in Florida." *Florida Historical Quarterly*, Vol. XXVII, No. 3, Jan. 1949. (2)

Smith, Mark A. "Engineering Slavery: US Army Corps of Engineers & Slavery at Key West." *Florida Historical Society*, Vol 86, No. 4. 2007.

Taylor, Robert A. "Cow Cavalry: Munnerlyn's Battalion in Florida, 1864-1865." *Florida Historical Quarterly*, Vol. LXV, No. 3, Jan. 1987.

Trifkovic, Srdja. "America's Dangerous Overreach." *Chronicles Magazine*, June 2021.

Warner, Frank. "The Civil War Divided Lehigh Valley." *The Daily Call*, May 16, 2013.

Waters, Zach C. "Tampa's Forgotten Defenders: Confederate Commanders of Fort Brooke." University of South Florida, Vol. 17, Art. 3.

Weinfeld, Daniel R. "Florida Jews & the Civil War." *Journal of Southern Jewish Historical Society*. Vol. 17, 2014.

Williams, Ames W. "Stronghold of the Straits, Fort Zachary Taylor." *Tequesta*, No. XIV, 1954.

Williams, Jr., Edward L. "Negro Slavery in Florida." *Florida Historical Quarterly*, Vol. XXVII, No. 2, Oct. 1949

Willings, David L. "Florida's Overseas Railroad." *Florida Historical Quarterly*, Vol. XXXV, No. 4, April 1957.

Wooster, Ralph A. "The Florida Secession Convention." *Florida Historical Quarterly*, Vol. 36, No. 4, April 1958.

Letters

Selected Letters of Salmon P. Chase, 1834-1867. PK Yonge Library of Florida History, University of Florida, Gainesville.

Letter from James Filor to Abraham Lincoln. Jan. 3, 1863, Abraham Lincoln Papers, Library of Congress.

Online Sources

Weaver, Jeff. "Confederate Cruiser Died a Long way from Her Element." *Bladen County Journal*, 2.22.2005 (accessed 2.23.2005)

Negus, Samuel. "A Notorious Nest of Offence: Neutrals, Belligerents and Union Jails." Academia.edu, accessed 2.15.22.

Bibliography

https://military-history.fandom.com/wiki/Company_K,_7th_Florida_Infantry_Regiment

FILOR v. UNITED STATES. | Supreme Court | US Law | LII / Legal Information Institute (cornell.edu)

www.oirf.org. Karl Reutling: Who Was William H. Ward? accessed 2.11.22.

Black Virginians in Blue accessed 1.23.22

www.find-a-grave.com Naugle, Claudia L., Henry Mulrennan. accessed 4.24.21.

www.SlaveryNorth.com, Harper, Douglas, 2003 Slavery in Pennsylvania, accessed 2.25.21.

www.KeysHistory.org Wilkinson, Jerry. Charles Howe. accessed 2.11.22

www.Wikipedia.com. Browne, Fielding Archer. accessed 2.11.22.

www.wfmz.com Allentown Black population, – accessed 12.12.20

http://slavenorth.com/pennsylvania.htm "Pennsylvania Slavery," Douglas Harper, accessed 11.27.21.

Civil War divided Lehigh Valley - The Morning Call (mcall.com) Frank Warner, (accessed, 7.6.21.

The Allentown Democrat: Feb. 11, 1863 : Allentown Public Library : Free Download, Borrow, and Streaming : Internet Archive WS_FTP\csn\sc (csnavy.org) Lt. William H. Ward, accessed 2.14.22.

http://rblong.net/sailor/a-1.html: Lt. George H. Arledge.

INDEX

Africans 7, 11, 63, 111, 141, 143, 145-147, 152, 159, 184, 210

Albury, Benjamin R. 82, 190

Allentown Democrat 65, 67, 70, 121, 124, 129, 137, 152, 166, 169, 171

Archer, Capt. Augustus A. 93

Arledge, George H. 81, 83

Atlantic, steamer 46, 48

Bahamas 13, 23, 47, 54, 57, 82, 84, 87, 91, 94, 97-98, 103-104, 142, 144-145, 177

Baldwin, John P. 47

Bartlum, Joseph S. 9, 223

Battery Buchanan 81, 83, 106, 173

Battery Campbell 81, 173

Bayview Park Memorial Pavilion 224

Berry, Charles H. 80, 131

Bethel, John A. 39, 112

Bethel, Winer 39, 112

bounties 128, 133-135, 138, 150-151, 153, 166, 189

Brannan, Capt. James 40, 148

Breckinridge, John C. 30, 32, 38, 177, 179, 227

Britain 152, 198-199, 202-203, 205, 207-208, 211

Browne, Fielding A. 3, 7, 31, 111, 219, 222, 229

Browne, Jefferson B. 3, 7, 31, 111, 219, 222, 229

Brownlow, Parson 57

Brown, Zachariah 26, 154

Buchanan, James iii, 205

Burns, Thomas 81

Calhoun, John C. 26-27, 31

Calusa 1

Canada 100, 151, 203, 207, 214

Canfield, Cyrus A. 19, 55, 104

Caribbean iii, 8, 11, 59, 65, 146, 158-160, 184, 197-198, 200-202, 207, 209-210, 214-215, 223

Cash, William D. 16, 75, 219, 221

Cass, Lewis 25

cayo hueso 1

Chapman, Charles H. 81

Charleston Mercury 34, 42

Chase, Salmon P. 97, 139, 177, 182, 185-186, 191-192

Chattahoochie, CSS 74, 81

Chebert, Jules 80

Chickamauga, CSS 94, 136

Clapp, James 18, 40, 47

Clayton-Bulwer Treaty 202

Cochrane, Vice-Admiral Sir Alexander 144

Cole, Joseph E. 80

colonization 65, 158-159, 184-185, 209-211, 223

Colored Troops, 34th US 155, 185, 193

Colored Troops, 2nd US 155, 185, 193

Colored Troops, 1st US 155, 185, 193

Colored Troops, General 155, 185, 193

Columbia, CSS 4, 81, 103, 220

Conchs iii, 3, 8-9, 23, 29, 54, 57, 80, 167, 227-228

conscription 127, 133-134, 137, 154, 164, 167, 209

contrabands 72, 95, 125-126, 146-148, 150, 155, 209-210

Cow Cavalry 168

Crusader, USS 11, 147

Crusoe, Peter 51-52, 104

Cuba 2-3, 10-11, 28, 52, 54, 56, 122, 142, 144-147, 160, 177, 179, 202, 205, 223

INDEX

Curry, Edmund 81, 119, 172, 223-224

Curry, Henry 81, 119, 172, 223-224

Curry, Joseph 81, 119, 172, 223-224

Curry, Samuel 81, 119, 172, 223-224

Curry, William 81, 119, 172, 223-224

Curtin, Gov. Andrew 62, 64, 68-69, 133-134, 136-137

Dana, Charles A. 170-171

Daniels, Enoch 164

Darien, Georgia 12, 82, 156

Davis, George 177, 179

De Ocha, Manuel Monte 94

deportations 53, 55, 162

Diaz, Francisco (Frank) 81, 172, 223

Dickison, Capt. J. J. 224

Dorsey, Edward 88

Douglass, Frederick 127

Drewry's Bluff 81, 89, 91, 94, 98, 103, 105, 174-175

Dunmore, Lord 143

Dupuy, John 81

Echo, Schooner 11

Fagan, Henry 81, 88

Fagan, Joseph 81, 88

Fales, Rofino 81, 89

Filor, James 31, 111, 132

Fingal steamer 83, 116, 168

Florida i, ii, iii, iv, 1-4, 8-17, 19, 22-45, 47-49, 51-53, 57, 59, 67, 73-74, 79-80, 82-84, 86-88, 91, 93-94, 96-99, 101, 103, 106-107, 111-113, 123, 125, 139, 142-145, 150-151, 153-155, 157-158, 161-165, 168-169, 171-172, 174-195, 197-201, 203, 212, 215, 218-219, 221-224, 227-229

Florida, Seventh Infantry iii, 4, 9, 12, 22, 24-25, 28, 40, 86-87, 93-94, 111, 142, 153-154, 185-188, 191, 198

Fontane, Philip J. 7, 13

Fort Fisher 81, 83, 89, 91, 94, 98, 102-103, 105, 172-173

Fort Jefferson 39, 43, 45, 59, 74, 79, 134, 146, 148, 165-166, 168, 175-176, 178, 197, 200, 207

Fort Pulaski 201

Fort Taylor ii, iii, 17-18, 35, 39-40, 42-48, 51-53, 56, 71, 74-75, 79, 82, 84, 99, 102, 107, 109, 112-113, 123, 130, 132, 140, 146-148, 164, 172, 175, 178, 197, 201, 218, 221

French, Maj. William 3, 47-48, 92-93, 113, 187

Good, Col. Tilghman 61

Gordon, Gen. John B. 95, 223

Hackley, William 5

Harris, Dr. Jeptha V. 222

Hilton Head 74, 76, 122, 124, 126, 150, 152-155, 157, 177, 185-186, 188, 191

Howe, Charles 15

Hunter, Gen. David 76, 123, 129, 153, 185

Hunts Merchant Magazine —

Huse, Caleb 14, 47, 77, 89-90

Indians 1-2, 80, 141-143

Isabel, steamer 4

Island Guards 42, 44, 49, 52, 79

Jackson Square i, 6

Josselyn, William A. 81, 90

Kerr, William 120

Key of the Gulf 5, 16, 30-31, 38-39, 46, 49, 73, 101, 113, 171, 219

Key West i, ii, iii, iv, 1-5, 7-19, 21-25, 27-32, 34-35, 37, 39-61, 64, 66, 69-99, 101-108, 110-112, 114-116, 118-121, 124-126, 130-133, 136, 138-139, 144-149, 152, 154-159, 162-179, 181, 183-184, 186-195, 197-201, 207-208, 211-212, 215, 217-225, 227, 229-230

INDEX

Key West Avengers iv, 73-74, 76, 79-80, 82-94, 96-98, 105-106, 115, 131, 136, 162, 166, 217, 223

Key West Gazette 5

Key West Inquirer 17

Knickerbocker, magazine 5

LaFayette Fire Department 7, 108

Lehigh Valley 61-62, 64-65, 68-70, 121, 124-125, 132, 134, 137, 139, 164, 167, 169, 171

Leopold, Newman 75

Lincoln, Abraham 70, 133, 171, 206, 215

Louisiana, CSS 31, 74

Lovitt, James 90

Lowe, Alfred P. 81, 88, 91, 96, 104-105, 172, 223

Lowe, Caroline 81, 88, 91, 96, 104-105, 172, 223

Lowe, John Thomas 81, 88, 91, 96, 104-105, 172, 223

Lowe, William 81, 88, 91, 96, 104-105, 172, 223

Lowe, William E. 81, 88, 91, 96, 104-105, 172, 223

Maffitt, John N. 11

Mail, Jacob 73, 92

Mallory, Ellen ii, 7, 12, 17-18, 23, 28, 47, 99, 108, 114, 228

Mallory, Stephen R. ii, 7, 12, 17-18, 23, 28, 47, 99, 108, 114, 228

Maloney, Jr., Walter C. 23, 104, 172, 219, 223

Maloney, Sr. Walter C. 4, 23, 38, 39, 42, 48, 82, 112, 123, 156, 219, 222, 229

Martello towers 61, 149, 154, 165, 197, 201, 207-208

Marvin, William 12-13, 42, 112, 179, 219

Massachusetts Idea 7, 141, 151

Maximilian, Ferdinand 211

McClune, Lt. H. H. 128

McKay, Capt. James 52-53, 56, 169, 174

Meares, William B. 227-228

Mexico iii, 8, 10, 15, 26, 58, 90, 197-199, 203, 206, 208, 211-212, 214, 223

Mississippi, CSS 31, 99, 115, 172

Monroe County i, iii, 4, 6, 12, 14, 16-18, 23-25, 28, 30-32, 38-39, 42, 51, 62, 67, 73, 84, 109, 112, 190, 219, 221, 227

Montgomery, Col. James 33, 46, 154

Moreno, Fernando 17

Morgan, Col. Joseph 75, 81, 124, 154, 172, 223

Morgan, Samuel 75, 81, 124, 154, 172, 223

Moss, Joseph H. 81

Mulrennan, Henry 8, 52, 201

Munnerlyn, Major Charles J. 168

Myers, Lt. Julian 174

Mystic, Connecticut 12, 14, 48, 107, 110, 120

Natural Bridge, battle of 174

New England secession 35

New York, 90th Regiment 11, 13, 38, 59, 73, 77, 89-90, 101, 147, 193

New York Herald 57, 60, 71, 74, 194

Ocean Pond, battle of 143, 175, 189, 193-194

Olivieri, Marcus 96

Pacetti, A.N. 82-96

Patterson, Alexander 6, 47

Pennsylvania, 47th Regiment 61, 73, 152, 171

Pennsylvania slavery 63, 126

Penn, William 62

Pent, John 223

Perry, Lt. Matthew 198

Philadelphia Inquirer 53-54, 71, 162, 167, 178

Index

Phipps, J. M. 223
Pickens Episode 35
Pinckney, Harriet 13, 17, 37, 84, 90, 112
Pinckney, William 13, 17, 37, 84, 90, 112
Plantz, Homer G. 181-182, 191, 194
Pocotaligo, South Carolina 69, 74
Rawle, William 41
refugees 139, 155, 161, 164-165, 174
Register, newspaper 5, 32
Rickards, George V. 104
Roberts, Capt. Richard 86
Rogers, Commodore John 145
Russell, John W. 223
Russia 3, 133, 202-203, 213-214
Saint-Domingue 144
Salas, Don Juan Pablo 2
Salvor steamer 52-53, 56, 107, 113
Sands, John B. 81
Sandy Cornish 145
Savannah, CSS 5, 23, 92, 106, 116, 118
Sawyer, Samuel Y. 19, 55, 81, 98, 104
Sawyer, William O. 19, 55, 81, 98, 104
Seminoles ii, 143
Senac, Felix ii, 17, 40, 101
Seward, William 159, 205
Shenandoah, CSS 178, 214
Simonton, John W. 3, 7
Slaves; Slave Trade 3, 7, 11, 13-14, 62-63, 71, 111, 118, 122, 141, 144-148, 152, 155, 159, 190, 202, 204, 210
St. Croix 159, 210
Stickney, Lyman D. 181-182, 184, 192-194
St. Marks 4, 87, 97, 142
Tattnall, Lt. Josiah. 198
Tift, Amos F. 7, 37, 39, 43, 48, 52, 56, 92, 107, 112, 120

Tift, Charles 7, 37, 39, 43, 48, 52, 56, 92, 107, 112, 120
Tift, Nelson 7, 37, 39, 43, 48, 52, 56, 92, 107, 112, 120
Tift's Wharf ii, 12, 114
Trent Affair 60, 121, 206, 208, 212
Union Volunteer Corps 15, 48, 82, 123
United Confederate Veterans 87-88, 91, 105, 223
United Daughters of the Confederacy 224
Veteran Volunteer 217
Wall, Lizzie 7, 100
Wall, William H. 7, 100
Ward, William H. 15, 25, 39, 43, 73, 77, 90, 106, 115, 159, 205
Ware, Eldridge L. 5, 8
Watlington, Francis B. 47
Watson, George 80, 88, 91, 172
Watson, Robert 80, 88, 91, 172
Weatherford, Jacob 81
Weyler, Gen. Valeriano 122
Whig party 12, 27, 29
Whitehead, William A. i, 6-7
Willemsen, John P. 80, 106
Woodbury, Gen. Daniel 168-169

Latest Releases & Best Sellers

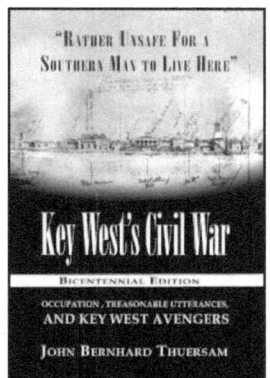

Over 70 unapologetic unreconstructed titles for you to enjoy

SHOTWELLPUBLISHING.COM

Free Book Offer

Visit **FreeLiesBook.com**

Sign-up for new release notifications and receive a **FREE** downloadable edition of:

*Lies My Teacher Told Me:
The True History of the War for
Southern Independence*
by Dr. Clyde N. Wilson

and

*Confederaphobia:
An American Epidemic*
by Paul C. Graham

You can always unsubscribe and keep the book, so you've got nothing to lose!

www.ingramcontent.com/pod-product-compliance
Lightning Source LLC
Chambersburg PA
CBHW020050170426
43199CB00009B/230